LIFE IN POETRY:
LAW IN TASTE

AMS PRESS
NEW YORK

LIFE IN POETRY:
LAW IN TASTE

TWO SERIES OF LECTURES DELIVERED

IN OXFORD

1895—1900

BY

WILLIAM JOHN COURTHOPE, C.B., M.A., Oxon.

HON. LL.D. EDINBURGH ; HON. D.LITT. DURHAM ; LATE PROFESSOR OF POETRY
IN THE UNIVERSITY OF OXFORD ; HON. FELLOW OF
NEW COLLEGE, OXFORD

London

MACMILLAN AND CO., Limited

NEW YORK : THE MACMILLAN COMPANY

1901

Library of Congress Cataloging in Publication Data

Courthope, William John, 1842-1917.
  Life in poetry.
    Reprint of the 1901 ed. published by Macmillan, London,
  New York.
    1. Poetry. 2. Poetry—History and criticism. 3. English
  poetry—History and criticism. I. Title. II. Title: Law in
  taste.
  PN1031.C6   1975   808.1   72-992
  ISBN 0-404-01785-1

Reprinted from the edition of 1901, London
First AMS edition published in 1975
Manufactured in the United States of America

AMS PRESS INC.
NEW YORK, N. Y. 10003

VIRO

QUI NUPER ARISTOTELIS περὶ ποιητικῆς LIBRUM,

PERBREVEM ILLUM QUIDEM SED VERE AUREUM,

RECENSUIT, ILLUSTRAVIT, COMMENDAVIT,

SAMUELI HENRICO BUTCHER,

TANTÆ PHILOSOPHIÆ INTERPRETI DIGNO,

AMICO

DE LITTERARUM REPUBLICA

EADEM SECUM VOLENTI EADEM NOLENTI,

HAS PRÆLECTIONES,

IN ORDINEM COACTAS,

JAM RUDE DONATUS,

DEDICAT PRÆLECTOR.

CONTENTS

PART I

INAUGURAL

	PAGE
LIBERTY AND AUTHORITY IN MATTERS OF TASTE	1

PART II

LIFE IN POETRY

LECT.		
I.	POETICAL CONCEPTION	37
II.	POETICAL EXPRESSION	63
III.	POETICAL DECADENCE	89
IV.	POETRY AND THE PEOPLE	123

PART III

LAW IN TASTE

I.	INTRODUCTORY	159
II.	ARISTOTLE AS A CRITIC	190
III.	THE IDEA OF LAW IN FRENCH POETRY	222
IV.	THE IDEA OF LAW IN GERMAN POETRY	252
V.	THE IDEA OF LAW IN ENGLISH POETRY	278
VI.	CHAUCER	299
VII.	MILTON	329
VIII.	POPE	360
IX.	BYRON AND TENNYSON	388
X.	CONCLUSION	419

PART I

INAUGURAL

LIBERTY AND AUTHORITY IN MATTERS OF TASTE

LIBERTY AND AUTHORITY IN MATTERS OF TASTE

EVEN those of my predecessors who have been called with higher qualifications than myself to discourse on Poetry before the University of Oxford must, on contemplating their duties, have felt that they had to face a problem of peculiar difficulty. The Professor of Poetry enjoys what I believe is the unique honour of being raised to his Chair by the vote of Convocation. Yet though he may thus be said to represent the oldest seat of learning in the British Empire on a subject of the deepest interest to the human imagination, he finds himself launched on this wide sea of thought without chart or compass or any kind of external instruction to guide him in the course which he is expected to steer. He is, indeed, bound to deliver three lectures yearly during his tenure of the Chair. But as to the subject-matter of these lectures he is under no obligation. Whether he should examine and discuss the general principles of poetry; whether he should rather dwell on the practice of individual poets; whether he should draw his illustrations exclusively from the acknowledged classics of literature, or should also handle the debateable questions of modern art; at all these points he is left entirely to his own discretion.

If he seeks for a solution of his difficulty in the definitions of language, he is at once met by an ambiguity of terms. We can have no doubt as to the meaning of the words Logic and Natural Science, nor as to the limitations imposed on those who give instruction in these subjects. But the word Poetry may be used to signify either the outward form in which imaginative thought is expressed by means of metrical language, or that inward conception of the mind preliminary to creation which is shared by the poets with the professors of the other fine arts. Thus we may without impropriety speak of the Poetry of Painting and even of the Poetry of Architecture.

Perhaps with natural piety the newly elected Professor of Poetry looks for guidance to the intentions or the character of the Founder of his Chair. But here too search is in vain: of him little is known that is definite, nothing that is remarkable. Henry Birkhead must have been born in the first quarter of the seventeenth century, for he took his degree of M.A. in 1639. He appears to have been affected by the religious difficulties of his time, for shortly after taking his degree he became a Jesuit, but, soon returning to the Church of England and to Oxford, he was elected a Fellow of All Souls.

He was known as a skilful philologist. He was also a writer of Latin verse, but there is no particular merit in the compositions of this kind which he has left behind him. When the Civil War broke out he was prominent among the little group of Oxford scholars and poets who attached themselves to the cause of the king, and the most distinguished of whom were John Cleveland and William Cartwright. The characteristic features in the poetry of these men are well known. They helped to develop what Addison calls the style of False Wit, and Johnson the school of Metaphysical Poetry. Their object was to give distinction to any theme, however trivial, by adorning it with a multitude of far-fetched metaphors, similes, and allusions. A specimen of their art survives in a small volume of poems, written by them in co-operation to celebrate the memory of Sir Bevill Grenvill, who was killed in a skirmish with the Parliamentary forces at Lansdown Hill. Birkhead's contribution to this poetical garland was not absolutely the worst; but he was the champion of a losing cause, alike in politics and in poetry. He saw the execution of the king for whom he had fought and written; the establishment of the Commonwealth; the Restoration of the Monarchy; the Revolution of 1688. Living till 1695, he witnessed the influence of the school of Cowley decline before the rising school of Dryden; and a Chair, which owed its existence to the liberality of one so deeply imbued with the spirit of the Middle Ages, was filled by its first Professor almost at the same time that English society began to listen to the criticism of the *Tatler* and *Spectator*.

The history of the Founder, then, throws no light on the duties attaching to this Chair. Nor can any clear notion of rule or system be gathered from the practice of those who have held it. The list of the Professors of Poetry indeed furnishes us with name after name intimately associated with great changes in the poetical taste of this country. Prominent in the early history of the Chair we observe the figure of Joseph Spence, author of the *Polymetis*, and of the better known *Anecdotes*, which so vividly illustrate the literary character of an age that found its standard in the poetry of Pope. Spence is followed after a short interval by Lowth, who enlarged the range of taste by his lectures on Hebrew Poetry, and attracted the attention of the world of letters by his dispute with Warburton, Pope's commentator and biographer. Later in the century appears Thomas Warton, the historian of English Poetry, and perhaps the earliest pioneer of the Romantic Revival, which refreshed with a new stream of thought and sentiment the exhausted classicism of those times. Coming to the present century, we admire the fine and balanced taste of Milman, the writer of the polished Newdigate prize poem on "The Belvedere Apollo," beginning:

> Heard ye the arrow hurtle through the sky?
> Heard ye the dragon monster's dying cry?

and containing the truly beautiful lines descriptive of the statue:

> For mild he seemed as in Elysian bowers,
> Wasting in careless ease the joyous hours,
> Haughty as bards have sung, with princely sway
> Curbing the fierce, flame-breathing steeds of day,
> Beauteous as vision seen in dreamy sleep
> By holy maid on Delphi's haunted steep,
> Mid the dim twilight of the laurel grove,
> Too fair to worship, too divine to love.

Next to Milman in point of succession, and equal to him in scholarship and refinement, the author of the *Christian Year* lent indirectly the aid of his criticism to the Lake School, then still struggling against the current of contemporary taste. Keble's *Prælectiones*, delivered as they were in Latin, appealed to a necessarily limited audience, but a new note was struck when Matthew Arnold, a name always cherished with affectionate admiration in Oxford, began to lecture in English. With him the classical genius of poetry revived under new auspices. The attention of the public at large was directed to the form of the Greek drama as a vehicle for the expression of modern thought. Attic wit amused itself with applying the standards of Hellenic culture to every department of English life. It seems to me but yesterday that I listened *in statu pupillari* to the famous dictum pronounced from this Chair, that "there were no Wraggs by the Ilissus." Nevertheless the stream of taste, diverted for the moment, has in our own generation shown a tendency to flow back into national channels, nor do I know of any book which has done more to accomplish this change than *The Golden Treasury of English Song*, a work of

Greek beauty, which will always remain as a monument of the critical refinement and the large sympathy of my predecessor, Francis Palgrave. When I consider all this ambiguity in the meaning of terms, this silence as to the intentions of the Founder of the Chair, this diversity of taste and practice among those who have held it, it appears to me that the first question to be decided is, how far it is possible to speak on Poetry with the confidence which is expected from one who discharges Professorial duties. I accordingly propose in this my Inaugural Lecture to ask my audience to consider with me the question of Liberty and Authority in Matters of Taste, so that we may determine from this point of view what limits Reason imposes on the Art of Poetry, and to what extent we can apply in the domain of Imagination those scientific methods which are properly applied to the objects of Sense. But I can imagine that an objection may be made on the very threshold of such an inquiry. It may be said: The question you raise is one that contains its own answer. There can be no established law in the sphere of Art and Taste.

> The Mind is its own place, and in itself
> Can make a Heaven of Hell, a Hell of Heaven.

In everything relating to $αἴσθησις$, taste, perception, the individual is free. Genius is the sole lawgiver in Art; and though the critic may serve the artist by sharpening the faculty of perception, yet if he attempts to measure works of art by any external standard, he ignores the proverbial and accepted wisdom of all ages: πάντων μέτρον ἄνθρωπος: *De gustibus non est disputandum.*

This is a formidable objection; the more so because it is an echo of the prevailing philosophy of the day which we recognise by the name of Culture. The philosophy of Culture is based on self-consciousness; that is to say, in this philosophy, the consciousness of freedom in the individual mind is made the standard and starting-point for all speculation about Religion and Art. Let me cite, as an example of what I mean by self-consciousness, a striking passage from the chapter in *Sartor Resartus,* called "The Everlasting No": "The Everlasting No has said: Behold thou art fatherless, outcast, and the Universe is mine; to which my whole *Me* now makes answer, *I* am not thine, but free and for ever hate thee." In the same spirit, though in a less obscure and poetical style, Matthew Arnold defines Criticism to be the free faculty that advances in the mind the growth of an inward Perfection; and, quite logically from his own premises, he identifies Poetry with the Idea as it exists in the individual mind and contrasts it with dogmatic Religion. "The future of poetry," he says, "is immense, because in poetry, where it is worthy of its high destinies, our race as time goes on will find an ever surer and surer stay. . . . Our religion has materialised itself in the fact, in the supposed fact, and now the fact is failing it. But for poetry the idea is everything, the rest is a world of illusion, of divine illusion. Poetry attaches its emotions to the idea; the idea is the fact. The strongest part of our religion to-day is its unconscious poetry."

But the opinion of those who hold with the maxim *De gustibus non est disputandum* is supported by a yet stronger ally in the prevailing taste of the age. It seems to be a necessary characteristic of a highly civilised society, that in proportion as it grows impatient of Authority in Belief it insists upon Novelty in Imagination. Everywhere we hear the question asked: May we know what this *new* doctrine whereof thou speakest is? And from all quarters, in satisfaction of the demand, comes the answer, in the revelations of the new Humourist, the new Dramatist, the new Woman. The same feeling is paramount even in those whose imagination is accustomed to dwell in the higher regions of art and taste, and I know not where it is more eloquently expressed than in the words of an Oxford scholar whose works live in the minds of many of us as his memory is fresh in our affections. "For us," says Walter Pater, "the Renaissance is the name of a many-sided but yet united movement in which the love of the things of the intellect and the imagination for their own sake, the desire of a more liberal and comely way of conceiving life, make themselves felt, urging those who experience this desire to search out first one and then another means of intellectual or imaginative enjoyment, and directing them not merely to the discovery of old and forgotten sources of this enjoyment, but to divine new sources of it, new experiences, new subjects of poetry, new sources of art."

What, then, is to be said in regard to this maxim, *De gustibus non est disputandum,* supported as it is by the philosophy of those who preach the gospel of self-culture, and impelled by the powerful current of the public taste? I do not think that there can be the slightest doubt as to the answer. To any one who raises such a preliminary objection as I have supposed, I would reply: You have stated strongly one side of the truth, but you have ignored, completely ignored, the other. You have asserted the claims of individual liberty, and up to a certain point I agree with you. I do not deny that spiritual liberty is founded on consciousness, and hence the self-consciousness of the age is part of the problem we are considering. I do not deny that the prevailing rage for novelty must also be taken into account. Liberty, variety, novelty, are all necessary to the development of Art. Without novelty there can be no invention, without variety there can be no character, without liberty there can be no life. Life, character, invention, these are of the essence of Poetry. But while you have defended with energy the freedom of the Individual, you have said nothing of the authority of Society. And yet the conviction of the existence of this authority is a belief perhaps even more firmly founded in the human mind than the sentiment as to the rights of individual liberty. If Henry Birkhead had not believed that the principles of poetry were, like those of all other arts or sciences, capable, up to a cèrtain point at all events, of definition and demonstration, would he, being in possession of all his senses, have bequeathed his property for the endowment of this Chair? If the University of Oxford, as a corporate body, had not shared his opinion, would it have accepted his benefaction? Could the long succession of those who have filled this Chair have been maintained, if the great majority of the Professors of Poetry, however various their opinions, however opposite their tastes, had not felt sure that there was in taste, as in science, a theory of false and true, in art, as in conduct, a rule of right and wrong? And even among those who have asserted most strongly the inward and relative nature of poetry, do you think there was one so completely a sceptic as to imagine that he was the sole proprietor of the perception he sought to embody in words; one who doubted his power, by means of accepted symbols, to communicate to his audience his own ideas and feelings about external things? Yet until some man shall have been found bold enough to defend a thesis so preposterous, we must continue to believe that there is a positive standard, by which those at least who speak a common language may reason about questions of taste.

There is no doubt a point at which the principle *De gustibus non est disputandum* must be strictly applied. Our English law recognises this. We know that when a man pursues his own taste so far as to publish in writing that which is decided to be contrary to the law of the land, the plea of the offender that he only wrote what seemed beautiful to him, or what he believed to be true, will not avail for his protection. Tastes of that kind we do not dispute about; we punish them. It is seldom indeed in England that any individual so far oversteps the large liberties allowed him by the law as to translate into action opinions which are recognised as dangerous to the community. But beyond those appetites which are proscribed as illegal there are secret proceedings of thought and perception which, while they elude the clumsy vigilance of the law, may poison the atmosphere about us—tastes that corrupt, sentiments that emasculate, affectations that debase, the whole spirit and character of society. To treat these with easy tolerance is only a sign of social cowardice. A nation which has a just sense of its own greatness and liberty must also have a sense of what is ideally noble and beautiful, and must not be afraid to condemn any departure from this standard. And indeed all experience shows that the instinct of every society impels it to assert its authority in questions relating to imagination and art. Nature bids us judge in matters of taste: the difficulty is how to judge rightly. Since, then, this is the object of our inquiry, I will ask you in the first place very briefly to glance at the different kinds of external tribunal by which Society has endeavoured to decide questions of taste, in order that we may see how far we can accept their authority.

Perhaps the form of external authority which most readily occurs to each of us is the Academy after the French model. No one will deny a grandeur to the constitution and history of this great body. You will remember what was the object of its creation as described by Richelieu, its founder: "The main function of the Academy shall be to work with all possible care and diligence at giving sure rules to our language, and rendering it pure, eloquent, and capable of treating the arts and sciences." And Renan, adding a slight emphasis to the idea of Richelieu, says: "The duty of the Academy is to preserve the delicacy of the French language." As far as regards the intellectual history of France, these strictly conservative duties have been performed with splendid fidelity and success. The Academy has admitted within its walls almost every great French writer since the day of its foundation, so that on literary grounds it may justly claim to speak with the representative authority of France. In the standard of taste which it has consistently upheld the French nation has seen the image of its own genius. One doubts whether to admire the Academy most for the thoroughness with which it has realised the idea of Richelieu, by carrying the rules of the French language through the anarchy of the Revolution, or for the courage with which it has maintained the standard of Renan, by preserving the delicacy of French thought in the days of M. Zola.

I do not wonder that so great a triumph should have profoundly impressed the imagination of English critics, or that we should frequently hear the opinion expressed, that it would be an excellent thing if we could have an institution of the same kind in England. Those who speak in this way usually support themselves by the authority of Matthew Arnold, and refer to a lecture delivered, I believe, from this Chair, on the Literary Influence of Academies. But they seem to me to misunderstand the mind of that eminent critic, because though all his arguments point to the foundation of an Academy in England, he concludes as follows: " An Academy quite like the French Academy, a sovereign organ of the highest literary opinion, a recognised authority in matters of intellectual tone and taste, we shall hardly have, and perhaps we ought not to wish to have it." That is the conclusion of common sense, and the most elementary considerations show why it must be so.

The French Academy is an effect, not a cause ; it is the product mainly of certain intellectual qualities of the French people. It was founded as an institution because, at a certain point of their history, the French people became conscious that they possessed these qualities, and a number of representative men began to form themselves into a society for the purpose of discussing questions of taste and expression. They had no intention of initiating or legislating: they came together to discuss and to judge. The English people do not possess that analytical and logical genius which would enable them to constitute a representative assembly for the same purpose.

But if the French Academy derives its representative character from the nature of the French intellect, the official prestige and authority it possesses come to it solely from a political source. It was, in fact, the offspring of the French Monarchy. It was established by the king; for a long time the king retained and exercised the power of veto in its elections: it would have been impossible to make it a really comprehensive and representative assembly if all the best minds of France had not first found a natural centre of attraction in the Court. Even therefore if the qualities of the English genius facilitated, instead of hindering, the constitution of an Academy like the French, the decentralisation of English institutions and our habits of individual liberty would necessarily prevent such a body from exercising any authority.

I might dwell on other Courts, of the nature of Academies, by means of which Society at different times has attempted to pronounce judgment in matters of taste. Such, for example, is the Coterie, which may be defined as a miniature Academy without official status, and which under various conditions has exercised great influence in Italy, France, and England. But as the Coterie represents no body of opinion beyond itself, and as it flourishes most in an aristocratic form of society, it is unnecessary to speak of it in detail, and I pass on to consider a tribunal with whose decrees we are all familiar, the Court of Public Opinion.

Public opinion delivers judgment either collectively, or representatively by means of an anonymous press. When it acts collectively it is certainly one of the most remarkable of human phenomena, and

I think that the spectacle of vast bodies of men giving simultaneous expression to their consciousness of what is right furnishes the strongest refutation that could be desired of the fallacy in the maxim, *De gustibus non est disputandum*. Such are the judgments pronounced by the spectators in a theatre, or by the audience at a public meeting when they express their approval of or dissent from the opinions of an orator. On these occasions the verdict of public opinion is, for the moment at least, irresistible. The dramatist is not obliged to regard it as final: he may reason with his judges, as Aristophanes did in the *Clouds*; he may even proclaim his contempt for their taste, as Ben Jonson did in his *Ode to Himself* after the failure of his *New Inn*; but he knows that there is no higher court to which he can appeal.

It must be allowed that, as a tribunal of taste, public opinion, or perhaps I should rather say popular opinion, possesses certain great virtues. For one thing, the taste of the people is almost always natural, and natural taste is the foundation of good taste. When a whole society—at least a society which is both historic and free—judges collectively, its instincts will not allow it to go very far astray. It will reject what is nasty and unwholesome; it will favour such tastes as are on the whole manly, and healthy, and vigorous. The judges in the gallery of a theatre, who hiss the villain of a play for his evil sentiments, are representatives of the authority of popular opinion. Critics of this stamp will also show themselves intolerant of such fundamental faults of taste as affectation and conceit, which pass unscathed the judgment, for example, of the Coterie. When a dramatist or any other kind of artist shows that he is thinking more of his own nature than of human nature, any large audience will be quick to find him out. Nor is the collective verdict of the public ever consciously unjust, because, as it judges in the mass, it is not affected by those petty personal motives of envy, jealousy, and resentment which so often disturb the reason of private critics.

But public opinion as a court of justice has certain obvious limitations and weaknesses. Like the old Teutonic assemblies of freemen which announced their decisions by the shouts of the multitude and the clashing of shields, its powers are restricted to simple approval or rejection. Moreover its judgments are always arbitrary, being founded on emotion, not on reason. The standard by which it judges may be constituted out of the merest prejudice and ignorance, yet as it knows of no other, it will regard its own canon as conclusive. In no other tribunal is the last word of the despot so decisively uttered: "Hoc volo, sic jubeo, stat pro ratione voluntas."

Again, even when it decides more deliberately through the anonymous criticism of the press, public opinion is subject to weaknesses, arising from hurry and superficiality, which lower its authority as a tribunal of taste. To judge rightly in matters of taste we must have time. An enduring work of art is the product of meditation and labour, and, from the nature of things, it cannot be measured by a mere ephemeral standard. The press can and does judge with admirable accuracy of the mass of novels, poems, plays, and pictures, which men read, glance at, talk about, and forget: its methods of swift intuition and generalisation are inadequate to estimate the work of a Raphael or a Milton.

I think that from the facts I have attempted to put before you two conclusions may safely be drawn. One is, that society in all ages has been constantly attempting to assert its authority in matters of taste; the other is, that no form of social organisation of which the world has had experience is likely to be accepted as a tribunal of taste in such a country as England. The Academy of the French pattern is defective because it is the offspring of centralisation; the Coterie is defective because it is not representative; Public Opinion is defective because it has no recognised standard of judgment, and also because its judgments are too rough and ready to be applicable to the higher creations of Art. It may indeed be doubted whether for such a society as ours, so full of self-consciousness and the spirit of individual liberty, so charged with party feeling, divided between so many sections and interests, any representative body could ever be formed which would be recognised as giving expression to the deliberate sense of the community on purely æsthetic questions. Yet one thing we may surely hope for—the growth of an educated Public Conscience in matters of taste which shall exercise a general influence on private judgment.

Perhaps the most signal of the services performed by Matthew Arnold was the constancy with which he insisted on the necessity of exercising right reason within the sphere of criticism. This is no mere rhetorical phrase. For not only is it possible to apply right methods of reasoning in art and taste, but certain evil consequences inevitably ensue when these methods are neglected. Every critic who attempts to decide a disputed point of taste must satisfy two conditions; in the first place he must judge judicially, that is to say, he must strive to regard the object of his criticism scientifically and apart from prejudice; in the second place he must verify his own conclusions by reference to some recognised standard of authority. This seems almost like the statement of a truism, and yet how rare it is to find both requirements fulfilled! How often, on the one hand, does private dislike and prejudice intervene to cut off the critic from the sight of his object; how often, on the other, is he satisfied with the unassisted decision of his own consciousness! And what are the consequences? Let me illustrate by two notable examples what happens when critics content themselves with satisfying one of the essential conditions of good criticism without attending to the other.

Probably no literary judgment ever produced more disastrous results in the interests of good taste than the article in the *Quarterly Review* on Keats's *Endymion*. Here the issue as between Liberty and Authority was raised in a very trenchant manner.

Keats was an innovator. Both in his treatment of his subject, in his diction, and in his versification, he came into violent collision with the canons of composition accepted in his day. Yet in the points of taste which called for a decision there was really nothing new. The question, for example, as to the right of coining new words or reviving disused words in poetry was as old as Horace; it had been debated in Italy by Castiglione in his *Courtier;* it had been raised in France by the Pleiad, and afterwards discussed by almost every French critic; it was familiar in England since the publication of Lyly's *Euphues.* The ruling on the point is given with admirable clearness in Horace's *Ars Poetica*—

> Multa renascentur quae jam cecidere, cadentque
> Quae nunc sunt in honore vocabula, si volet usus,
> Quem penes arbitrium est et jus et norma loquendi.

Usus; usage; the genius of the language; there was the law. The sole question was whether Keats had violated the law, and if so, with what amount of justification. Nothing could have been simpler than to apply the test of right reason. But how did Croker deliver judgment? In the first place he announced that he had only read one book of *Endymion,* which was quite enough for him. In the next place, as to the particular point at issue, he decided as follows :—

"By this time our readers must be pretty well satisfied as to the meaning of Mr. Keats's sentences and the structure of his lines. We now present them with some of the new words with which, in imitation of Mr. Leigh Hunt, he adorns our language. We are told that 'turtles *passion* their voices;' that an arbour was *nested;* and a lady's locks *gordianed up;* and to supply the names of the nouns thus verbalised, Mr. Keats with great fecundity spawns new ones: such as 'men-slugs and human *serpentry*'; the *honey-feel* of bliss; wives prepare *needments;* and so forth."

Now as to the substance of this judgment we cannot doubt that Croker was right. He had satisfied one of the conditions of sound criticism in referring to a positive standard of authority, and, like all sane critics before him, he had taken usage as the standard of measurement. Keats had offended against the genius of the English language with crudeness, violence, and affectation. But could anything be more unjudicial than the manner in which Croker told him so, without making any allowance for the fact that he was a young man, and evidently a young man of genius? More unfortunate still in the interests of criticism was the fact that Croker's judgment, besides being offensive and contemptuous in tone, was in certain points incorrect. The standard of usage by which he measured was simply the standard recognised in his own day without reference to the historic growth of the language, and he showed ignorance in supposing Keats to have been merely coining new words. Hence the " cockney school " as he called the innovators, while they justly complained of his manners, could also point to his mistakes.

They hardened themselves in impenitence, and began to criticise by rules of their own the practice of the prevailing school, whom, with a ludicrous self-importance, they called the disciples of "one Boileau." The general reader was puzzled with the dispute, but when he turned to *Endymion*, and found there such an exquisite passage as

> Whence come ye, jolly Satyrs, whence come ye,
> So many, and so many, and such glee?

he was amazed at the blindness of the Quarterly Reviewer, and concluding that he must be entirely wrong, rejected his whole standard of measurement —though it was really a just one—to the irreparable damage of good taste and common sense.

This is an example of the consequences of not judging judicially. As an illustration of the results of judging by a merely private standard, I think I shall not be mistaken in citing Matthew Arnold's lecture on the Literary Influence of Academies. You will remember that he there criticises a great number of English authors, amongst others Addison, Jeremy Taylor, Burke, and Mr. Ruskin, from whose works he quotes passages as samples of bad taste in writing. It is plain that Matthew Arnold is here judging judicially. All the examples he produces are really examples of bad taste. All of them are selected with great fineness of perception and great accuracy of instinct. But whereas the kind of taste they exhibit is extremely diverse, specific, and characteristic of the individual, Matthew Arnold chooses for his own purposes to ascribe their defects to one single source, and that a national one. He says: "Adopting Dr. Newman's expressive word, I say that in the bulk of the intellectual work of a nation which has no centre, no intellectual metropolis like an Academy—like M. Sainte-Beuve's 'sovereign organ of opinion,' like M. Renan's 'recognised authority in matters of tone and taste'—there is observable a note of provinciality. Now to get rid of provinciality is a certain stage of culture, a stage the positive results of which we must not make of too much importance, but which is nevertheless indispensable; for it brings us on to the platform, where alone the best and highest intellectual work can be said to begin." There have been some who shrank from bringing an indictment against a whole nation. Matthew Arnold had no such diffidence. But what is the supposed standard by which he judges? The note of provinciality? How can the genius of a great nation be called provincial? Of what central society is a nation a province? Is it not plain that, when Matthew Arnold produces a rhetorical effect by a phrase like this, he is judging by a measure recognised only by himself? The world would not have accepted Quintilian's judgment on Seneca's style as conclusive, if he had not criticised it by canons which the world could understand.

Thus then we are brought to the practical question —What is the final authority to which right reason should refer in judging of matters of taste? I do not think that we can be in doubt about the answer.

In every art the standard is the example of the great artist, the practice of those who are acknowledged to be masters in the art. Not, however, because they are arbitrary dictators. There are, I think, two paramount reasons why the standard must be settled by them. One is that argument from antiquity which is so admirably stated by Sir Joshua Reynolds in his *Discourses on Painting*. He says: " The modern who recommends himself as a standard may justly be suspected as ignorant of the true end, and unacquainted with the proper object, of the art which he professes. To follow such a guide will not only retard the student but mislead him. On whom then can he rely, or who will show him the path that leads to excellence? The answer is obvious: those great masters who have travelled the same road with success are the most likely to conduct others. The works of those who have stood the test of ages have a claim to that respect and veneration to which no modern can pretend. The duration and stability of their fame is sufficient to evince that it has not been suspended upon the slender thread of fashion and caprice, but bound to the human heart by every tie of sympathetic approbation."

But there is, it seems to me, another reason even more powerful than the argument from antiquity, though it merely presents a different side of the same truth : great artists are the standards of art, because they are old no doubt, but also because they are representative. I take all great poetry to be not so much what Plato thought it, the utterance of individual genius, half inspired, half insane, as the enduring voice of the soul and conscience of man living in society. The great poets and orators of Greece and Rome are justly accepted as our masters in eloquence, because their works present in an ideal form lasting records of the thoughts and emotions which the human heart experiences in the various vicissitudes of active life. For example, Milton says, in words which are a living part of our language,

> Fame is the spur that the clear spirit doth raise
> (That last infirmity of noble mind)
> To scorn delights and live laborious days.

But is it not a striking thought that, between two and three thousand years before, the same sublime logic should be found in the words with which Homer makes Sarpedon animate the courage of Glaucus, and which have scarcely lost anything of their original nobility, in the version of Homer's English translator?

> Could all our care elude the gloomy grave
> Which claims alike the fearful and the brave,
> For lust of fame I would not vainly dare
> In fighting fields to urge the soul to war.
> But since, alas! ignoble age must come,
> Disease, and death's inexorable doom,
> The life that others pay let us bestow,
> And give to Fame what we to Nature owe.
> Brave though we fall, and honoured if we live,
> Or let us glory gain, or glory give.

We watch the conflict between divine and human law in the *Antigone* of Sophocles, and we realise the eternal truth of the dramatic situation when we pass to the history of England and see it repeated in the tragedy of Alice Lisle. How intelligible seems the dispute between the Just and Unjust Argument in the *Clouds* of Aristophanes to the old English Tory! Why do we in this country feel a peculiar sublimity in the famous oath of Demosthenes on the souls of those who fought at Marathon and Salamis? Is it not because we cherish the memories of the men who perished under Nelson and Wellington in a later defence of European liberty? And when we read the ever memorable lines of Virgil,

> Tu regere imperio populos, Romane, memento ;
> . . . . .
> Hae tibi erunt artes, pacisque imponere morem,

what Englishman is not proud to feel how justly they may be applied to those who administer the government of India?

I conceive that it is this political spirit—I use the word *political* in its wide Greek sense—which has given a special character to the study of the classics in the English Universities since the days of Erasmus and Colet, of Cheke and Ascham. Our ideal of classical education differs alike from the æsthetic ideal of the Italian Humanists, who deified the ancients as absolute lawgivers in the sphere of abstract form, and from the scientific ideal of the German Universities, which regard the dead languages as one of the many departments of abstract knowledge. We in England, on the contrary, look on the classics as a great school of taste, and we consider the education of taste itself as a means to a practical, a political end. We have not allowed the necessarily Pagan genius of the Greek and Roman writers to undermine the foundations of the Christian faith, but treating their works as living creations of humanity, interpreting their spirit and character with the kindred sympathy of freemen, we have familiarised ourselves for centuries with the principles that governed their imagination. We appreciate their singular felicity in the choice of subject, the chastened elegance of their composition, the harmonious purity of their style.

Testimony is borne to the efficacy of this system of University education by the most illustrious of those who have pursued a different object. "The office of the English Universities," says Döllinger, "is by means of the study of classics and mathematics, combined with logic and moral philosophy and a college education to turn out for the benefit of the State and Society the cultivated and independent gentleman. I will not conceal the fact that these renovated and improved editions of the old and unfortunately extinct German bursaries, the colleges of Oxford and Cambridge, have many a time as I observed their working on the spot awakened in me feelings of envy, and led me to long for the time when we might again have something of the kind; for I could plainly perceive that their effect was to make instruction take root in the mind, and become a part of it, and that their influence extended beyond the mere communication of knowledge, to the ennobling elevation of the life and character."

What member of the English Universities, above all what member of the University of Oxford, would wish to see an education which has borne such fruit as this displaced in favour of a system calculated to promote mere self-culture? Year by year the Universities send to the Bar, to the Public Services, to the great army of Journalism, bands of recruits who diffuse the influence of their own tastes, and help to direct the movements of popular opinion. Were there to be any breach between the educated taste of the Universities, and the natural taste of the public at large, the whole system of irrigation in English æsthetic culture would be tainted at its source. The taste of the Universities would become more monastic, more epicurean; the taste of the public would grow more rude, more barbarous. It should surely therefore be the object of all patriotic endeavour to strengthen the established principle of authority in matters of taste, and to widen its base so as to meet the necessities of our imperial society.

A great opportunity of advancing in this direction seems to be offered by the foundation of the new Oxford School of English Language and Literature. For while the ancient classics must always remain our primal authority in determining what are the principles of good taste, it is in the classics of our own country that we can best study the manner in which these principles have been and should be applied. The tablets of the English School are still almost a blank: it will depend upon the first teachers and examiners what shall be written in them. You may make it a genuine school of taste, which shall show the student what is the true standard of excellence in English writing, and how he may measure for himself the aberrations of eccentric genius. In that case the School will follow the lines of *Literæ Humaniores*. You will cause the greatest English writers to be studied mainly for the purpose of understanding their spirit and character; you will show each of them in his just proportions, and the place which he occupies in our literature as a whole; how he was affected by, how he represented, and how he himself influenced, the movement of his own age. In such a school the exact study of language will be, as it is in *Literæ Humaniores*, of the highest value in helping to unlock the secrets of thought, and in exhibiting the orderly development of the laws of taste and harmony. Language is the instrument of thought, and, like the winged sandals of Mercury, it may aid the mind to mount into the higher regions of thought and imagination. But it would be an error to take Mercury's sandals as the source of his divinity, and something of the kind would happen, if, as might be done in the English School, the study of language were allowed to predominate over the study of literature. The study of language in itself is, like every branch of science, of the highest intellectual interest. But were it to be raised above literature, or even studied apart from literature, I venture to say that you would be wasting an unequalled opportunity; for you would be introducing a foreign educational principle which can never acclimatise itself in the genius of England and Oxford. You might under such conditions get a school of archæological research, which would doubtless be of use and interest to the special student; but you would not get, what you may still get, a school capable of exercising a national influence in the discipline of English taste.

I have now arrived at something like a practical conclusion to the inquiry with which I started. A question is naturally raised by the scepticism of an old society, whether any law or authority can be recognised as binding in matters of taste. The universal instinct, which in every society prompts men to insist on their right of judging in such matters, seems to point to the existence of some principle of authority in the constitution of human nature. But in what way can this authority be enforced? I have shown that it is idle to expect Englishmen to submit their private liberty of judgment to any external tribunal of taste. It would appear, however, to be a less hopeless task, by close attention to great works of art, to create a consciousness of what is truly beautiful, and so to form a canon of taste which shall impose itself on the individual judgment. A public conscience of this kind must be the product of education, and the education which is required is precisely that which has been long established in the English Universities.

As for the particular functions of this Chair in promoting the education of taste, several conditions have to be regarded. I do not think that the duties of a Professor of Poetry lie mainly in the illustration of technical principles; for in poetry, even less than in the other arts, is great work the result of mere attention to rules; it is the result of the inspiration, corrected by the severe self-discipline, of genius. Moreover, the rare occasions on which the Professor of Poetry makes his appearance in the lecture-room must preclude him from giving that minute and systematic instruction in the subject which is rather the function of a resident Professor of Literature On the other hand, there are questions of taste constantly and naturally rising out of the doubts of a self-conscious society—conflicts between Liberty and Authority, between Novelty and Tradition— which suggest subjects that may be profitably considered from this Chair. I shall therefore hold myself at liberty to treat Poetry in that wide and general sense of the word which makes it coextensive with the creative power of the Imagination, and I shall devote my lectures mainly to examining the laws and conditions on which the life of Poetry depends. This may be done in a variety of ways: by dwelling on the principles of great poetry; by observing the manner in which these have been applied by great poets; by analysing the causes of national movements of imagination; and by tracing the development of individual genius. Much also may be learned from the fate of poets, who in all ages have fallen victims to Affectation, Exaggeration, Conceit, False Wit, False Sentiment, in a word to all the immortal fallacies by which the fascination of novelty bewitches the inexperience and credulity of taste. I am aware that the task I propose to myself is one of great difficulty. To define the laws of Good Taste becomes always harder as civilised society moves farther away from the primal sources of poetical inspiration. But at least we shall be looking in the right direction if we take for our standard the principle which Pericles recommended to the Athenians—φιλοσοφοῦμεν ἄνευ μαλακίας : We pursue culture in a manly spirit.

PART II

LIFE IN POETRY

I

POETICAL CONCEPTION

THERE is a certain irony in the relation between art and criticism. The artist under the impulse of imitation within him follows the lead of Nature, and brings his imaginative idea into being guided only by instinct and judgment. At a later stage in the history of society, perhaps after creative energy has ceased, comes the critic, and traces the idea backward as far as he can through the artist's mind, always stopping short, however, of the real sources of life. Then deeming that he has penetrated the secret of art, the critic begins to lay down the law for the artist, and his law is usually wrong.

Wrong, indeed, he is almost bound to be, because he has followed the order not of Nature but of logic. Yet, so vast is the persuasive power of logic, that deductive criticism, *a priori* criticism, has had an appreciable influence on the course of literature, has, in fact, been the parent of all the Academies. And it is observable that this kind of criticism flourishes most in societies in which the spirit of political liberty has been, or is being, extinguished. Academies began to thrive in the Italian Republics after they had lost their freedom, in France when the nation was tending towards absolute monarchy. As regards the art of poetry, those who helped to found the Academies submitted themselves without reservation to the authority of Aristotle. Misconstruing the text of the *Poetics*, they deduced from their own misunderstanding of the philosopher a code of supposed artistic necessity, which had no basis in the nature of things. They succeeded in getting recognition for a set of rules which Corneille, while submitting to them in theory, was obliged to disregard in practice, and which were of such stringent logic as to convince Voltaire and Frederick the Great that Shakespeare was a barbarian and a bungler.

Criticism, in my opinion, is only of value so long as it follows an inductive method. As I said in my inaugural lecture, the sole authorities in the art of poetry are the great classical poets of the world: the business of the critic is to infer from their work the true means of producing lasting pleasure. I propose, therefore, in a series of lectures to discuss the question of life in poetry, regarding it in three aspects: (1) Poetical Conception; (2) Poetical Expression; (3) Poetical Decadence. In my present lecture I shall endeavour to trace the course of an imaginative creation from the moment when a design first begins to shape itself in a poet's brain. I shall ask to be allowed to make but one assumption—one, indeed, which has been regarded as self-evidently true by all sound critics from the time of Aristotle—namely, that the end of the fine arts is to produce enduring pleasure for the imagination. With the help of this I shall then attempt to frame a working definition of poetry, and shall inquire from the nature of the art what must necessarily be its fundamental principles. These I shall verify by applying them to poems which are allowed to have attained the position of classics, as well as to others which, after enjoying a temporary popularity, have fallen into neglect. Finally, after establishing my conclusions, I shall consider what practical bearing they have on the production of poetry in our own day.

With respect to life in poetry, as distinguished from life in the other fine arts, it is plain, in the first place, that poetry takes a distinct way of its own to produce pleasure. It proceeds differently from music, because that is an art which appeals to the emotions through the ear, and, except when it is joined to words, seldom raises ideas and images in the mind. It differs again from painting and sculpture, for, though these can suggest ideas and images, they can do so only through the associations of sight. Painting and sculpture can represent movement and action, but their representation is limited to a single moment of time. For instance, in Raphael's great picture of the Fire in the Borgo, there is an extraordinary suggestion of life and passion. You see a mother just handing her child out of a window; a young man in the act of letting himself drop from a roof; other persons energetically striving to save their goods from the flames; and others again, whose property has been consumed, prostrated with despair. But the infant is never actually rescued; the young man remains suspended; we know not how much salvage is effected, or what becomes of the homeless refugees.

Another aspect of this arrested life in painting and sculpture is expressed in Keats's fine Ode on a Grecian Urn :

> Heard melodies are sweet, but those unheard
> Are sweeter : therefore, ye soft pipes, play on ;
> Not to the sensual ear, but more endeared
> Pipe to the spirit ditties of no tone.
>   Fair youth, beneath the trees thou canst not leave
>   Thy song, nor ever can these leaves be bare ;
>   Bold lover, never, never canst thou kiss,
> Though winning near the goal—yet do not grieve :
>   She cannot fade, though thou hast not thy bliss :
>   For ever wilt thou love, and she be fair.

Poetry can represent ideal life of this kind, but it can do much more. It can call up before the mind, by a kind of inward painting, images of outward forms which the act of sight has stored in the memory; and though some critics, like Sir Philip Sidney, have thought that poetry can be dissociated from metre, still the practice of the greatest poets shows that it is the nature of the art to produce pleasure by means akin to music. Beyond this, however, poetry, working through language, can free itself, as painting and sculpture cannot, from the limitations of time and space, and can represent in words, what music cannot, a series of connected actions.

But this is not all. Poetry differs from its sister arts not only in the variety of its means but in the diversity of its effects. Since it reaches its ends through instruments so complex as thought and language, it comprehends many styles; unlike painting, for example, in which Sir Joshua Reynolds admits only one legitimate method; insisting — whether rightly or wrongly I do not presume to question—that the single aim of every great painter must be the Historic or grand style. In poetry, on the contrary, the Epic, the Dramatic, the Ethical or Satirical modes of composition are all distinct: each is capable of producing a different kind of pleasure: and any attempt to introduce the style proper to one department into another would be a sign of incapacity in the poet. Suited to different moods of the mind, these various kinds of poetry adapt themselves to the wants of opposite conditions of society. Satire, that peculiarly Roman form of poetry, found a congenial soil in the manners of the City under the Empire, when the epic, dramatic, and lyric motives of composition all languished. In England, after the Restoration, the questions which most strongly stirred men's imaginations were of a religious and political kind. To satisfy this taste the representative poet of the day produced works like *Absalom and Achitophel*, *The Medal*, and *Religio Laici*, defending his style on the plea of its fitness for his artistic needs:

> And this unpolished rugged verse I chose,
> As fittest for discourse and nearest prose.

You will observe that Dryden says *nearest* prose; not actually prose; meaning that his style suited his subject, and that this, though akin to matter usually treated in prose, had in itself an element of imagination and emotion which adapted it for expression in metre. When Matthew Arnold, looking to the comparatively matter-of-fact nature of their thought, says that Dryden and Pope are not classics of our poetry, but classics of our prose, he is the victim of a verbal fallacy. For if the end of poetry be to produce enduring pleasure for the imagination, and if Dryden and Pope, adopting the usual machinery of poetry, satisfy this end, these writers cannot be denied a place among our poets merely because their subjects are less imaginative than is the case with metrical writers of another kind. We may, I think, be content to define poetry as the art which produces pleasure for the imagination by imitating human actions, thoughts, and passions, in metrical language. The life of poetry is in fact that which is beautifully described by Spenser in his *Ruins of Time:*

> For deeds do die however nobly done,
> And thoughts of men do as themselves decay,
> But wise words, taught in numbers for to run,
> Recorded by the Muses, live for ay,
> Ne may with storming showers be washed away,
> Ne bitter-breathing winds with harmful blast,
> Nor age, nor envy, may them ever waste.

Passing on from our definition to consider the nature of Poetical Conception, we have to remember that Fine Art does not, like photography, imitate real Nature, but the idea of Nature existing in the mind. Ideal Life is subject to laws of its own, and Horace, in his *Ars Poetica*, says very justly: "Painters and poets have always been allowed a just freedom of conception: this is an admitted fact, and the critic grants the indulgence that the poet asks." All that the poet is required to do is to create a perfect illusion; to produce what Aristotle calls τὸ πιθανόν, the effect of poetic probability; or, in other words, that idea of unity which is the essential condition of organic life.[1] When he is successful in doing this he reaches the standard of the true poet described by Pope in one of his *Imitations of Horace:*

> 'Tis he can give my heart a thousand pains,
> Can make me feel each passion that he feigns;
> Enrage, compose, with more than magic art;
> With pity and with terror rend my heart;
> And snatch me through the earth or in the air,
> To Thebes or Athens, when he will and where.

To produce this effect of organic ideal life is difficult, because in the mind Reason acts against Imagination, and because, in critical ages, men apply to poetic inventions standards of judgment proper only to scientific analysis. Aristotle, for example, cites some of the criticisms passed in his day even on the *Iliad*. Such and such a thing in the poem, said one, was contrary to fact; something else, said another, was impossible by the laws of Nature; this and that a third

---

[1] πρός τε γὰρ τὴν ποίησιν αἱρετώτερον πιθανὸν ἀδύνατον ἢ ἀπίθανον καὶ δυνατόν. Aristotle, *Poetics*, xxv. 17.

declared to be opposed to experience. But, as the philosopher shows, these objections were all ill-grounded, because—such is his vigorous phrase—"Homer tells lies as he ought."[1] He is not to be judged by the laws of material Nature; his conception is poetically true. Our imagination moves easily through his ideal world. We readily grant him his whole stock of marvellous hypothesis—gods, giants, celestial arms, and talking horses—because we feel that it proceeds from a living source in his own mind. Yet, if a sophisticated poet were to force himself to invent such things, merely to gratify our taste for the wonderful, it is certain that every intelligent reader would reject his conception with indignation and disgust.

In every genuinely inspired poetical conception there are, as Aristotle and Horace both tell us, two elements of life, one universal, the other individual. The universal element is the idea of the subject, whatever it may be, as it exists in an undeveloped state in the human mind; the individual element is the particular form and character which is impressed upon the subject by the creative genius of the poet. As regards the process of creation by which these two elements are fused into organic life, we cannot do better than attend to what is said by Horace, a poet who attempted various styles of poetry and succeeded in them all. First, says Horace, there must be complete union between the imagination of the poet and the subject he selects. "All you who write"—such is his advice in his *Ars Poetica*—"choose your subject in

[1] Aristotle, *Poetics*, xxv.

accordance with your powers; turn over in your mind what your shoulders can bear and what they cannot. The poet whose subject is completely assimilated to his genius will not fail in point of eloquence and lucid order." Every word of this advice is pregnant with thought. There is a modern school of poets which insists that all poetic creation is the work solely of the poet's mind: form, they tell us, is everything, matter nothing. But here you have one of the classic poets of the world declaring that a large portion of the life, and even of the form, of every poem is contained germinally in the subject matter. Artistic creation is not the mere act of the artist's will; the first movement of inspiration comes to him from outside; hence the solemn invocations of the greatest poets for divine aid in their undertakings; as, for example, at the opening of *Paradise Lost:*

> And chiefly thou, O Spirit, who dost prefer,
> Before all temples, the upright heart and pure,
> Instruct me, for thou knowest; thou from the first
> Wast present, and, with mighty wings outspread,
> Dovelike, satst brooding o'er the vast abyss,
> And madst it pregnant; what in me is dark
> Illumine; what is low raise and support,
> That to the height of this great argument
> I may assert Eternal Providence,
> And justify the ways of God to men.

And so too Dante, in the quaint but impressive appeal to Apollo in his *Paradiso*: "Divine Virtue, if thou wilt but inspire me to make manifest the shadow of the blessed realm which is stamped upon my brain, thou wilt see me come to the tree that thou lovest, and crown myself there with the leaves of which my *matter* and thou will make me worthy."¹ The reality and power of this inspiration from without are attested by the fact that, in many of the great poems of the world, the form appropriate to the subject has not been stamped at once upon the poet's conception. You will remember that *Paradise Lost* first suggested itself to Milton in the form of a miracle play, modelled after the Greek drama, with the accompaniment of a chorus. In the execution of this design he proceeded some way, and wrote, among other passages, Satan's speech to the Sun, which is now embodied in the Fourth Book of *Paradise Lost*. Long meditation and fresh inspirations from without were required before the poet saw why the dramatic form was unfitted to his subject, and in what mould poetic necessity demanded that his conception should come into being.

Not very different was Scott's experience in the conception of the *Lay of the Last Minstrel*. A lady asked him to write an imitation of an ancient ballad. Then, says Lockhart in his very interesting narrative: "Sir John Stoddart's casual recitation of Coleridge's unfinished *Christabel* had fixed the music of that noble fragment in his memory; and it occurs to him that, by throwing the story of Gilpin Horner into somewhat similar cadence, he might produce such an echo of the later metrical romance as would seem to connect his conclusion of the primitive *Sir Tristrem*

¹ Dante, *Paradiso*, i. 22-27.

with the imitation of the popular ballad in the *Grey Brother* and *Eve of St. John*. A single scene of feudal festivity in the Hall of Branksome, disturbed by some pranks of a nondescript goblin, was probably all that he contemplated; but his accidental confinement in the midst of a volunteer camp gave him leisure to meditate his theme to the sound of the bugle; and suddenly there flashes on him the idea of extending his simple outline so as to embrace a vivid panorama of that old Border life of war and tumult and all earnest passions with which his researches on the minstrelsy had by degrees fed his imagination, until every the minutest feature had been taken home and realised with unconscious intensity of sympathy, so that he had won for himself in the past another world hardly less familiar or complete than the present. Erskine or Cranstoun suggests that he would do well to divide the poem into cantos, and prefix to each of them a motto explanatory of the action, after the fashion of Spenser in the *Fairy Queen*. He pauses for a moment and the happiest conception of the frame-work of a picturesque narrative that ever occurred to any poet, one that Homer might have envied, the creation of the ancient Harper, starts to life. By such steps did the *Lay of the Last Minstrel* grow out of the *Minstrelsy of the Scottish Border.*"[1]

But besides this instinctive, unconscious union between the imagination of the poet and his external subject, the poet's conception, when born into the

---

[1] Lockhart's *Life of Scott*, vol. ii. p. 24 (1837).

world, must be qualified to live in the imagination of his audience. On this point too let us hear Horace. "It is difficult," says he, "to clothe universal abstract ideas with individual life and character, and you would do better to ground a play on some story as old and familiar as the *Iliad*, than to seek credit for originality by representing something that nobody has heard or thought of before." Yes, and why so? Because as the subject matter fitted for art exists in embryo in the mind in general, and not merely in the mind of the poet, the poet must satisfy those conditions of ideal life which prepare the imagination of the audience for the reception of his thought. If he attempts to conjure up an ideal situation entirely out of his own consciousness, it is almost certain that his creation will have a lifeless or mechanical appearance, or will provoke an instinctive opposition in the reader's sense of probability. If, on the other hand, he seeks to vitalise the inorganic matter already existing in general conception, his audience will, as it were, conspire with him in the act of creation, and the general pleasure his work will arouse will insure for it immortality. For this reason the greater Greek dramatists grounded their plays on the popular mythology, while the Elizabethan poets took their plots, as a rule, from novels or histories with which their audience were already familiar.

We conclude, then, with Horace that the secret of life in poetry lies in the power to give individual form to universal ideas of nature adapted for expression in any of the recognised classes of metrical composition.

Let us now look at the question from another side, and apply this law to poems whose position has been finally settled by the judgment of mankind. Why, for example, is the *Iliad* so full of life? Mainly because the subject of the poem was very much alive in Homer's own imagination: everything in it seems to be of a piece, and to be said naturally and without conscious effort. It must, however, also be admitted that Homer enjoyed an immense advantage over all his successors by starting in almost complete unity with his theme. When he composed the *Iliad* the poetical mode of conceiving things was the natural mode of conception; so that we may almost say the image of the poem pressed itself on his mind from the outside ready made, and all that he had to do was to find an adequate mould for the expression. In his verse the commonest objects and actions—a ship being rowed over the sea; a banquet; a sacrifice —are described in a manner at once grand and simple; not, I imagine, merely because Homer was a great poet, but because, in his age, almost everything was conceived as having a divine life of its own. Inability to conceive of Nature in the same spirit of childlike poetry extorted from Wordsworth his passionate cry of regret:

> Great God! I had rather be
> A Pagan suckled in a creed out-worn,
> So might I, standing on this pleasant lea,
> Have glimpses that would make me less forlorn,
> Have sight of Proteus rising from the sea,
> Or hear old Triton blow his wreathèd horn.

As regards the individual element in his poem, therefore—the union, that is to say, between the poet's imagination and his subject — Homer had everything in his favour. What is to be said, however, of the union between his imagination and the imagination of his audience? Think how much there is in the *Iliad* to militate against the production of the desired effect! A scheme of theology which more than two thousand years ago was repudiated by the philosopher; a view of Nature which is to-day incredible to the schoolboy; a representation of warfare which must seem ridiculous to the soldier; and a recital of methods of killing and wounding which, since the invention of firearms, has lost its interest even for the surgeon. What is it, then, in Homer's poetry that produces such unequalled pleasure? It is the element of the Universal. Nowhere else, except in Shakespeare, will you meet with so many characters which are immediately perceived to be living imitations of mankind; so many sentiments which at once move the affections; so many situations of elemental interest and pathos;—nowhere else will you find the images of things adapting themselves so readily to the movement of verse whose majestic roll seems animated by the very life of Nature, and yet is found on examination to be the product of idealising Art.

In the *Æneid* we perceive the case to be quite different. Here we have evidently a sharp separation between the subject and the mind of the poet, and we understand that Virgil's matter must have been long meditated, assimilated, and transmuted, before the

poem was ready to be born into the world. The
hero of the *Æneid* is, comparatively speaking, a poor
creature; the sentiments and manners represented in
the poem, far from making us breathe a naturally heroic
atmosphere, provoke question and criticism; many of
the incidents appear improbable, being in fact trans-
ferred from Homer, and having lost some of their life
in the passage. We feel through the last six books of
the epic that the poet is only carrying on the action
because the machinery of his work requires him to
do so. Nevertheless from the very first the *Æneid*
has been alive; it is alive still. What is the secret of
its vitality? Partly, no doubt, the fact that Virgil
was able to impregnate his subject with certain
qualities of his own nature in which no poet has ever
equalled him, piety, gravity, sweetness. But partly
also the fact that he has developed out of his subject,
with unrivalled art, the elements that it contains of
the Universal. We know how the *Æneid* appeared
to Virgil's contemporaries. They hailed it as some-
thing greater than the *Iliad*. "Nescio quid majus
nascitur Iliade," said Propertius; and though this
sounds like patriotic exaggeration, there is a sense
in which it is true. For the *Æneid* is *par excellence*
the epic of Civil Life. It is the poem of a Roman,
having for its theme the foundation of the Roman
Empire, and reflecting at every point the majesty
of the Roman character. That was the special
quality in it which so deeply influenced the genius
of Dante; and wherever the civilising power of the
Roman Empire has been felt, that is, over the whole

of modern Europe, there will this element of life in the *Æneid* continue to produce sublime pleasure.

But there is a wider, a more human sense, in which the *Æneid* may be said to be greater than the *Iliad*, and that is in the conception of the pathetic. Not, of course, that Homer is wanting in pathos; he covers a larger surface of the pathetic than Virgil; but at certain points Virgil goes deeper. His great poetical principle is embodied in the line, " Sunt lacrimae rerum et mentem mortalia tangunt," which a modern poet has beautifully rendered :

> Tears waken tears, and honour honour brings,
> And mortal hearts are moved by mortal things.[1]

Inadequate as the character of Æneas is on the heroic side, it is exceedingly human, and the poet has sounded the deepest feelings of our kind in the description of his hero's adventures and misfortunes. The narrative of the fall of Troy, the death of Dido, the meeting of Æneas and Anchises in the lower world, the deaths of Nisus and Euryalus, these things will move the hearts of men through all time. Virgil in such passages has individualised the Universal; his images live for ever in a stream of verse as deep and full as Homer's is swift and brilliant.

Let me now, by way of contrast, refer to a poem which having once enjoyed great popularity has long passed, not indeed into oblivion, but neglect. When the *Thebais* was first published, we know from Juvenal that it was received with general enthusiasm,

---

[1] F. W. Myers, *Classical Essays*, p. 120.

and even in the Middle Ages the reputation of Statius was so great—mainly no doubt on account of his legendary Christianity—that Dante assigns him a place in his *Purgatory*. To-day he is known only to professed scholars. Why? If we try to realise the manner in which the *Thebais* came into existence we shall be able to account for its literary fate. Statius so far complied with Horace's advice in the *Ars Poetica* as to choose a subject not less well known to his audience than "the tale of Troy divine." Unfortunately it had no special elements of interest which could touch his heart as a man and a Roman; hence his subject never really passed into his own imagination; he hatched it, so to speak, like an artificial incubator. Let us try to watch him composing the Fourth Book, which is much the best in the poem. Here his business was, in some way or other, to conduct Polynices and the Argive army to Thebes, where Eteocles had usurped the government. Statius sets to work in a style which is eminently logical, and, in a way, scientific. He starts his expedition with stir and bustle, and tells us of all the rumours which the news of the invasion set in circulation at Thebes. Then he appears to have said to himself, "Now what effect would these rumours have had on the mind of Eteocles?" Eteocles is conceived as a gloomy tyrant. Of course, then, his bad conscience would drive him to consult the prophet Tiresias. Here came a splendid opportunity for what Horace calls "a purple patch." Tiresias practised magic in a wood; the wood must therefore be described; and described it is with great effect, and so are the magical incantations. Next it is necessary to learn the future from Laius, the founder of the ruling family, who must be brought from the infernal regions according to the precedent of Æneas, when he went thither to seek the spirit of Anchises. Statius seems to have thought within himself: "How can I have a novel and effective other-world scene, something different from Homer's and Virgil's?" and so full is he of this idea, that he puts it into the mouth of his imaginary characters. Tiresias, being blind, has to be helped in his incantations by his daughter Manto, who, after she has performed the necessary rites, informs her father that hell is in view; but, says she, "what is the use of bringing up the monsters of Erebus, the idly raging Centaurs, the Giants, and all the rest of them?"[1] In other words, Homer and Virgil have done all this kind of thing before. "Quite true," observes the practical prophet, "everybody knows about the rebounding stone of Sisyphus, and the fleeing waters of Tantalus, and the wheel of Ixion: let us, for a change, have the spirits of the wicked Argives and Thebans."[2] And accordingly up come these from the nether world, one after another, "stern Abas, and guilty Prœtus, and mild Phoroneus, and mutilated Pelops, and Œnomaus all bestained with cruel dust."[3] Laius appears the last, and delivers himself of an oracle so judiciously obscure that, for all the information it affords his hearers, they and the poet might have spared

[1] *Thebais*, iv. 534-536. [2] *Ibid.* 537-544. [3] *Ibid.* 589-591.

themselves the trouble they took to procure his advice. Whoever compares this with the Sixth Book of the *Æneid* will see the difference between Life and Machinery in poetry. Statius is full of cleverness and learning; he is careful to follow poetical precedents; but his creation is not alive; he himself did not care about it; his Roman audience did not care about it, though they applauded it; it is vain therefore to expect an audience to care about it in the nineteenth century.

How admirable is the reasoning of Juvenal in the matter! "These things," he says in substance, "have no life. I must have life in my poetry: I shall accordingly write Satire, and shall deal with matters that really do interest us: every sort of human action and passion, wishes, fears, anger, pleasure, joy, philosophy, these are my subjects."[1] Hence, though he is only a satirical poet, Juvenal, having this strong individual element in himself, and the element of the Universal in his theme, has contrived to produce permanent pleasure for the imagination; while Statius, with his grandiose subject and his sounding verse, has fallen into neglect. Juvenal makes us see, as if they were things of to-day, the perils of the streets in ancient Rome;[2] the "bald Nero" and his flatterers in council over their turbot;[3] the Trojan-born aristocracy cringing for the rich parvenu's doles;[4] the bronze head of Sejanus's statue turned into pots and pans.[5]

[1] Juvenal, *Sat.* i. 85-6.   [2] *Ibid.* iii.   [3] *Ibid.* iv.
[4] *Ibid.* i. 99-100.   [5] *Ibid.* x. 61-64.

And when a satirist is full, like Juvenal, of universal interest, we can listen to him even though he talks mainly of himself. Witness the opening of Pope's *Epistle to Arbuthnot*, where every word seems to throb and tingle with sensitive life:

> Shut, shut the door, good John! fatigued, I said,
> Tie up the knocker, say I'm sick, I'm dead.
> The dog-star rages, nay, 'tis past a doubt,
> All Bedlam and Parnassus is let out.
> Fire in each eye, and papers in each hand,
> They rave, recite, and madden through the land.

And so on, through all the poet's interviews with his literary tormentors, till we reach the climax in the portrait of Atticus, where universal truth lives as lastingly as in the characters of Achilles and Hamlet:

> Peace to all such! But were there one whose fires
> True genius kindles and true fame inspires;
> Blest with each talent and each art to please,
> And born to write, converse, and live with ease;
> Should such a man, too fond to rule alone,
> Bear like the Turk no brother near the throne;
> View him with scornful yet with jealous eyes,
> And hate for arts that caused himself to rise;
> Damn with faint praise, assent with civil leer,
> And, without sneering, teach the rest to sneer;
> Willing to wound, and yet afraid to strike,
> Just hint a fault, and hesitate dislike;
> Alike reserved to blame and to command,
> A timorous foe and a suspicious friend;
> Dreading e'en fools, by flatterers besieged,
> And so obliging that he ne'er obliged;
> Like Cato give his little senate laws,
> And sit attentive to his own applause;

> While wits and Templars every sentence raise,
> And wonder with a foolish face of praise :
> Who but must laugh if such a man there be ?
> Who would not weep if Atticus were he ?

Even in lyric poetry, which seems above all other forms of the art to be the vehicle of individual feeling, if the verse is to have enduring life, the universal must be present either in the simplicity of the emotion or in the common interest of the theme. No better illustration of this truth can be found than Gray's *Elegy*, a composition which has perhaps produced more general pleasure than any in our literature. Take the last line of the first stanza : " And leaves the *world* to *darkness* and to *me*," where two of the most abstract words in the language are combined with the most personal. Or again, the closing stanza, in which the epitaph on the individual is brought to a climax in the most universal idea that the human mind can conceive :

> No further seek his merits to disclose,
>   Or draw his frailties from their dread abode,
> (There they alike in trembling hope repose)
>   The bosom of his Father and his God.

Difficile est proprie communia dicere. Difficult indeed ! But to overcome the difficulty is the triumph of art. And here the triumph is complete. How simple and obvious are all the reflections, and yet how individual they seem in the form in which the poet presents them ! A single familiar image is selected as the centre of a group of truths which every man acknowledges, and, as a rule, forgets ; each stanza seems to condense in words the experience of human society; and breathes in its solemn harmony the catholic teaching of the grave.

If then we are justified in believing this law of life in poetry to be what we have described it, we may draw some practical conclusions from it with regard to the poetry of our own day. For is not one of the most striking characteristics in modern poetical conception the exaggeration of the individual element and the neglect of the universal? Many of the spiritual forces in our society—notably reaction from materialism, vulgarity, commonplace—impel the imagination towards a state of transcendental monasticism, thrusting the mind inward upon itself, and urging it to the contemplation of its own ideas without considering them in relation to the ideas of others. Poetical conception so formed will, by its own innate force, command attention and respect from those whose spiritual experience has been in any way similar, and yet, as it has been framed without reference to the wants of human nature at large, will necessarily lack the main element of enduring life. This is the danger that in my opinion threatens the position of one of the most eminent metrical composers of our own generation; I need hardly say that I refer to Robert Browning. No one who is capable of appreciating genius will refuse to admire the powers of this poet, the extent of his sympathy and interest in external things, the boldness of his invention, the energy of his analysis, the audacity of his experiments. But so absolutely does he exclude all consideration for the reader from his choice of subject, so arbitrarily, in his treatment of his themes, does he compel his audience to place themselves at his own point of view, that the life of his art depends entirely on his individuality. Should future generations be less inclined than our own to surrender their imaginations to his guidance, he will not be able to appeal to them through that element of life which lies in the Universal.

If it is an error to look for the life of poetry exclusively in the mind of the poet, it is no less an error to derive its sources from the current tastes of the people. What is universal is always popular in the true sense of the word; but what is popular is not necessarily universal. Yet the modern poet is under a strong temptation to adapt his conceptions to the fashion of the moment. Modern invention and science occupy the imagination with a dissolving panorama of passing interests; and to embody these in a striking form is the proper end of the art of journalism. The ability and success with which the journalist discharges his functions naturally excite emulation among those who practise the fine arts. They imitate his methods. Hence they are led to Realism in the choice of subject, Impressionism, Literary Paradox, and all those other short cuts in art through which seekers after novelty attempt to discover nine-days wonders for the imagination. By the very hypothesis of fine art such methods must necessarily be fallacious; because, when the temporary conditions to which they owe their being pass away, the pleasure they excite perishes with them.

The abiding life of poetry must be looked for far beneath the surface of society: it should be the aim of the poet first to divine the true *character* of his age, as distinct from the shows and illusions of things, and then to discover which of the great moulds of poetry corresponds most closely with the nature of his thought. This is a truth written on every page of classic English poetry. In the reign of Elizabeth the life of the nation had its centre in the Crown, and poetical energy found its natural expression in the drama. The eighteenth century was an age of aristocracy and philosophic thought; accordingly the characteristic poetry of that era was ethical or elegiac. With the French Revolution began the great democratic movement which has prevailed for a hundred years, and from that time to this the dominant note in poetry has been lyrical.

I think that one difficulty in the way of forming a poetic conception of Nature and Society in our own day arises from our adhering too tenaciously to a poetical tradition which no longer corresponds with the life and reality of things. Poetry, like politics, is an outward mode of expressing the active principle of social life, and for three generations the master-spirit in social action has been Liberty. In politics we have seen Liberty embodying itself in all that we understand by the word Democracy; sweeping away privilege, test, restriction; widening the basis of government; wakening the energies of free thought; shaking the foundations of faith and authority. In poetry the same principle has found utterance in the varied emotions we comprehend under the name of Romance. Romance was heard in the voice of Wordsworth sending out his thought into the heart of Nature; in the voice of Byron rebellious against the laws of Society; in the voice of Shelley dreaming of the destinies of humanity; in the voice of Tennyson penetrating the depths and intricacies of private sorrow. For universal conceptions such as these Romance has been the fitting vehicle of expression. But alike in politics and in poetry, the productive power of Liberty seems to have reached its natural limits. Can Democracy, apart from hereditary Monarchy, solve the problems it has itself created? civilise the swarming populations of the city? bind the young and vigorous colony more closely to the venerable Mother Country? charm away the demon of social envy? curb the fury of political faction? Or is Romance the poetical form that can most fitly reflect those scientific ideas of Nature and Society which press so powerfully on the modern imagination? It is just because Romance is unable to do this that the school of poetry which has adhered most faithfully to the romantic tradition now sounds in its art the note of lyric pessimism.

There is surely an analogy in the tasks that lie respectively before the modern statesman and the modern poet. It is the part of the one, rising above the pettinesses of party, to lead, to construct, to consolidate in an imperial spirit. Not very different should be the aim of poetry. The romantic poet regards himself as "the idle singer of an empty day": is it, however, just to charge the age with emptiness merely because it affords no materials fitted for expression in a particular poetical mould? The art of poetry has many mansions; and it does not follow that, if one mode of conceiving Nature has become trite and mechanical, the resources of Nature herself are exhausted. Sound reasoning would seem rather to point to the conclusion that, since the subjective and lyrical forms of poetry languish, the sources of life are rather to be sought on the objective side, and in the dramatic, ethical, and satiric forms of the art.

But perhaps to speculate precisely on this point is to fall into the very error of academic criticism which we started with condemning. It will be best to conclude with reiterating the truth that, while the force of individual liberty and genius is absolutely necessary to inspire poetic conception with the breath of life, obedience to the law of the Universal in Nature is no less needful, if the life thus generated is to be enduring.

II

POETICAL EXPRESSION

EXPERIENCE shows me that, in England, it is unsafe to suppose that the most elementary truths of criticism will be accepted as self-evident, or that the most familiar terms can be left without explanation. In opening this series of lectures on "Life in Poetry," I began, as I was bound to do, with a definition. I said that " Poetry was the art which produces pleasure for the imagination by imitating human actions, thoughts, and passions in metrical language." Since poetry had been regarded as an imitative art by a hundred well-known critics from Aristotle downwards, and since not only Aristotle, but such modern and Christian critics as Wordsworth and Coleridge, had agreed that the end of poetry was to produce pleasure for the imagination, I fondly hoped that what I called a "working" definition might pass without argument. But what happened? A critic in a weekly paper of high standing supposed that by using the word "imitation" in relation to poetry I must necessarily mean the photographic reproduction of external objects, and that the word "pleasure" must by implication carry with it some low and materialistic sense. Reasoning on this hypothesis, he contrived, in the first place, to misinterpret the argument in my lecture to an extent which, in my vanity, I had hoped to be impossible, and, further, to convince other people, as appeared from the correspondence which ensued, that I was not only an ignorant but an immoral person.

As I shall need my definition for the purposes of my present lecture, let me say at starting that I regard poetry as a fine art, and therefore subject to the operation of laws which, like those of the other fine arts, are capable of explanation; that I call it an imitative art because its function is to find beautiful forms for the expression of ideas existing universally, but embryonically, in the human imagination; that while I consider the end of poetry, as of all the fine arts, to be, to produce pleasure for the imagination, this idea of pleasure includes rapture, enthusiasm, even pain of the kind intended by Aristotle, when he says that Tragedy effects a purgation of Pity and Terror by means of those passions. I must apologise to my present audience for an explanation which they will probably find superfluous, but as I desire to make my argument as clear and convincing as is possible from the nature of the subject, it is best to proceed by the ordinary course of dialectic.

My last lecture was devoted to an investigation of the law of poetical conception, which may be called the soul of poetical life. We sought for the universal conditions under which an idea must germinate and come into being in the imagination of the individual poet, in order afterwards to enjoy immortal life in the imagination of the world. I shall deal to-day with the laws of poetical expression, in other words, of the outward form or body in which the poet's conception is manifested. And just as in human beings it is the complete union of soul and body which constitutes the harmonious life of each person, so in poetry the beauty and propriety of the imaginative form will proceed from the organic unity of the imaginative conception. This is a truth which requires to be thoroughly realised, and I think I cannot make it clear to you better than by reverting to the words of Horace I have already cited:

> Cui lecta potenter erit res,
> Nec facundia deseret hunc nec lucidus ordo.

I do not understand Horace to mean that just conception in poetry necessarily inspires the poet with the best form of expression. Such an opinion would be contrary to experience: the history of poetry shows that many true poets, especially young poets—men like Persius and Oldham, for example— have wanted the perfect art which is needed to do justice to their thoughts. Thus Dryden, in his lines on the death of Oldham, asks:

> O early ripe, to thy abundant store
> What could advancing age have added more?
> It might—what Nature never gives the young—
> Have taught the numbers of thy native tongue:
> But Satire needs not those, and Wit may shine
> Through the harsh cadence of a rugged line.

Horace is speaking rather of the inward conditions that must be satisfied before a poetical conception can be animated with the spark of life. What are they? First of all, *res*; the poet must be sure that he has something poetical to say. Next, what he has to say must be *lecta potenter*, chosen suitably or according to capacity,—a phrase which, I think, has a double meaning. The subject must be treated in accordance with the powers of the poet, and conformably with what its own nature requires. Poets are often anxious to excel in styles of poetry for which nature has not qualified them. Tennyson, for example, constantly attempted the poetical drama, but never with success. Keats and Shelley failed conspicuously whenever they aimed at comic humour. Again, the subject must be treated in the manner which its inherent nature and the circumstances of the age demand. *Paradise Lost*, as we have already seen, required epic treatment; it could not have properly taken a dramatic form, at least in Milton's time. On the other hand, when the conditions of just conception have been satisfied; when the fruitful subject has been selected; when its true poetical character—be it epic, dramatic, or satiric—has been realised; when the poet has allowed the subject in all its bearings to blend and harmonise with his own imagination; then, as Horace says, he will find himself provided, as if by Nature herself, with the richness of language and the lucid arrangement of thought necessary to give to his conception the appearance of organic life.

We have seen that in every just poetical conception there are two indispensable elements of life— one individual, one universal. Both of these elements must therefore reappear in the form of poetical expression in which the poetical conception is given to the world. The individual element in every great poem is imparted to it solely by the genius of the poet. It includes everything relating to the treatment of the subject, all that helps to produce the organic effect; the just distribution of the matter, the particular methods of diction, the peculiar combinations of metrical movement; whatever, in fact, constitutes the distinction, the character, the style of the work. All this resembles the individuality of the human body, and indeed the style of every genuine poet may be compared to that total effect of personality produced by the combination of feature, the expression of the countenance, the complexion, the shape, which makes each single member of the human race in some respect different from every other member of it. To lay down laws of style for poetry is to attempt the impossible. What form other than that of the *Divine Comedy* could have expressed the universal idea contained in the subject? Yet what critical analysis could ever have arrived at the form invented by the genius of Dante? In Dante doubtless there is a strong lyrical note; in the epic and dramatic forms of poetry, on the contrary, the universal element predominates; but even in these the individual genius of the poet will always make itself felt by some characteristic mode of expression. The treatment of a tragic subject by Ben Jonson differs from the treatment of Shakespeare; Shakespeare's manner is equally distinguishable from Fletcher's; Pope's satiric style is unlike Dryden's, and Byron's stands apart from both.

We cannot go beyond the simple principle of Horace, which says that the right form of expression will spring naturally out of a just mode of conception. In all that portion of the art of poetry which relates to the treatment of the subject, the sole guide of the poet must be his own judgment: the extent of his success in the expression of his ideas will be principally determined by the possession of a quality which, as a factor of composition, is not less important than imagination and invention.

But while the genius of the individual poet enjoys this large freedom, there are certain universal laws of expression, proper to the art of poetry, which no individual poet can disregard with impunity; and as to the nature of these I think it is perfectly possible, by the inductive method of criticism, to arrive at positive and certain conclusions. I have said that, in my opinion, poetry necessarily produces its effects by means of metrical language. But upon this point there is a dispute; and the question which I am now going to put before you for consideration is, Whether metre is necessary for poetical expression, and, if so, whether this necessity binds the poet to use forms of diction which, even apart from metre, are different from the forms of prose?

Now as to the first of these questions very opposite opinions have been advanced, according to the view which has been taken of the nature of poetry; it has been said, on the one hand, that poetry is merely versification, and, on the other, that verse is not necessary for poetry. The former opinion had its advocates as early as the days of Aristotle, who shows us that certain authorities, of whom he does not speak without respect, considered that poetry consisted in putting words together in a certain order determined by the quantity of their syllables, one critic going even so far as to say that it would be quite easy to make poetry if you were allowed to lengthen or abbreviate syllables at will.[1] Opposed to this opinion is one equally extreme, but recommended by the eminent names of Sir Philip Sidney and Shelley. Sidney says, in his *Apology for Poetry*:

> The greatest part of poets have apparelled their poetical inventions in that numberous kind of writing which is called verse. Indeed but apparelled, verse being but an ornament and no cause to poetry, since there have been many most excellent poets that have never versified, and now swarm many versifiers that need never answer to the name of poets. For Xenophon, who did imitate so excellently as to give us *effigiem justi imperii*, the portraiture of a just empire under the name of Cyrus (as Cicero saith of him), made therein an absolute heroical poem.

And Shelley says, in his *Defence of Poetry*:

> It is by no means essential that a poet should accommodate his language to the traditional form, so that the harmony which is its spirit be observed. The practice is indeed convenient and popular and to be preferred, especially in such composition as includes much action: but every great poet must inevitably innovate upon the example of his predecessors in the exact

[1] Aristotle, *Poetics*, xxii. 5.

structure of his peculiar versification. The distinction between poets and prose writers is a vulgar error. . . . Plato was essentially a poet . . . the truth and splendour of his imagery and the melody of his language are the most intense that it is possible to conceive. . . . Lord Bacon was a poet. His language has a sweet and majestic rhythm which satisfies the sense no less than the almost superhuman wisdom of his philosophy satisfies the intellect.

What Aristotle thought on the matter is not quite clear. He extends the idea of poetical "imitation" so as to include certain compositions in prose; but his argument is directed against those who think that poetry lies solely in versification; he does not attempt to prove that metre is not a necessary accompaniment of the higher conceptions of poetry.[1] This great critic, therefore, cannot be ranged with those who support that extreme opinion, and the arguments of Sidney and Shelley will not stand examination. The fallacy of the examples given by each of these critics is, that they do not take into account the different aims of the writers they cite. The end of Xenophon in the *Cyropædeia* was not to please but to instruct; if he produced an image pleasing to the fancy, it was only by accident. Shelley's reasoning is still more inconsequent. It does not follow, because the versification of every great poet innovates on the practice of his predecessors, that versification can therefore be dispensed with in poetry. Nor does it follow, because the truth and splendour of Plato's

[1] See Aristotle, *Poetics*, c. i. 6-8. A correspondence with Professor Butcher, the eminent editor of Aristotle's *Poetics*, convinces me that by ψιλοί λόγοι the philosopher means compositions in prose, and not, as I was at first inclined to think, metrical words unaccompanied by music.

imagery are the most intense that it is possible to conceive, that he was therefore "essentially a poet"; the same might be said of the imagery of a great orator; yet oratory is not poetry. The end of Plato was to convince by dialectic, and though for this purpose he may have resorted to rhetorical and poetical methods of persuasion, that does not take him out of the class "philosopher," and transplant him into the class "poet." The most that Sidney and Shelley prove is, what every sensible critic would be ready to grant without argument, that poetry does not lie in metrical expression *alone*.

Against the *obiter dicta* of these two writers, distinguished as they are, I put the universal practice of the great masters of the art, and I ask, Why have poets always written in metre? The answer is, Because the laws of artistic expression oblige them to do so. When the poet has been inspired from without in the way in which we saw Scott was inspired to conceive the *Lay of the Last Minstrel*—that is to say, when he has found his subject-matter in an idea universally striking to the imagination, when he has received this into his own imagination, and has given it a new and beautiful form of life there, then he will seek to express his conception through a vehicle of language harmonising with his own feelings and the nature of the subject, and this kind of language is called verse. For example, when Marlowe wishes to represent the emotions of Faustus, after he has called up the phantom of Helen of Troy, it is plain that some very rapturous form of expression is needed to convey an adequate idea of such famous beauty. Marlowe rises to the occasion in those "mighty lines" of his:

> Was this the face that launched a thousand ships,
> And burned the topless towers of Ilium?

But it is certain that he could only have ventured on the sublime audacity of saying that a face launched ships and burned towers by escaping from the limits of ordinary language, and conveying his metaphor through the harmonious and ecstatic movements of rhythm and metre.

Or, to take another instance, Virgil more than once describes the passion of the living when visited by the spirits of those whom they have loved and lost, and he invented a metrical form of expression for the feeling, which he knew to be so beautiful that he used it twice. Expressed in prose, the passage runs thus: "Thrice he there attempted to throw his arms round her neck; thrice embraced in vain, the phantom glided from his grasp; light as the empty winds, likest to a fleeting dream." There is pathos in this; but now listen to the verses:

> Ter conatus ibi collo dare brachia circum,
> Ter, frustra comprensa, manus effugit imago,
> Par levibus ventis volucrique simillima somno.

What infinite longing, what depths of sorrow, are expressed in the selection and collocation of the words, and the rhythmical effect of the whole passage! How profound a note of melancholy is struck in the monosyllables with which each line opens! How wonderfully is the fading of the vision symbolised in the dactylic swiftness with which the last line glides to its close!

Or, yet once more : you remember how Prospero breaks off the marriage pageant in the *Tempest* to deal with the conspirators, and the splendidly abrupt transition of feeling with which he reminds his audience of the end of all mortal things :

> And, like the baseless fabric of this vision,
> The cloud-cap't towers, the gorgeous palaces,
> The solemn temples, the great globe itself,
> Yea, all which it inhabit, shall dissolve;
> And, like this insubstantial pageant faded,
> Leave not a rack behind. We are such stuff
> As dreams are made of, and our little life
> Is rounded with a sleep.

I think no critic in his senses would say that the full effect of this passage could be given in prose.

Nevertheless, though the necessity of metre to poetry would thus appear to be proved by reason and by the practice of the greatest poets, it has been denied by one who was undoubtedly a master in the art. In the well-known preface published with his poems in 1805 Wordsworth asserts that the poet is under no obligation to write in verse, and that he himself only does so on account, partly, of the additional pleasure afforded by metre, and, partly, of certain technical advantages to be derived from the practice. He defends his theory as follows :

> From the tendency of metre to throw a sort of half-consciousness of unsubstantial existence over the whole composition, there can be little doubt but that more pathetic situations and

sentiments—that is, those that have a greater proportion of pain connected with them—may be endured in metrical compositions, especially in rhyme, than in prose. . . . This opinion may be illustrated by appealing to the reader's own experience of the reluctance with which he comes to the representation of the distressful parts of *Clarissa Harlowe* or *The Gamester;* while Shakespeare's writings in the most pathetic scenes never act upon us as pathetic beyond the bounds of pleasure—an effect which in a much greater degree than might be imagined is to be ascribed to small but continual and regular impulses of pleasurable surprise from the metrical arrangement.

I think Wordsworth's analysis of emotion is clearly wrong. The reason why the harrowing descriptions of Richardson are simply painful, while Shakespeare's tragic situations are pleasurable, is that the imagination shrinks from dwelling on ideas so closely imitated from real objects as the scenes in *Clarissa Harlowe*, but contemplates without excess of pain the situation in *Othello*, for example, because the imitation is poetical and ideal. Prose is used by Richardson because his novel professedly resembles a situation of real life; metre is needed by Shakespeare to make the ideal life of his drama real to the imagination. Wordsworth, if I may say so, has put the poetical cart before the horse.

It may be admitted, however, that if Wordsworth's theoretical principles of poetical conception were just, he would not only have been under no necessity to write in metre, but he would have been wrong to use it at all. He says of his own method:

> The principal object proposed in these poems was to choose incidents and situations from common life, and to relate or

describe them throughout, as far as was possible, in a selection of language really used by men, and, at the same time, to throw over them a certain colouring of the imagination whereby ordinary things should be presented to the mind in an unusual aspect; and further, and above all, to make these incidents and situations interesting by tracing in them truly, though not ostentatiously, the primary laws of our nature: chiefly as far as regards the manner in which we associate ideas in a state of excitement.

Now, whether this method of composition can or cannot be regarded as falling legitimately within the art of poetry, it is at least certain that it is opposed at all points to the mode of conception adopted by the greatest poets of the world, as this has been already described. It does not involve inspiration by the universal idea from without, and the recreation of the universal idea within, the mind of the individual poet. It implies, on the contrary, that the inspiration proceeds from the poet's own mind; that the poet can make even common things poetical by throwing "over them a certain colouring of the imagination;" the process of conception described is one not so much of imaginative creation as of imaginative analysis; and to express quasi-scientific truths of this kind the metaphorical forms of language peculiar to metrical writing are certainly not *required*.

But, more than this, it can be shown that, in endeavouring to put the particular conceptions he speaks of into metre, Wordsworth was adopting a wrong form of expression. Let me not be misunderstood. Wordsworth, I need hardly say, often wrote very nobly in metre; but when he did so, he did none of those things which, according to his own theory of poetry, he ought to have done. For it is quite certain that neither in *Laodamia*, nor in the *Ode on Immortality*, nor in the lines about skating on Windermere in the *Prelude*, nor in those about the "lively Grecian" in the *Excursion*, nor in those describing the Yew Trees of Borrowdale, nor in the Sonnet on the Dawn on Westminster Bridge, nor in that on Liberty, nor in a hundred other places, is there anything of that analytical process of conception on which he sets so high a value. In all of the examples I have mentioned there is the *res lecta potenter*; that is to say, an idea of universal interest. This universal idea is assimilated with the poet's imagination, and it is expressed in what is universally felt to be a noble and beautiful form of words. But sometimes Wordsworth really does work in the way which he says is the right way. The whole conception and construction, for example, of the *Prelude* and the *Excursion* are founded on a subject-matter which is private to the poet himself, and consists for the most part of conversational discourse about external matters not of universal interest. Here undoubtedly the whole process of imagination is analytical, and consequently the forms of expression used are, for the most part, prosaic. Take, for example, the following lines, which are neither better nor worse than hundreds, probably thousands, in these poems:

> These serious words
> Closed the preparatory notices
> That served my Fellow Traveller to beguile
> The way while we advanced up that wide vale.

Who does not perceive that the man who wrote this was not, at the time he wrote it, in the right mood for poetical expression? And accordingly, as he chooses to express himself in metre, he often uses wrong forms, as, for example, in a passage like this, describing his residence in London:

> At leisure then I viewed from day to day
> The spectacles within doors, birds and beasts
> Of every nature, and strange plants convened
> From every clime; and next those sights that ape
> The absolute presence of reality,
> Expressing, as in mirror, sea and land,
> And what earth is, and what she has to show:
> I do not here allude to subtlest craft,
> By means refined attaining purest ends,
> But imitations, fondly made, in plain
> Confession of man's weakness and his loves.

Observe that Wordsworth is here working on a subject of his own choosing—an "incident and situation from common life,"—and he is trying to make it fit matter for poetry by showing its relation to his own mind, and yet, for all this, he does not contrive to present his thought in what he calls "a selection of language really used by men." For if he had done this, he would simply have said: "Every day I was accustomed to go to a natural history museum, or a picture gallery, in which scenes from nature were exactly imitated;" that is to say, he might have expressed in twenty-four words what he actually expresses in eighty-one. You see, too, that Wordsworth, as he chooses to write in metre on such a subject, is, in spite of himself, forced to use a kind of poetical diction, which makes his style pedantic and obscure. For what man in real life, wishing to describe what he had seen at Kew Gardens, would say that he had "*viewed* strange plants *convened* from every *clime*"? Or who would think it worth while to say that the Panorama of Niagara was an exhibition that "*apes* the absolute presence of reality"?

I think that what I have said serves to show that the propriety of poetical expression is the test and the touchstone of the justice of poetical conception. Like all sound principles, Horace's maxim about the right selection of subject is capable of being reversed. Poetry lies in the invention of the right metrical form—be it epic, dramatic, lyric, or satiric—for the expression of some idea universally interesting to the imagination. When the form of metrical expression seems *natural*—natural, that is, to the genius of the poet and the inherent character of the subject—then the subject-matter will have been rightly conceived. When, on the other hand, it is found to be prosaic, obscure, strained, or affected, then we may be sure either that the subject has not been properly selected by the poet, or that the individuality of the poet has, in the treatment, been indulged out of due proportion to the universal nature of the subject.

Apply this test of what is natural in metrical expression to any composition claiming to be poetically inspired, and you will be able to decide whether it fulfils the universal conditions of poetical life, or whether it is one of those phantoms, or, as Bacon calls them, idols of the imagination, which vanish as soon as the novelty of their appearance has exhausted its effect. For instance, the American poet, Walt Whitman, announces his theme, and asks for the sympathy of the reader in these words:

> Oneself I sing, a simple, separate person,
> Yet utter the word Democratic, the word En Masse.
> Poets to come, orators, singers, musicians to come,
> Not to-day is to justify me and answer what I am for.
> But you, a new brood, native, athletic, continental, greater than before known,
> Arouse! for you must justify me!
> . . . .
> I am a man who, sauntering along without fully stopping, turns a casual look upon you and then averts his face,
> Leaving it to you to prove and define it,
> Expecting the main thing from you.
> Thou, reader, throbbest life, and pride, and love, the same as I:
> Therefore for thee the following chants.

To this appeal I think the reader may reply: The subject you have chosen is certainly an idol of the imagination. For if you had anything of universal interest to say about yourself, you could say it in a way natural to one of the metres, or metrical movements, established in the English language. What you call metre bears precisely the same relation to these universal laws of expression, as the Mormon Church and the religion of Joseph Smith and Brigham Young bear to the doctrines of Catholic Christendom.

Again, we have the poetical ideal of the graceful poet whose recent loss we in England have so much cause to deplore. Mr. William Morris's aim in poetry was to revive the spirit and manner of the past in opposition to the spirit of the present. He says, in his *Earthly Paradise:*

> Of Heaven and Hell I have no power to sing;
> I cannot ease the burden of your fears;
> Or make quick-coming death a little thing;
> Or bring again the pleasures of past years;
> Nor for my words shall ye forget your tears,
> Or hope again for aught that I can say,
> The idle singer of an empty day.
>
> But rather when, aweary of your mirth,
> From full hearts, still unsatisfied, ye sigh;
> And feeling kindly unto all the earth,
> Grudge every minute as it passes by,
> Made the more mindful that the sweet days die;
> Remember me a little, then, I pray,
> The idle singer of an empty day.
>
> The heavy trouble, the bewildering care,
> That weigh us down, who live and earn our bread,
> These idle verses have no power to bear,
> So let us sing of names remembered,
> Because they, living not, can ne'er be dead,
> Nor long time take their memories away
> From us poor singers of an empty day.

Of this we must say that it is tender, charming, even beautiful, and under existing circumstances peculiarly pathetic; but still a poetical idol. We feel that the form of expression in metre is not quite natural; the artifice is apparent. It bears the same relation to the life of poetry that mere Ritualism bears to Religion.

The language does not proceed from the source of life that inspired the poetry of Chaucer, Mr. Morris's professed master. Chaucer would never have spoken in this morbid way about life, and death, and action; he would never have regarded poetry as an opiate for the imagination. His mode of conception was masculine, humorous, dramatic; he drew his inspiration from the life about him, and accordingly the metrical forms he used sprang naturally out of the idiom of his time.

Once more, there is an idol of the art of poetry which suggests that the source of poetical life is to be found in words rather than in ideas. This is of all poetical idols the most seductive, because it presents strongly one side of the truth, and because it is recommended by many brilliant poetical *tours de force*. Coleridge defined prose to be words in the right order, poetry to be the best words in the right order. And, doubtless, the mere sound of words has the power of raising imaginative ideas, as we see from Keats's lines—

> Forlorn! the very word is like a bell,
> To toll me back again to my sole self!

and we know that the word "nevermore" inspired Edgar Poe with his remarkable poem, *The Raven*. But words, apart from things, can, as a rule, suggest only fragmentary conceptions of life and nature. What can be more delightfully suggestive of coming poetry than the opening of *Kubla Khan*?

> In Xanadu did Kubla Khan
> A stately pleasure-dome decree:

> Where Alph, the sacred river, ran
> Through caverns measureless to man
> Down to a sunless sea.

But, as we know, Nature never provided the completion, nor could she have done so, of that wonderful fragment of poetry. Sometimes, indeed, a whole poem containing a definite idea may be constructed on this principle, and a very fine example is furnished by Mr. Swinburne's *Dolores*, where the aim of the poet has, apparently, been to group a variety of images round the single central phrase, "Our Lady of Pain." Many of the stanzas in this poem completely satisfy Coleridge's definition of poetry, "the best words in the right order," but, on the other hand, as the inspiration proceeds from words rather than ideas, there are many other stanzas in it which have no poetical *raison d'être*, and which diminish the effect of the whole composition. This mode of expression belongs to the art of music rather than to the art of poetry. Horace's rule is inverted: the eloquence and order of the metrical arrangement suggest the idea, not the idea the verse. I do not say that such a method of composition is illegitimate; but it must be evident that the inspiration is of the most fortuitous kind, and that one might as well attempt to make oneself dream the same dream twice over, as to find a regular principle of poetical expression in the metrical combination of words and metaphors.

Few indeed are the metrical compositions that will stand the test I propose, few the poems that answer perfectly to Spenser's description of life in poetry:

> *Wise* words, taught in numbers for to run,
> Recorded by the Muses, live for ay.

But this being so, we may well ask ourselves the question, Why is verse so abundantly produced in our time? Why do we so often find men in these days, either using metre, like Wordsworth in the passages I have cited, where they ought to have expressed themselves in prose, or expressing themselves in verse in a style so far remote from the standard of diction established in society that they fail to touch the heart?

I think the explanation of this curious phenomenon is that, though metre can only properly be used for the expression of universal ideas, there is in modern society an eccentric or monastic principle at work, which leads men to pervert metre into a luxurious instrument for the expression of merely private ideas. The metrical form of expression is the oldest form of literary language that exists. In the early stages of society it is used for two reasons, first because, as writing has not been invented, it is the only way of preserving memorable thoughts, and secondly because in primitive times what may be called the poetical or ideal method of conceiving nature predominates over the scientific method. Imagination is then stronger than reason, and the poet is at once the story-teller, the theologian, the historian, and the natural philosopher of society. As society emerges from its infancy more scientific habits of thought are gradually formed; the art of writing is invented; and men find the means of preserving the records of ordinary observation and experience in prose. Science is always withdrawing fresh portions of nature from the rule of imagination; and no one who is animated by a scientific purpose, and understands how to use language properly, thinks any longer of composing a treatise on astronomy or an historical narrative in verse.

Yet, in spite of these achievements of civilisation and science, it would be a vast mistake to suppose that society in its later stages can dispense with the poet and the art of metrical composition. The deepest life of society is spiritual, ideal, incapable of analysis. What binds men to each other is the memory of a common origin, the prospects of a common destiny, common perceptions of what is heroic in conduct, common instincts as to what is beautiful in art. The unimpassioned language, suitable to law and science, suffices not for the embodiment of these great elemental ideas. The poet alone possesses the art of giving expression to the conceptions of the public conscience, and he is as much bound to interpret the higher feelings of society in the maturity of its development, as the scald or minstrel was bound to act as interpreter for the imagination of the primitive tribe. No other defence of the art of poetry is needed than this, that, only in imaginative creations, metrically expressed, can society behold the image of its own unity, and realise the objects of its own spiritual existence.

But since this is so, to pursue any other ideal is "to speak things *un*worthy of Phœbus," and to misapply the purposes of the art. Nevertheless it cannot be denied that contrary views of the end of poetry have asserted themselves in this generation. The vulgar idea of poetry is, that it is something private, peculiar, and opposed to common sense. We have been taught by the poets themselves that the source of poetry lies solely in the mind of the individual poet, and that the life of poetical expression is to be found apart from the active life of society. Philosophers have encouraged this belief. John Stuart Mill attempts to draw a sharp distinction between the genius of the orator and that of the poet; the one, he says, speaks to be heard, the other to be overheard.[1] I venture to say that a more false description of the life and nature of poetry has never been given to the world. At no great epoch of poetical production was the art of the poet ever entirely separated from that of the orator. Did Homer, Pindar, the Greek tragedians, and Aristophanes not speak to be heard? Were the Trouvères, the Troubadours, the Ballad Singers, the Elizabethan dramatists, the English satirists of the Restoration and the Revolution, not dependent on an audience? There have been, it is true, epochs when the private literary motives approved by Mill have prevailed in poetical composition—Alexandrian periods of literature, when the poet, abandoning the representation of the great themes of action and passion, and sick

[1] *Dissertations and Discussions*, i. 71 (1859).

of self-love like Malvolio, has indulged himself in the pleasures of soliloquy. But these were also the ages in the history of the world when men for the sake of life had destroyed the causes of living, when a petty materialism had dwarfed their conception of the sublime and the heroic, when liberty had perished, and art languished in decay.

On this subject I propose to speak more fully in my next lecture on Poetical Decadence. Meantime the course of our argument brings me round to a re-statement of the law of poetry, as it is declared by Horace, and illustrated in the practice of all great classic poets. The secret of enduring poetical life lies in individualising the universal, not in universalising the individual. What is required of the poet above all things is *right conception* — the *res lecta potenter* of Horace—a happy choice of subject-matter which shall at once assimilate readily with the poet's genius, and shall, in Shakespeare's phrase, " show the very age and body of the time his form and pressure." The poet must be able not only to gauge the extent of his own powers, but to divine the necessities of his audience. He must realise the nature of the subject-matter which, in his generation, most needs expression, and know whether it requires to be expressed in the epic, dramatic, lyric, or satiric form. When the subject has been rightly conceived, then, as Horace says, it will instinctively clothe itself in the right form of expression, according to the laws of the art. The poet's theme being of a universal nature, Wordsworth was right in demanding that his diction should not be very remote from "the real language of men"; but as the poet's thought is conveyed in verse, the expression of his ideas must accommodate itself to the laws of metre, and these exact a diction far more radically distinct, than Wordsworth imagined, from the forms of prose. As to the more particular character of poetic diction, everything will depend on the individual genius of the poet: the beauties of style must be studied in the works of the great classic poets. Shakespeare has furnished a thousand examples of poetic diction suitable to the requirements of the romantic drama; the style of *Paradise Lost*, peculiar as it is, is exactly appropriate to what Pope calls the out-of-the-world nature of the subject; Dryden's character of Zimri, and Pope's lines on the death of Buckingham, reach the highest level of poetic diction in satire; and, lest I should be thought to depreciate the poetry of our own day, let me cite one out of many suitable passages from Tennyson's *In Memoriam*, to exemplify the perfection of lyrical composition. The lines are those in which the poet is describing the loss of the individual human life in the total life of nature:

> Unwatch'd, the garden bough shall sway,
>   The tender blossom flutter down;
>   Unloved, that beech will gather brown,
> This maple burn itself away;
>
> Unloved, the sun-flower, shining fair,
>   Ray round with flames her disk of seed,
>   And many a rose-carnation feed
> With summer spice the humming air;

> Unloved, by many a sandy bar
>   The brook shall babble down the plain,
>   At noon or when the lesser Wain
> Is twisting round the polar star;
>
> Uncared for, gird the windy grove,
>   And flood the haunts of hern and crake;
>   Or into silver arrows break
> The sailing moon in creek and cove;
>
> Till from the garden and the wild
>   A fresh association blow,
>   And year by year the landscape grow
> Familiar to the stranger's child;
>
> As year by year the labourer tills
>   His wonted glebe, or lops the glades;
>   And year by year our memory fades
> From all the circle of the hills.

There is but one phrase in this passage which I could wish to see altered. "*Twisting* round the polar star" is a mode of expression too fanciful and particular, in my judgment, to blend with the chaste simplicity of the other images. But with this exception the poetical effect is produced by rendering a general idea into language which differs from the ordinary idiom only in the elegance and refinement of the words chosen, and in the perfect propriety with which they adapt themselves to the movement of the verse. Horace's principle is vindicated in practice; the eloquence and lucid order of the versification prove the justice and universality of the thought.

III

POETICAL DECADENCE

In my last two lectures I traced the conditions under which Poetry comes into existence in the mind of the poet, and the manner in which it clothes itself with external form. I showed that it was the product of the harmonious fusion of two contrary elements, the Universal and the Individual. By the universal element I mean what we often call by the name Nature: whatever is furnished naturally to the poet's conception by forces outside himself; the sources of inspiration springing from the religion, tradition, civilisation, education of the country to which he belongs; the general mental atmosphere of the age in which he lives; the common law of the language in which he composes. By the individual element I mean what we usually call Art; including all that is contributed by the genius of the poet, and that helps to constitute the characteristic form or mould in which the universal idea is expressed.

I shall in my present lecture go further, and try to pursue the course of Life in Poetry in the history of the art, because the Art of Poetry has a life of its own, exactly analogous to the life of individual men and of States, proceeding from infancy to maturity and from maturity to decay. Great poetry of any kind is, as a rule, produced within certain well-defined periods of a nation's history, and the culminating point in every such kind of poetry is reached by a gradual ascent to the work of some great representative or classic poet. When this point has been reached we generally find an equally regular course of declension, represented by poets not without genius, but whose work is always characterised by certain common defects, which denote the exhaustion of the art and give warning of its approaching end.

In the Greek epic, for example, Homer, marking the zenith of the art, has for his successors the literary composers of the Alexandrian period; and these again have their epigoni in poets like the Pseudo-Musæus. In the history of the Attic drama, the movement of decline begins almost insensibly with Euripides, but proceeds with increasing speed in Agathon and other tragedians, whose names Time has not cared to preserve. Pastoral poetry has still to be invented, but the epigrammatists of Alexandria are the only representatives left, after the fourth century, of all the lyric singers of the free Greek cities; and thus by degrees the voice of Greek poetry dies into silence. Latin epic poetry declines from the height to which it has been raised by Virgil, through Lucan to Statius, from Statius to Claudian, from Claudian to nothingness. The English poetical drama, culminating in Shakespeare, moves downward to Massinger, and expires in the rhyming tragedies of Dryden and Lee. The ethical and didactic poetry of England, arriving at its grand climacteric in Pope, shows a dwindling force in Johnson and Goldsmith, and reaches its last stage of senility in the sounding emptiness of Erasmus Darwin.

Now, this law of progress and decline, which is common to all the fine arts, may, I think, be formulated as follows. In the infancy of poetry or painting the universal element of life predominates over the individual; men's imaginative conceptions, as we see in the work of Giotto and Chaucer, are stronger than their powers of technical expression. In the maturity of art there is a perfect balance of the two opposing elements, as shown in the works of Raphael and Sophocles and Shakespeare. In the decadence of art, the individual overbalances the universal: we come to the stage either of insipid mannerism, exemplified in the paintings of Carlo Dolci and the poetry of Rogers; or of violent exaggeration, such as we find in the pictures of Michael Angelo Caravaggio, and in tragedies like those of Seneca and Nathaniel Lee.

I shall ask you therefore to consider the symptoms that betoken the decline of poetry from its culminating point; and I shall take my illustrations from different periods, which, by universal critical consent, are periods of decadence. The subject is indeed a vast one, but I think I shall be able to establish the truths which I am anxious to impress upon you, by presenting the matter in three aspects: (1) The Decline of the Universal in Ages of Poetical Decadence. (2) The Exaggeration of the Individual in such ages. (3) The Abdication by Society of its right of judgment in questions of Poetry and Art.

(1) As regards the Decline of the Universal, the most vivid examples of this phenomenon are furnished by the history of Greek poetry, because the Greek genius was so comprehensive that there was no form of poetical expression in which it did not produce work of the highest excellence. Let us in the first place make our observations on the ground of the Greek drama. Probably few critics would care to contest the opinion that the culminating point of Greek tragedy is to be found in the *Œdipus Rex*, and indeed the reason for this is plain. In the early days of the Greek drama the universal predominated strongly over the individual. Every one who listens to me knows that the form of Greek drama was worked out almost instinctively by means of a union between the Greek myths and the Chorus, which was the original mouthpiece of the worship of Dionysus. Now, the essence of the drama lies in the exhibition of action; but, even as late as the time of Æschylus, the religious, or didactic, or universal element in tragic conception was so powerful that, in plays like the *Agamemnon* and the *Eumenides*, though the course of the action is well defined, the Chorus seems to be a more important part of the whole structure than the actors themselves. In the *Œdipus Rex*, on the other hand, there is a perfect balance between

Nature and Art; the moral of the play is expressed mainly by means of the action. Pity and terror are aroused by the tragic order in which the events are made to succeed each other; the elevation to which the hero is raised by his genius and wisdom before the great περιπέτεια to which he is exposed; the irony which makes the whole horror of the situation apparent to the spectators, while the person most affected remains unconscious of the truth; the crash of ruin in which he is involved by the antecedent sins of others rather than by his own—all this is as much in accordance with the Greek sense of religion as are the doctrines of the Chorus in the tragedies of Æschylus; and it is more in harmony with the nature of the drama as a form of poetic art.

But when we come to Euripides, with whom begins the period of tragic decadence, the state of the ideal atmosphere has manifestly changed. Poet and audience have both lost much of their old religious belief, and this mental change brings with it a corresponding change in the form of the drama. The Chorus, no longer the natural mouthpiece of the universal feeling of awe and reverence, dwindles into a mere instrument for the invention of new melodies; on the other hand, the story is not arranged for the purpose of bringing out the ideal significance of the situation, but to display the poet's ingenuity in the construction of his plot, or some other kind of artistic cleverness. And this tendency was doubtless strongly developed by Agathon, who, if there is any truth in Aristophanes' representation of him in the *Thesmo-*

phoriazusae, must have been a typical representative of those who follow art for art's sake.

Let us next turn to the Greek epic, and contrast the work of its maturity and decadence as illustrated respectively in the *Iliad* and the *Argonautica* of Apollonius Rhodius. One of the most striking characteristics in Homer's poetry is the richness and variety of its materials, the universal nature of its interest. The poet is at once a theologian, a statesman, a moralist, and—observe this particularly—a painter. There is scarcely an object in nature which he does not represent; and yet so perfect in him is the balance between the universal and the individual, that each of his conceptions is placed in its just relation for the purposes of art. Those exquisite touches of pathos, seeming to spring instinctively out of the narrative; those lofty strokes of rhetoric, so proper to the occasion; those detailed descriptions which embody the very genius of painting—all is adapted to elevate, to humanise, to relieve the progress of the action.

How different is the case with Apollonius Rhodius! The master from whom Virgil learned so much was no mean poet; but in him whatever is excellent comes scarcely at all from the universality of human interest which abounds in the *Iliad:* almost everything depends on the ingenuity of the artist. I do not remember in the *Argonautica* a single passage of deep natural pathos, a single general reflection or observation universally true, a single effort of soul-stirring rhetoric. All these elements have disappeared from the life of the epic; what remains to it is the genius of painting. Apollonius's descriptions are admirable, whether he exerts himself to paint the external symptoms of love in Medea, or to heighten a scene of romantic adventure. As a specimen of his powers in the latter class take his description of Medea hypnotising the snake that guarded the Golden Fleece,[1] which may be translated thus:

> When to his ears the sweet enchantment came,
> A languor shuddered through the serpent's frame.
> Through all his length the soothing influence rolled,
> And loosed the spiry volumes fold on fold;
> As swells a single wave mid Ocean's sleep,
> Sullen and soundless, through the stagnant deep:
> Yet, though the powerful charm benumbed the rest,
> High o'er the ground up-towered his grisly crest:
> Wide gaped his jaws to seize their prey. But now
> The dauntless maiden dipped her charmèd bough
> In the fell broth, and on his eye-balls flung
> The magic dew, and, while she sprinkled, sung;
> Till, 'neath the charming voice and odours shed
> From the drugged potion, sank the languid head,
> And through the trunks, inert and brown as they,
> The lifeless coils stretched rood on rood away.

This reminds one of Turner's picture of Apollo killing the Python. It is the work of a great painter. And yet how inferior to Homer is Apollonius even on his own ground! Homer will often stand still to breathe his imagination, in the midst of his rapid narrative, by elaborating a simile beyond what is required for the likeness itself; but he never does this without making the simile really illustrate the action. For instance, he illustrates his account of

[1] *Argonautica*, book iv. 149-161.

Agamemnon watching the mustering of the troops of the two Ajaces by the following simile: "As when from a rock a herdman sees a cloud coming over the sea before the blast of the west wind, and as he stands afar off, it seems to be rushing across the sea blacker than pitch, carrying with it a mighty whirlwind; as he looks he shudders, and drives his flock under a cave."[1]

Apollonius admired and imitated Homer's manner of painting: he is even more picturesque than Homer himself; but there is this difference between them, that the poet of Alexandria introduces similes that do not illustrate anything, merely for the sake of the painting. Here is a characteristic example. "As when a sunbeam plays on the side of a house, reflected from water which has just been poured into a cistern, or perhaps a pail: hither and thither it dances on the quick eddy; even so"—What? "even so the maiden's heart in her breast was tossing, and tears of pity flowed from her eyes."[2] Or take this, which is still more elaborate: "As when a poor working woman heaps straws under a burning log, while she is at her task of spinning wool, that she may make a blaze for herself at night beneath her roof, waking betimes; and the flame rising wondrously from the little log consumes all the straw." A very charming and pathetic picture! But what do you suppose this poor working woman is like? Strange to say, like Medea in love! "Even so," says the poet, "beneath her breast cruel love burned always secretly, and he changed her

---

[1] *Iliad*, book iv. 275.   [2] *Argonautica*, book iii. 756-761.

tender cheek from red to pale by reason of the anguish of her mind."[1]

Now, to measure the decay of the universal in Greek epic poetry by a positive standard, the best way is to compare this kind of thing, which is really the best that Apollonius Rhodius can give, with the contrast between the eloquence of Menelaus and Odysseus as described by Antenor. You may feel the greatness of Homer in Pope's version:

> When Atreus' son harangued the listening train,
> Just was his sense, and his expression plain,
> His words succinct, yet full, without a fault,
> He spoke no more than just the thing he ought:
> But when Ulysses rose, in thought profound,
> His modest eyes he fixed upon the ground;
> As one unskilled or dumb, he seemed to stand,
> Nor raised his head, nor stretched his sceptred hand;
> But when he speaks, what elocution flows!
> Soft as the fleeces of descending snows,
> The copious accents fall, with easy art,
> Melting they fall, and sink into the heart.[2]

Thus we find in Greek poetry the drama declines and disappears: the epic declines and disappears. For a moment you have a flash of fine inventive genius in the Idylls of Theocritus. But where does Theocritus go for his invention? Though the inspiration of poets in the great days of Greek art proceeded essentially from civic sources, Theocritus has to go into the country, and to refresh the jaded imagination of the effete Alexandrians with the rustic melodies of shepherd life.

[1] *Argonautica*, book iii. 291-298.   [2] *Iliad*, book iii. 213.

At last there is no distinctive form of poetry left to the Greek muse but the epigram. I am tempted to linger for a moment over this form of the Greek poetic genius: there is something in it so beautiful, so brilliant, and so tasteful, that, even at the very last, it seems wrong to think of decay in connection with the immortal freshness of the race. On whatever subject Greek epigrams are written, they contain a touch of poetry or graceful ingenuity that is not to be found in the similar work of any other people. Who does not feel, for example, the Universal in the epigram assigned to Plato?—

ἀστέρας εἰσαθρεῖς, ἀστὴρ ἐμός· εἴθε γενοίμην
οὐρανός, ὡς πολλοῖς ὄμμασιν εἰς σὲ βλέπω.

Dost gaze on stars, my star? That I might be
Yon heaven, to gaze with myriad eyes on thee!

Or in the beautiful and deeply pathetic elegy of Callimachus on the poems of his dead friend Heracleitus?—

εἶπέ τις Ἡράκλειτε τεὸν μόρον, ἔς δέ με δάκρυ
ἤγαγεν, ἐμνήσθην δ᾽ ὁσσάκις ἀμφότεροι
ἥλιον ἐν λέσχῃ κατεδύσαμεν, ἀλλὰ σὺ μέν που
ξεῖν᾽ Ἁλικαρνασσεῦ τετράπαλαι σποδιή·
αἱ δὲ τεαὶ ζώουσιν ἀηδόνες, ᾖσιν ὁ πάντων
ἁρπακτὴρ Ἀίδης οὐκ ἐπὶ χεῖρα βαλεῖ.

They told me, Heracleitus, you were dead:
Tears filled my eyes, to think, in days long fled,
How oft we two talked down the sun; but thou,
Halicarnassian friend, art ashes now![1]

[1] I have a vague recollection of having seen the rendering of this couplet somewhere, but, if I have taken it from anybody, I cannot discover, after long search, to whom I owe it.

Yet live thy nightingales, and on that band
All-robbing Death shall never lay his hand.

In the vein of pure wit, the following is probably unmatched:

χρυσὸν ἀνὴρ εὑρὼν ἔλιπεν βρόχον, αὐτὰρ ὁ χρυσὸν
ὃν λίπεν οὐχ εὑρὼν ἧψεν ὃν εὗρε βρόχον.

I doubt if any other language could tell the story so naturally and pointedly in two lines. Ausonius gives it in four, in order to make the situation clear, and, even with this license, his version is extremely flat and prosaic.[1] Dr. Johnson's rendering is clever:

Hic aurum ut reperit, laqueum abjicit, alter ut aurum
Non reperit nectit quem reperit laqueum.

But his "alter ut aurum non reperit" is not so clear as the Greek, and he avoids a difficulty by putting all his verbs into the present tense. The following is the best I can make of it in English:

Tom meant to die, but, finding gold, found for his noose no use;
But Dick, his gold who could not find, used what he found, the noose.

But when all is said, such clear-cut and perfect jewels of individual thought do not compensate us for the loss of the spontaneous treasures of creative imagination, poured forth by the Greek mind in the great days of its liberty, like gold brought down on the stream of the Pactolus.

[1] Thesauro invento qui limina mortis inibat
Liquit ovans laqueum quo periturus erat.
At qui quod terra abdiderat non repperit aurum
Quem laqueum invenit nexuit et periit.

Not essentially different is the lesson derived from the history of Latin poetry. The Roman genius—or at least the art—of poetry rises in an ascending scale from Lucretius and Catullus to Virgil, from whom it moves in a declining course through Lucan to Ausonius. In Lucretius there is an abounding source of native energy, a rush and volume of inspiration which almost swallows up art, though of this, as Cicero says, there are many traces in the *De Rerum Natura*. Something of the Universal, something of poetic energy, had been consciously lost even in Virgil's time, as we see from his complaint at the opening of the third *Georgic*:

> Cetera quae vacuas tenuissent carmine mentes
> Omnia jam vulgata.

But Virgil knew how to repair the loss; and having selected such a truly Roman theme as the *Georgics*, he produced, in his treatment of it, that complete balance between the Universal and the Individual which Lucretius had failed to attain. When we come to Ausonius, on the contrary, we find that the universal element has almost vanished: there is, for example, in his very charming poem on the Moselle, as compared with the *Georgics*, a loss of poetical life almost exactly analogous to that which occurs in Greek poetry between the period of Homer and the period of Apollonius. The *Georgics* are full of beautiful pictures, but they are also full of the genius of Roman action, and of the Roman imperial spirit; while the poem on the

Moselle depends for its charm entirely on its landscape-painting.

I come to our own country. Did time permit it would be easy to show in detail that an exact parallel exists between the rise and decline of the poetical drama in Athens and in England. In England, as in Athens, the idea of tragedy arose out of the religion of the country. Shakespeare's tragedies are a direct development of the miracle plays and moralities, just as the tragedies of Æschylus and Sophocles are the final results of the evolution of the drama from the rude exhibitions given by Thespis at the festival of Dionysus. The history of the tragic principle is the same in England and in Greece. In the Attic drama the universal underlying idea of the greater tragedians is Misfortune, necessarily entailed on families and peoples by the curse of hereditary sin : this idea was derived from the popular myths on which the drama was founded. In the Shakespearian tragedy the fundamental idea is Misfortune, brought about by the weakness and corruption of the human will; and this idea of conflict between good and evil, the natural product of the Christian faith, was also the central principle determining the action of all the ancient miracle plays and moralities. It may be said therefore to be the universal idea of tragedy in the mind of the English people, and, in one shape or another, it survived on the English stage so long as the poetical drama continued to flourish. When the stage was revived after the Restoration, this fundamental idea had vanished as a motive of tragedy.

Plays were then written to embody some abstract idea of romantic love, or honour, or absolute monarchy, favoured by the Court, but not indigenous in the mind of the people. The universal element in the poetic drama was extinct; and the poetic drama itself, having no root, withered away.

It is the same with our epic poetry. The English idea of epic action was composite, made up of many contrary elements — ecclesiastical, chivalric, civic, Christian and Pagan—and it was long before these elements could find the right form of organic expression. We see them trying to struggle into poetic life in the *Faery Queen*, a poem which is overflowing with imaginative matter; but they fail to assume in it a perfectly consistent and intelligible shape; the English epic does not settle into its ideal unity until a mould is found for it in *Paradise Lost*, where all the elements treated by Spenser are mixed with each other in such right proportion that the just poetical balance is attained. After Milton, the universal idea of the epic so rapidly dwindles that it has no exponent in English poetry but Sir Richard Blackmore, who, as Dryden says, "wrote to the rumbling of his chariot wheels."

(2) I pass on to consider the second symptom of poetical decadence, namely the exaggeration of the individual element, which is the necessary result of the decline of the universal. As the sense of poetry dwindles in society at large, as people less and less care for and believe in what is beyond and above themselves, the poet endeavours more and more to

fill up the gap in imagination by novelty in art. Observe how this was the case on the stage at Athens. It is evident that neither Euripides himself nor a very considerable portion of his audience cared anything for the myths which formed the subject of the tragic drama, except in so far as they provided a groundwork of supposed fact on which plays could be artistically constructed. The moral sentiment counted for nothing; what Euripides wanted above all things was a subject that had not been treated in poetry before. Hence he chose just those myths for representation which his greater predecessors had left untouched, and he defended his practice on the ground that he was only representing realities. You know how Æschylus deals with his argument in *The Frogs*. Euripides asks (I use Frere's translation):

> But after all what is the horrible mischief?
> My poor Sthenobœas, what harm have they done?

Æschylus replies:

> The example is followed, the practice has gained,
> And women of family, fortune, and worth,
> Bewildered with shame, in a passionate fury,
> Have poisoned themselves for Bellerophon's sake.

Euripides: But at least you'll allow that I never invented it;
Phædra's affair was a matter of fact.

Æschylus: A fact with a vengeance! but horrible facts
Should be buried in silence, not bruited abroad,
Nor brought forth on the stage, nor emblazoned in
    poetry.
Children and boys have a teacher assigned them;
The bard is a master for manhood and youth,
Bound to instruct them in virtue and truth,
Beholden and bound.[1]

[1] Aristophanes, *Ranæ*, 1049-1057.

Euripides again, if he chose an old myth, cast about in all directions for a new way in which to treat it. Æschylus and Sophocles roused pity and terror by the ideal nature of the tragic situation: Euripides sought to rouse the feeling of compassion by stage effects, making his characters poor and lame, dressing them in rags, and, generally speaking, reducing the myth as far as possible to the level of actual life. He endeavoured also to attract attention and excite wonder by novelties of thought and expression, making his *dramatis personae* say things which he knew would shock the prejudices of the majority of his audience, and would please the cultivated and clever minority: "Who knows whether living is not the same as dying?" "The tongue swore, but the mind remained unsworn," and the like.

Still, when all is said, Euripides was a great poet, and his art was kept within due bounds by the sense of the Universal still surviving in his audience. If we wish to study the exaggeration of the Individual in poetry, the most striking examples of it are to be found in the plays of Seneca. All Seneca's plays are founded on Greek myths; and of course these myths were in themselves nothing to him: they did not in any way form part of the Roman conscience; moreover, his plays were never meant for acting; hence the sole motive of their composition was his desire to match himself as a poet with the tragedians of Athens, and to do something in tragedy which they had not done. Observe then how he goes to work. In his *Phaedra* he enters into competition with Euripides. Euripides, though he overstepped due bounds in the selection of the subject, treated it with tragic instinct, and invested the character of Phædra in his *Hippolytus* with dignity and nobility. Seneca aimed solely at giving an exhibition of frenzied female passion, and his representation of Phædra's character is so horrible that I cannot use it for the purposes of illustration. Again, in his *Oedipus*, Seneca matches himself with Sophocles, and of course the result is still worse. You can imagine for yourselves the lengths to which exaggeration carries him from the single fact that, after the awful περιπέτεια in the story, he positively ventures to imagine a meeting and a dialogue between Œdipus and Jocasta. In the *Trachiniae* Sophocles represents the terrible death of Hercules by means of a poisoned garment, which has been sent to him by Deianira, under a misconception. The hero in the midst of frightful suffering meets his end with manly resolution; but all that Sophocles makes him say is—I use the excellent translation of Mr. Lewis Campbell:

> Stubborn heart, ere yet again
> Wakes the fierce rebound of pain,
> While the evil holds aloof,
> Thou, with bit of diamond proof,
> Curb thy cry, with forced will
> Seeming to do gladly still.

In his *Hercules Oetaeus*, Seneca supposes that the garment was sent to Hercules by Deianira in a moment of mad jealousy. His mother Alcmena exhorts him to die with fortitude, to which the hero makes the following reply : " If Caucasus exposed me to be feasted on by the beak of the greedy vulture, though all Scythia groaned, no tear or groan should be wrung from me. If the wandering Symplegades should crush me between their rocks, I would flinch not from the dread of each returning shock. Let Pindus fall upon me, and Hæmus, and Athos who breaks the Thracian waves, and Mimas shaking off the thunderbolt of Jove. Nay, mother, though the world itself should fall upon me, and on the world the chariot of Phœbus all in flames should fire my couch, no coward shriek should subdue the will of Hercules. Let ten thousand wild beasts descend and rend me all together. Let the Stymphalian bird on one side with fierce yells, and on the other the bull with all the terrors of his neck batter me; let all the monsters Earth breeds and dreadful Sinis hurl themselves on my limbs. Though I be dragged in pieces I will keep silence."[1] But if he means to keep silence, why so many words? Absence of inspiration, exaggeration of art!

It will suffice if I give you one more example of the exaggerated art which arises out of the exhaustion of nature. It is perfectly plain that both Dante and Cowley derive their poetical ideas from the same source, namely, the Scholastic Philosophy, though one wrote when that philosophy had reached its zenith, and the other when it was in the last age of

[1] *Hercules Oetaeus*, 1378-1396.

decline. Each of these poets makes use of objects of sense, in order to convey to the mind of the reader an image of some unseen spiritual form of life. Dante gives his reason for this practice, which is as follows: "It is necessary to speak thus to your wit, since only from an object of sense does it apprehend what it afterwards makes the subject of understanding. Hence the Scripture condescends to your capacity, and attributes feet and hands to God, meaning something else; and Holy Church represents to you in human likeness Gabriel, and Michael, and the other who made Tobias whole again."[1] See how real this universal belief makes Dante's imagery. Describing the appearance of certain souls whom he met in the moon's sphere, he says: "As through glasses transparent and polished, or through waters clear and calm, not so deep as to make the bottom dark, the lines of our faces are so faintly returned that a pearl on a white forehead comes not with less force against our eyes; so saw I many faces ready to speak."[2] Judging these to be reflections, he turns his head behind him to see the objects from which they proceed; but Beatrice, "with a smile glowing in her holy eyes," explains to him that these appearances are true substances. Compare with this Cowley's description of the Tree of Knowledge:

> The sacred tree midst the fair orchard grew;
>   The phœnix Truth did on it rest,
>   And built his perfumed nest,
> That right Porphyrian tree, which did true logic show:

[1] *Paradiso*, canto iv. 40.   [2] *Ibid.* canto iii. 10.

> Each leaf did learnèd notions give;
> The apples were demonstrative:
> So clear their colour and divine,
> The very shade they cast did other lights outshine.

Clearly there is nothing natural here; the poet merely wants to make a display of his art—art which is in itself poor, because its mechanism is glaringly apparent: nothing is required but to think of the ideas suggested by "tree," "leaf," and "apples," and to couple them in a verse with the ideas suggested by "logic," "learned notions," "demonstrations."

(3) The last symptom of poetical decadence which need be considered is the Abdication by Society of its right of judgment in matters of Art and Taste. In all great periods of poetical production this right is freely exercised. Sometimes the people criticises in public, as at Athens, where judges representing the spectators decided, rightly or wrongly, on the merits of the dramatists who competed before them for the prize. Sometimes the standard of taste is determined by the voice of a few literary critics who are felt to represent the sense of the community, men like the Quintilius Varus spoken of by Horace, who could say to the poet, "Correct this and that," because as both had the same universal idea in their minds, the critic could point out to the poet the places in which his expression fell short of what was ideally right. But when this universal sense of law in art decays, then the average man begins to doubt about the truth of his own perceptions; and the strong-willed artist introduces such novelties as he

may choose. The individual becomes despotic, and, like all despots, he instinctively fortifies himself with a bodyguard, consisting partly of fanatical admirers, partly of those who find their account in imposing on the public.

This is the origin of the Coterie, which in all ages of artistic decline is a powerful factor in directing the fashion of taste. The poetical decadence of Greece enjoyed a comparative freedom from the plague, because the Greek genius was so richly endowed that an idea of truth and nature survived the loss of political liberty; yet in Alexandria the coterie of Callimachus was able to prevent Apollonius Rhodius from obtaining a hearing. The coterie throve at Rome in the Silver Age of Latin Literature; and from the letters of Pliny the younger we can easily divine how the machinery of admiration was prepared beforehand, and worked by a *claque* at the public readings and recitations. When the last of the great mediæval Italian poets had said his say, a hundred literary academies began to squabble over the rival merits of Ariosto and Tasso. In France the decay of mediæval Romance was emphasised by the enthusiasm with which it was cultivated in Mademoiselle Scudéry's little literary circle; and the Précieuses went on copying the obsolete fashions of the Troubadours till they were extinguished by the ridicule of Molière. In England the poetical barrenness of the last quarter of the eighteenth century was illustrated in the notorious coterie of Della Crusca, who, with Laura Maria and Anna Matilda, attitudinised before a gaping public, and fell at last too easy victims to the somewhat laboured satire of Gifford.

This brings me naturally to the conclusion I desire to draw from my argument. You will have observed that all my examples of poetical decadence have been taken from the historic periods of literature, and that I have said nothing about the art and poetry of our own day; had I attempted to do so I should have been in fault, because that would have involved the assumption that we are living in an age of artistic decline. Whether this is or is not the case, posterity alone can decide with certainty; but meantime it is of the highest importance that we should be able to form an opinion on the matter, since we have Matthew Arnold's authority for the statement that "in poetry, when it is worthy of its high destinies, our race, as time goes on, will find an ever surer and surer stay." Poetry which is to fulfil a duty of that kind must not be of a decadent order.

Now modern society finds itself face to face with this phenomenon, that the present creative tendency in all forms of art is opposed to tradition. The Preraphaelite movement in English poetry and painting; the movement of the Symbolists in French poetry; the revolution effected by Wagner in German music—all of which claim to be the determining factors in the art of the future—agree in this, that they have broken with the artistic principles of the past. Moreover, the ideas involved in these movements have given rise to a most interesting dispute between the representatives of science and the votaries of art. On the one side the artists say to society: "There is coming a new heaven and a new earth. Old things have passed away; all things have become new. Religion is powerless: Science is 'bankrupt'"—that is their phrase: "Art alone, mystical, symbolic, spiritualistic art, can supply the void in the human imagination." On the other side come the men of science, represented by Herr Max Nordau, a name of European reputation, and they say: "Do not trust these artists; they are charlatans, who, so far from being Apostles and Prophets, are to be classed as 'Mattoides,' 'Circulars,' 'Graphomaniacs,' and other varieties of hysterical patients." Who shall decide when doctors disagree?

I confess that, when I read Herr Nordau's book on "Degeneration," from which I have extracted these names, and which is full of vigorous and vivacious thought and admirable literary criticism, I thought that he was intending to take a humorous revenge on the artists, for having called him a member of a "bankrupt" company; and that he had hit on the happy device of the philosopher who, having fallen into a dispute with a voluble fishwife, reduced her to silence by calling her "an isosceles triangle." But closer study showed me that the book was written with true Teutonic seriousness. Frivolous observers may regard art and poetry as the product of mere fashion and whim. Not so the man of science, who treats them as belonging to the department of pathology. "The physician," says Herr Nordau, "recognises in the tendencies of contemporary art and poetry, in the style of the creators of mystic, symbolic, decadent works, and in the attitude of their admirers, in the æsthetic impulses and instincts of fashionable society, a concurrence of two well-defined pathologic states with which he is perfectly well acquainted, degeneration and hysteria; the lower degrees of which are called neurasthenia."

Do you ask how this is proved? The late M. Paul Verlaine, the poetical chief of the French symbolists, wrote an Art of Poetry, in which he lays down rules very much opposed to those of Horace. M. Verlaine's portrait shows, it appears, that the shape of his skull resembles that of the degenerate hysterics whom Lombroso classifies as born criminals. What then can be more reasonable than to conclude that the new French Art of Poetry is the product of hysteria? Again, in one of his poems, M. Verlaine calls very frequently on the name of the Virgin. Of course, says Herr Nordau; exactly the same symptoms were noted by Dr. Legrain in an omnibus driver suffering from hereditary mania. Mr. Rossetti, in a ballad, employs a burden, which is certainly as senseless as it is ugly, "Eden bower's in flower," and "O the flower and the hour!" Clearly, Herr Nordau thinks, this is a case of *echolalia*, a mode of utterance which seems to prevail among imbeciles and idiots.

Now, when these pathological methods of judgment are applied to works of art, I think we may venture to say, even to men of science, *Ne sutor supra crepidam.* The methods are unscientific. Unless Herr Nordau can prove that he has followed all the operations of a poet's brain when he is composing, it is not scientific to couple his case with that of the madman or idiot, whose symptoms can be watched in the ward of a hospital. And, again, unless his investigations in the history of poetry have been very much more extensive than I imagine, it is not scientific to ascribe the practice of a poet to a physical cause, when it may have been the result of mere literary imitation. Will Herr Nordau, for instance, venture to say that, when Shakespeare introduces such a line as, "With hey, with hey ! the thrush and the jay !" into a song, he does so under the influence of hysteria ? Or when he finds, as he may, examples of *echolalia* in the poetry of the Greeks and the Romans, has he evidence to show that these people were widely afflicted with neurasthenia ?

There is indeed something of question-begging in Herr Nordau's whole argument. "The ancient Northern myth," says he, "contained the frightful dogma of a Twilight of the Gods. In our days the finest imaginations are haunted with the sombre apprehension of a Twilight of Nations, in which sun and stars are gradually extinguished, and in the midst of a dying Nature men perish with their institutions and works." In other words, the whole of modern society is incurably afflicted with hysteria : hence all modern art and poetry must necessarily reflect the universal disease.

Conclusions of this kind are not very respectful

to the human race, to the judgment of which even men of science must submit their opinions; and perhaps they are somewhat premature. It may be, of course, that time will justify Herr Nordau's forebodings, and that the historian—if any historians are left—will be able to trace the ruin of a perished society to the ravages of hysteria. Meantime we, who live in the present, are bound to regard the artist, the individual who receives pleasure from art, and the organised body of individuals who judge of art, as responsible beings, who have as natural a capacity for deciding what is good or bad in the principles of taste as for perceiving what is right or wrong in the practice of morals. And hence, when the modern painters and poets and musicians come to us, telling us that the principles of ancient art are obsolete, and that they themselves can supply us with new sources of imaginative pleasure, and even fill the void caused by the loss of religion, it is not sufficient to dismiss them as "mattoides," or "graphomaniacs," or "circulars," even though they may have fairly provoked this kind of retaliation by speaking of the "bankruptcy of science." On the other hand, they can hardly expect us to accept their own estimate of themselves without examination. We ought to consider patiently what they have to tell us; and my main object in this series of lectures is to suggest a method of induction from experience and observation, by which society may be able to test the quality of the pleasure which modern artists are offering to our imagination.

I have shown in my earlier lectures that all poets whose works have provided the world with enduring pleasure have followed a universal mode of conception, and have conformed to certain invariable laws of expression. I have shown to-day that the work of all poets produced in periods of undoubted decadence is distinguished by other characteristics also invariable, also universal. In support of my argument I have not relied upon a single opinion that has not received the critical consent of ages, or cited a single fact that is not capable of positive verification, in so far as the subject admits of this. I think therefore that, in judging of the value of any modern poem, I have the right to infer that, in so far as it is conceived or expressed in a manner fundamentally different from the great living poems of the world, it is unlikely to contain the principle of enduring life; while in so far as it reproduces those particular features we have been considering to-day, it is in all probability the fruit of poetical decadence.

Let me apply this test, as a crucial instance, to the principles and practice of modern French poetry, because in France, as is usual, the leaders of the new School of Art defend their innovations on the ground of logic. Speaking of right aim in poetry, M. Mallarmé, one of the leaders of the French symbolists, says: "To name an object is to destroy three-quarters of the enjoyment of a poem." From this we see that the new school of Poetry agrees with the old school in holding that the end of poetry is to produce pleasure for the imagination; but if M. Mallarmé's words mean anything, they must mean that, when Homer named the wrath of Achilles, or Milton the loss of Eden, as the subjects of their poems, these poets at once destroyed three-quarters of the pleasure that their art might have produced. M. Mallarmé goes on to say: "The true goal of poetry is suggestion. Symbolism consists in the artistic employment of this mysterious principle; in evoking, little by little, an object, so as to indicate a state of soul, or, conversely, to choose an object, and to disentangle from it a state of soul by a series of decipherings."

This, you may say, is a little obscure. But we may divine M. Mallarmé's meaning from M. Paul Verlaine's *Art Poétique*, a poem containing very many charming ideas that could have occurred only to a man of genius, however perversely that genius may have been employed. He says:

> Il faut aussi que tu n'ailles point
> Choisir tes mots sans quelque méprise :
> Rien de plus cher que la chanson grise,
> Où l'Indécis au Précis se joint.
>
> C'est des beaux yeux derrière des voiles,
> C'est le grand jour tremblant de midi,
> C'est par un ciel d'automne attiédi,
> Le bleu fouillis des claires étoiles !
>
> Car nous voulons la Nuance encor,
> Pas la Couleur, rien que la nuance !
> Oh ! la nuance seule fiance
> Le rêve au rêve et la flûte au cor !

I do not pretend to understand what M. Verlaine meant by these last two lines: probably he would have admitted that he did not know himself. But the drift of his advice is quite intelligible. Like M. Mallarmé, he says, "Do not choose definite subjects: what we want in poetry is not expression but suggestion; neutral tints, not positive colours." His *Art Poétique* is therefore naturally opposed to the *Ars Poetica* of Horace :

> Cui lecta potenter erit res
> Nec facundia deseret hunc nec lucidus ordo.

M. Verlaine would maintain that Horace's principle, "Denique sit quidvis simplex duntaxat et unum," would not produce the effect that he himself desired. Nor would it; but why? Because Horace and M. Verlaine each aim at producing pleasure of a different kind. Horace aims at pleasing the imagination with ideas, at creating an illusion of organic ideal life, outlined with all the clearness of sculpture, but animated with the breath of human sympathy. M. Verlaine and M. Mallarmé seek, by means of metrical language, to evoke moods of the soul. Horace strives to produce pleasure that may satisfy the philosopher; the pleasure desired by M. Verlaine is the intoxication of the opium-eater. A poetical idea is enjoyed as a thing of beauty by one generation after another, *semper, ubique, ab omnibus;* the mood of the individual soul evaporates with the fumes of the intellectual drug by which it is called into being.

The French symbolists are therefore opposed to the classical poets both in their ends and means;

but these are in full accord with the ends and means of the poets of decadence. For observe that their symbolism is quite of a different kind from that of Dante, who, perhaps above all other poets, aimed at the *facundia* and *lucidus ordo* desired by Horace. Dante's symbolism was based on the scholastic philosophy, when that system was universally accepted as the key to the interpretation of Nature. When this philosophy ceased to satisfy the intellect, then it also lost its poetical power, and, as we see from the lines of Cowley I have already cited, fell, for poetical purposes, into complete decay. Modern symbolism or mysticism, which aims in poetry at suggestion rather than expression, is in reality identical with the taste for enigmas and obscure thought represented in the style of Lycophron of Alexandria, surnamed ὁ σκοτεινός, whose *Cassandra* is composed with a riddle in every line. And who that is not a German now knows anything of Lycophron except his name?

Again, one of the distinguishing marks of great classical poets, like Sophocles and Virgil, is their reticence and reserve. The chief characteristic of poetical decadence, as we see in Seneca, is lawlessness in the choice of subject and violence of expression. M. Rollinat, who is said to enjoy a high reputation among his countrymen, is probably one of the few poets in the world who can boast of having surpassed Seneca in these qualities. Here are the titles of some of his poems: *Buried Alive; The Soliloquy of Tropmann; Putrefaction; Rondeau of the*

Guillotined; and the following is the only quotable portion of a composition describing the embalming of a dead woman's body: "To snatch the dead one, fair as an angel, from the cruel kisses of the worm, I caused her to be embalmed in a strange box. It was a night in winter." Then the whole process of embalming is minutely painted.

One more example will suffice. All great classic poetry reflects in an ideal way the active life of the society in which it is composed. The *Iliad* breathes in a heroic style the spirit of Greek warfare. Æschylus, who fought at Marathon, Sophocles, who served as a general with Pericles, fill their tragedies with the patriotic sentiment of their age: the old Attic comedy found its matter in contemporary social interests: Shakespeare's chronicle plays popularise half the history of England : the satires of Dryden and Pope are the monuments of once living manners. But the French symbolists—whose aim it is to evoke moods of the soul—dread nothing so much as any form of social activity. "Art for Art's sake!" is their cry. There is something pathetic in the earnestness with which M. Charles Morice, the chief philosopher of the school, utters his lamentations over the exacting tyranny of public duties. "To think," he cries, "that the poet should be obliged to break off in the middle of a stanza in order to go and complete a period of twenty-eight days' training in the army!" Poor fellow! And again: "The agitations of the streets; the grinding of the Government machine; journals; elections; changes of administration—never has there been such a hubbub; the turbulent and noisy autocracy of commerce has suppressed in public preoccupations the preoccupation of Beauty; and trade has killed whatever might have been allowed by politics to live on in silence." One feels sad as one thinks of the happiness and quietism which might have been the lot of this forlorn soul in some other period of poetical decadence. We imagine, for example, that he might have obtained from one of the Ptolemies, say in the second century B.C., the post of sub-librarian at Alexandria, and we fancy him composing some afternoon, in a cool portico, without any interruption from the drill-sergeant, the pentameter of the epigram which he had begun in the morning. Or he might have lived at Rome under the placid reign of Domitian, free from all such disturbance as the clamour of a vulgar newsboy, bawling over the Palatine the latest stages of a ministerial crisis, and breaking in on his preoccupation, as he put together some tuneful trifle on a Greek subject, or prepared for public recitation a flattering elegy on Cæsar's pet bear.

I have confined my observations to the modern French School of Poetry, because I find there the philosophy of a widespread movement put forward in the most frank and lucid form. But, in fact, the features which this school presents are repeated with variations in the contemporary literature of every country in Europe. For the moment, at least, life in poetry is no longer looked for in that perfect balance between the universal and individual elements which is the essence of all classical art. The aim of the poet is not now to create the natural in the sphere of the ideal, the image of

> Nature to advantage dressed,
> What oft was thought but ne'er so well expressed.

The essence of Life in Poetry and in all the arts, according to the new philosophy, is Novelty. And whence are the sources of this new life to be derived ? The answer is, that each of the arts is to borrow some principle from the others; the painter aims at effects which have hitherto been attempted only by poetry; the poet devotes his efforts to imitate in words ideas which are more naturally expressed by means of forms and colours, or indefinable emotions like those which are aroused by the notes of music; the musician tries to combine with the resources of his own art the beauties peculiar to poetry and painting. I do not deny that, when these experiments are made by men of genius, the artistic result produced is often striking, and for a time even pleasurable. But when it is claimed by the pioneers of the new movement—by the brotherhoods, the societies, the coteries, which organise their efforts to impose the new doctrines on the taste of a bewildered world—that this confusion of the boundaries of art is the beginning of a fresh and vigorous outburst of artistic life, experience says, No! The things that are being attempted are as old as civilised society. The poet-musician who endeavours to create a new kind of pleasure, by combining on the stage the principles of poetry, painting, and music, is only doing what was done two thousand years ago by Agathon and the late Attic tragedians. The poet who exalts the element of painting inherent in his art above the principle of action is following the example of Apollonius Rhodius. The poet who tries to attract attention to himself by an ideal representation of extravagant and unnatural passion is modelling himself upon Seneca. And Agathon, and Apollonius Rhodius, and Seneca, are all poets of decadent ages.

Now, if we are living in an age of poetical decadence, it is a very serious matter, and questions arise which urgently demand an answer. Is this decadence confined to the genius and methods of the poets themselves? or does it extend to the taste of that portion of society which the poets are specially anxious to please? or does it imply a failure of the sources of life in the nation at large? These are problems of the profoundest interest, and I shall attempt to deal with them in the lecture with which I propose to conclude this series — namely, on the relations that exist between the Life of Poetry and the Life of the People.

IV

POETRY AND THE PEOPLE

HAVING noted the symptoms that universally accompany poetical decadence, and having observed the appearance of many of these symptoms in the poetry of every country of modern Europe, I asked, with practical reference to the contemporary poetry of England, whether this decadence had its sources merely in the art itself; whether it was the result, as Herr Nordau seemed to think, of the decay of society; or whether it was due to some transitory conditions of taste which might be removed by the influx of fresh elements of imaginative life. Before I attempt to answer these questions, let me consider an initial objection which has been made to my treatment of the subject. A writer in the *Spectator*—whom I take to be the same courteous, but somewhat unsympathetic critic who previously censured, without understanding, my use of the word " imitation " in defining Poetry—says : " We may say that the very same poet, and sometimes even a great poet like Goethe, has had both a fresh and a decadent period in his own poetry." In illustration of his point the critic cites Scott's lines, "To a Lock of Hair," and observes: "This passionate outpouring of Scott's momentary despair should show us how dangerous it is to trace what seems to be decadence in any one poet to general, social, and political causes. We never know whether that which drives one poet into artificial and morbid strains, into histrionic attempts to simulate passions which he does not really feel, may not drive another into those "fresh woods and pastures new" which renew a decadent world. Scott became the originator of a great and healthy literature through an attack of melancholy due to a personal grief."

Now of this I am afraid I must say that the critic has made no attempt to understand the sense of my terms or the nature of my argument. I have nowhere used the word "decadence" as signifying the decay of poetical power in the individual poet as compared with himself. Had I done so, I should doubtless have committed myself to many a proposition as utterly incapable of proof as the assertion that "Scott became the originator of a great and healthy literature through an attack of melancholy due to a personal grief." I have put forward no opinion in these lectures which does not appear to me to be established by history and experience. The subject of them has been "Life in Poetry." By these words I mean the qualities in poetry, whatever they are, whencesoever they are derived, which have the power of producing enduring pleasure; and I have attempted to ascertain their nature by examining the works of poets who have been acknowledged, *semper, ubique, ab omnibus,* to be the living poets of the world. By " Decadence in Poetry " I mean poetical work which, though it may have qualities capable of exciting temporary pleasure and admiration, has not sufficient vitality to continue to produce pleasure for posterity; and here, again, I have endeavoured to arrive at positive conclusions by investigating the qualities of poets who are admitted to be the representatives of recognised periods of poetical decline. Whether my conclusions are right or wrong can be determined only if my critics will condescend to examine what my terms and arguments really mean, and will deal with them on their own ground.

Using the word "decadence," then, in the sense in which I have been using it all along, inductive criticism will, I think, furnish us with a decided answer to the first of the questions I have proposed. Experience makes it probable that the symptoms of decadence in contemporary art and poetry are produced, not simply by a failure of imaginative power in artists and poets, but by the exhaustion of some active principle of life in society at large. There is, in the first place, the fact that, in all previous periods of poetical decadence, artistic decline has proceeded *pari passu* with political decline. The decline of Greek poetry began with the decline of the Greek city states towards the close of the Peloponnesian

War: the decline of Latin poetry advanced with increased speed after the death of Augustus, when the life of the old Republic dwindled away under the Cæsars: the decline of the distinctive forms of mediæval poetry became rapid after the Council of Trent, when the principles of Catholicism and Feudalism had also lost much of their vitality.

In the second place, it is evident that this joint failure of social and imaginative life proceeds from a common moral cause. The highest form of social activity is reached when a state finds the true balance of Liberty and Authority: the highest form of Life in Poetry consists in the harmonious fusion of the universal and individual elements of imagination: in other words, when the individual poet embodies the general consciousness of society as to what is sublime and pathetic, noble and beautiful, in some organic ideal creation which seems to be a true imitation of nature. In both cases the just equilibrium is obtained by obedience to laws above the will of the individual and the majority of the moment, which laws constitute the sources of life in society itself. The greatest artists have shown themselves well aware of this connection between the ἦθος or characteristic life of the people and the life of art; hence Æschylus and Sophocles are, each in their own way, profoundly conservative in matters of faith and morals; they regard the legendary and traditional religion of the State as something established, something not to be touched with profane hands, but to be exalted and sanctified by all the ennobling powers of poetry; hence, too, the bitter criticisms of Aristophanes on the analytical, sceptical, and individualising methods of Euripides, to whom nothing was sacred that gave him an opportunity of displaying his own cleverness. We may conclude, then, with confidence that whatever failure of life may be observed in modern art and poetry is connected with some failure of life in the people.

But the answer to the second question, namely, whether this decadence in art proceeds from the decadence of society as a whole, is far more complex and difficult, and cannot be given with the confidence which is expressed in some quarters. No man alive is in a position to view modern civilisation from the heights on which Gibbon surveyed the Decline and Fall of the Roman Empire; no inhabitant of contemporary Europe, certainly no Englishman, can look on the life of his own country as Machiavelli did on the life of Florence, and say, "Virtue has passed away from us." Experience is wanting. For if we look to the civilisations of Greece and Rome we see that the conditions of public life in those communities were quite different from our own. Then the Law and Religion of the State were inextricably blended with the life of the individual, and when the ἦθος of the State decayed there was no power of recovery; in a moral sense, the community and the individual, liberty and art, all degenerated together. But in modern European civilisation the sources of public life are far more numerous; religious life is not so completely fused with political life as in the states of antiquity. International Life and Law are preserved by the rivalry of evenly-balanced nations; in each nation the antagonistic interests of separate classes help to keep alive the activity of the community as a whole. Beyond this, the moral, social, and intellectual life of each Christian nation is recruited by the art and civilisation of the Pagan world. Hence the fountains of national life are less easily exhausted in modern than in ancient times, and even if the symptoms of modern Poetry indicate decadence in the art, it does not follow that they are also the imaginative reflection of general and inevitable social decline.

All through the history of England, for example, we see a tendency in the life of the nation to concentrate itself in some particular part of the constitution, or in some particular class, which becomes for the time being the sovereign power, rallies round itself all the faculties of the people, represents them to the world, and at last falls into a state of exhaustion. Thus, in the sixteenth century, the centre of English national life was undoubtedly the Crown. The Crown, acting through the Court, was the main instrument in transforming the manners of the nation in the period of transition from feudal custom to civil law and order. The Crown, through the Episcopacy, was the means of regulating, retrenching, and defining the external modes of religious life rendered necessary by the separation of England from the Papacy. The Crown was also the protector of the infant commerce of the nation, and its defence against all the foreign powers that menaced its independence. And yet, while all things seemed to make for the establishment of Absolutism, the onward movement of national life was exhausting the power of the Crown, as the cocoon which guards the chrysalis disappears when it has prepared the organism for a new era of existence.

English poetry in the sixteenth and seventeenth centuries is but the imaginative reflection of the active movement in the heart of the nation, and exhibits in itself that remarkable phenomenon of simultaneous Decadence and Revival which seems to perplex the critic of the *Spectator*, to whom I have before alluded. He observes, for instance, that Cowley, who was certainly a poet of Decadence, was also a contemporary of Milton; and he asks, therefore, rather triumphantly, How can you speak of an age which produced Milton as being an age of Decadence? The answer is obvious. As far as the poets of the seventeenth century in England embodied simply and solely the exhausted spirit of the Middle Ages, to that extent theirs was an age of Decadence. Donne was a contemporary of Shakespeare; and yet almost all the motives of Donne's poetry are of a decadent order, because he fixed his attention mainly on the waning scholastic principle in the national life, instead of on the active civic principle; and just in the same way Cowley went on vainly clothing his thoughts in feudal and mediæval forms, while Milton, breathing into his soul all that was energetic and life-giving in the social atmosphere about him, was qualifying himself to reproduce this in the organic epic form of *Paradise Lost*.

Carry on this idea of the intimate connection

between national life and national poetry into the periods following the Revolution of 1688, and you will see that it helps to explain the changes of taste in the imagination of the people. Look at the history of the eighteenth century. The feudal Monarchy has disappeared : the aristocratic families of England have, to a very great extent, taken the place of the Monarchy as the governing power in the country : the semi-Catholic theology of the seventeenth century is overlaid by the latitudinarian reasoning springing out of the philosophic Humanism of the Reformation. Does not the characteristic poetry of the period faithfully correspond with the political, religious, and social state of things ? It is not such a great school of poetry as that of the Elizabethan dramatists and Milton, because it does not embrace so many elements of imagination ; it cuts out the mediæval and romantic principles : nevertheless, it is thoroughly successful in fusing the universal springs of inspiration that remain, namely, the Humanistic and the National. The imaginative product is those admirable pictures of life and manners, and that beautiful and perfect form of social expression, which characterise literary style from the times immediately preceding the Revolution of 1688 down to the death of Pope. But as these aristocratic forms of life are dependent mainly on but two sources, the period of aristocratic decadence sets in more quickly than was the case with the mediæval styles of poetry. The aristocratic principle inspires poems like the *Rape of the Lock*, the *Epistles* and *Satires* of Pope, and *The Essay on Man;* it is still strongly felt in such works as *The Deserted Village* and *The Traveller*; but it becomes pompous and grotesque in Darwin's *Botanic Garden*, tame and mannered in *The Pleasures of Hope* and *The Pleasures of Memory*. Here, too, we see that the decline of the Classic style in poetry is coincident with the decay of aristocratic supremacy which was terminated by the Reform Bill of 1832.

This aristocratic decline was due to an exaggerated conception of the principle of Constitutional Order; and the exaltation of the principle of authority in politics finds its analogy in literature, in the predominant attention paid by the aristocratic writers of the period to correctness of style. The rise of the Middle Classes, on the other hand—of the Classes, whose political influence has, on the whole, now been paramount for more than sixty years—was characterised by a passionate devotion to the principle of individual liberty. At first allying themselves with the Whig section of the aristocracy, the Middle Classes advanced cautiously, qualifying the principle of commercial liberty, for example, as Adam Smith did, with a defence of the Navigation Laws, and contenting themselves with such measures of Reform as might be conceded by a leader like Lord Grey. But as their political power increased, each of the sections of which the Middle Classes are composed showed a tendency to pursue its own ideal of Freedom—Freedom of Thought, Freedom of Speech, Freedom of Trade—without reference to the order of the corporate life of the nation; and hence the general effect of national policy since 1832 has been at once to promote all the activities of personal life—Money-making, Journalism, Mechanical Invention—and to resist any interference on the part of the State with the freedom of the individual. The net result of the habit has been a decline in the influence of central authority.

Now it is well worth observing what a close relationship there is between this political tendency in the history of the Middle Classes, as the governing power of the country, and the movement in the sphere of taste and imagination which has accompanied it. Since the close of the last century the main current of taste has run in strong antagonism to the aristocratic principles established after the Revolution of 1688. So long as the dominant motive of the new school of poetry was, in one form or another, the sentiment of *action* inspired by the French Revolution, the chief poets of the early part of the present century, Byron, Shelley, and—when he was not misled by his own theories—Wordsworth, sought mainly to amplify and extend universal modes of poetical expression sanctioned by generations of usage. Very soon, however, the centrifugal, individualising tendencies of the time disclosed themselves in two theories of poetry which, while sharply opposed to each other in their results, were agreed in placing the source of Poetry solely in the mind of the individual poet, and in disregarding the continuity of tradition in the art itself. One of these was headed by Wordsworth, who taught, first, that the poet can make all things poetical by his own imagination, and hence that the selection of distinctively imaginative subjects is not essential in poetry; secondly that, as the proper language of poetry is the language actually used by simple men, all traditional distinctions between the language of poetry and the language of prose are false and arbitrary. The other movement originated with Keats, who, shrinking from the forms of vulgarity and meanness visible in the actual life of his time, sought for the life of poetry in abstract beauty of form. In both directions there has been a withdrawal from those universal sources of imaginative life that inspire the action of the nation, and a corresponding exaggeration of individual consciousness; the followers of Wordsworth carrying Poetry into the sphere of Philosophy, Analysis, Psychology, with an almost complete disregard of the universal requirements of art; and the disciples of Keats seeking to identify the art of Poetry more and more with the arts of Painting and Music.

Similar symptoms, as I showed in my last lecture, manifest themselves in all historic periods of Poetical Decadence. If it be asked how I connect these symptoms with the characteristic taste of the Middle Classes, I answer: First, the impassioned pursuit of Liberty has encouraged an enormous growth of self-consciousness, which accounts for the exaggeration of the individual element in modern poetry; secondly, the sectional tendencies in the Middle Classes have helped to disintegrate that union of primal forces on which the ideal life of the nation so largely depends;

and this accounts for the decay of the universal element.

The Middle Classes have always played a great and valuable part in English History by balancing and reconciling conflicting principles in the nation, but they have not been themselves strongly in sympathy with any one of these. The Middle Class, as such, has been opposed to the life of ecclesiastical Catholicism by reason of its Puritanic instincts; it has been opposed to the life of Feudalism in consequence of its commercial instincts; mainly inspired by the practical object of the moment, it has little sympathy with the tradition of classical culture; while its own worship of personal liberty naturally tends to weaken the life and action of the nation as a whole. Intellectually eager, and of a boundless private benevolence, its imaginative interest is excited by the novel and curious rather than by the beautiful, just as its most practical virtues are those which radiate from the centre of home, independently of the larger interests of the State. It is a rare thing to find an average Englishman of the Middle Class submitting the freedom of his individual impulses to the control of any reasoned ideal, divine or human. But this habit of mind does not take us into the region of the Universal, or quicken that historic conscience which is, on the one hand, an essential condition of social order, and, on the other, a necessary element in the life of poetry. And hence, now that the Middle Classes find themselves confronted with collective ideals of Order or Disorder, opposed to their own notions of Individual Liberty—the ideal of Socialism; the aggressive ideals of other Nations; the ideals of the Greater Britain beyond our own islands—they are bewildered and perplexed; and the exhaustion of their capital stock of beliefs reflects itself in the anarchical conflict of ideas embodied in contemporary Fiction and Poetry.

History, however, shows us that the political decline of a single class need not involve decadence in the people; and it cannot be said that there has been a lack of ideals—of attempts to recover the idea of the Universal in our national life and poetry—originated by men of genius with a view of staying the contemporary movement of imaginative exhaustion in the Middle Class. I propose to consider briefly three such ideals, because they seem to me to represent characteristically the main tendencies which, during the present generation, have been operating in the governing portion of society; and if I examine them with strictness, and even severity, I would ask my hearers to believe that it is not because I do not sympathise with much of what is proposed, or because I wish to depreciate the genius of those who propose it, but because I am trying to test the adequacy of the one, and the authority of the other, by a standard which is above and beyond that of any individual, namely, the ideal life of England itself.

The first ideal which I will consider was put forward from the midst of the Middle Class, and by one whose name is eminent among the holders of this Chair; I need hardly say that I allude to the ideal of culture as defined by Matthew Arnold. Matthew Arnold enjoys the rare distinction of having been the first to oppose the imaginative self-satisfaction of the Middle Classes; his portrait of Bottles, as the self-satisfied Englishman, is in its way a creation; his playful vein was never more happily employed than in commenting on such watchwords as the " Dissidence of Dissent"; he showed courage in criticising the self-conscious swagger of anonymous journalism. Many of his favourite phrases, "Right Reason," "Our better Selves," "Perfection," seem to involve the recognition of some positive and universal standard of authority by reference to which the soundness of all private ideals may be tested. He uses language which shows his sense of the necessity of the Universal as an element in the Life of Poetry : " We are sure," he says, " that the endeavour to reach through culture the firm intelligible law of things, we are sure that the detaching ourselves from our stock notions and habits, that a more free play of consciousness, an increased desire for sweetness and light, and all the bent which we call Hellenising, is the master-impulse now of the life of our nation and of Humanity—somewhat obscurely perhaps for the moment, but decisively for the immediate future—and that those who work for this are the sovereign educators." This sounds well. But the moment these phrases are examined, it is seen that they have no reference to the Universal, as manifested in our English life, but are, in fact, the quintessence of Individualism, the climax of Negation.

The free play of Consciousness which is recommended is in reality only the analysis of Self-Consciousness. The idea of Perfection is derived from a comparison of self with the imperfection of one's neighbours. Asked what ideal of national *action* he desires to promote, Matthew Arnold replies: " Because machinery is the bane of politics, and an inward working, and not machinery is what we most want, we keep advising our ardent young Liberal friends to think less of machinery, to stand more aloof from the arena of politics at present, and rather to try and promote with us an inward working." In fact, Matthew Arnold, in respect of all that concerns life and action, seems to be in pretty general agreement with that melancholy apostle of Poetical Decadence, M. Charles Morice, whose opinions I noticed in my last lecture. I do not understand very readily how either Politics or Poetry can dispense with the aid of machinery. Of Poetry at any rate we may say that all the great forms of enduring Poetry, Epic, Dramatic, Lyric, are essentially based upon action; and it is therefore a significant illustration of the Individualism, which is a sign of Decadence, that Matthew Arnold should define Poetry as the *Criticism* of Life.

Again, if we test the ideal of self-conscious Culture by its practical results, we find that it offers very unsatisfactory remedies for those excesses of Middle Class Individualism which it justly criticises. I know of no more salutary corrective for the vanity of the criticism which trusts solely to the infallibility of its own intuitions, than a comparison of the principles recommended by Matthew Arnold with his practical application of them. For example: "To reach through Culture the firm intelligible law of things." Think then of Matthew Arnold's application of this principle to English society, and "the law of things" which was disclosed to his perception; his division of his own nation into Barbarians, Philistines, and Populace—could any phrases and terms be found to-day more esoteric, more unmeaning, more obsolete? Or again: "An increased desire for sweetness and light." Was it sweetness and light that suggested to Matthew Arnold's imagination the simile of the three Lord Shaftesburys? Or: "All the bent which we call Hellenising." Hellenising, nevertheless, was of no avail to prevent that fine and beautiful taste which once embodied itself in *The Scholar Gipsy* and *Thyrsis* from conceiving and committing to print the following sentence: "From such a spectacle as that of poor Mrs. Lincoln—a spectacle to vulgarise a whole nation—aristocracies undoubtedly preserve us!" A form of Culture which is constantly violating the first principles of good breeding will scarcely enable us to renew the decadent life of Poetry.

Another ideal of Life and Poetry is offered to us by Mr. Swinburne. Mr. Swinburne has, in one respect, taken his torch from the hand of Matthew Arnold. His is "the bent which we call Hellenising." But he understands the word in a different sense from that of his predecessor. Hellenising with Mr. Swinburne means ideas drawn exclusively from the fountain of the Classical Renaissance, a tributary of

English poetry undoubtedly full of life and freshness, but which, unless it is merged with the other waters of the national imagination, soon swells into revolution. From the first his most characteristic poems have been those which, like *Atalanta in Calydon*, have been inspired by recollections of Greek mythology and the Greek drama. The effect of this source of inspiration has been to give his genius great largeness of idea and great swiftness of movement; and the influence of these qualities on the art has been beneficial, because they have helped to deliver imagination from Wordsworth's fatal heresy, that there is no distinction between the diction of poetry and the diction of prose. Mr. Swinburne has done more than any living poet to prove the intimate connection between Poetry and Oratory; and when he lights on a theme worthy of his genius, no man has shown a greater mastery of the traditional style of English lyric verse: witness his very fine lines on Greece in *Songs before Sunrise*:—

> There where our East looks always to thy West,
>   Our mornings to thine evenings, Greece to thee,
> These lights that catch the mountains crest by crest,
>   Are they of stars or beacons that we see?
> Taygetus takes here the winds abreast,
>   And there the sun resumes Thermopylæ;
> The light is Athens where those remnants rest,
>   And Salamis the sea-wall of that sea;
> The grass men tread upon
> Is very Marathon;
> The leaves are of that time unstricken tree,
>   That storm nor sun can fret,
>   Nor wind, since she that set,

> Made it her sign to men whose shield was she:
> Here, as dead Time his deathless things,
> Eurotas and Cephisus keep their sleepless springs.

The weakness of Mr. Swinburne's ideal is that it is not drawn from the active traditional Life of the People. It was well to replenish Poetry from the spring of classical culture, the loss of which, under the influence of Middle Class taste, was starving the stream of English poetical conception, just as the loss of the mediæval spring diminished the volume and energy of the aristocratic style in the last century. But it was not well to isolate the tributary of the Renaissance from the current of the national thought and language, in which it had been historically blended with other influences, and, by a violent reaction from the tastes of the Middle Classes, to set up the ideal of Paganism as something opposed to the ideal of Christianity. The consequence of the separation has been that, though the idea of the Universal enters into Mr. Swinburne's poetical conceptions, it is of an abstract character, and does not spring out of the ἦθος and tradition of the people: having its source rather in the self-consciousness of the poet than in the widely diffused consciousness of society, it can be apprehended by the intellect, but does not often touch the heart. Mr. Swinburne's abstract mode of poetical conception reflects itself vividly in his modes of poetical expression. His verse is of a fine oratorical order, but the oratory is of a kind which appeals only to those who can follow the train of ideas set in motion by a particular keynote. Picturesque phrases, detached from books, provide themes for metrical composition; the imagery of the Bible, separated from its religious associations, is transferred into the sphere of Revolutionary politics; the words employed, instead of being suggested by the spontaneous energy of thought, seem to fall into their places through some prearrangement of rhythmical melody. But these as I have already urged are methods better fitted for the arts of Painting and Music than for Poetry, and hence the pursuit of Abstract Ideal Form seems a principle as inadequate as the Criticism of Culture for supplying the universal element needed to counteract the decadence of poetical Life.

The poetry of Mr. Rudyard Kipling, on the other hand, supplies many of the elements of life and action which are wanting in Mr. Swinburne's poetry. Mr. Kipling has learned much from Mr. Swinburne in the way of versification—swiftness, energy, freedom of style; and he has applied these qualities to subjects taken directly from the life of the people. Wherever he looks he finds something to interest his imagination; his motto is *Quidquid agunt homines.* Indian Mythology; Suttee; the Parnell Commission; American humour; elementary instincts of race and nation; the simple yet unerring intuitions of the Barrack room; all these supply him with themes for verse; and he generally treats them in the form of the Ballad, often with admirable effect. Those of my audience who may have read a poem called *An Imperial Rescript*, ridiculing from the popular point of view the nebulous philanthropy of schemes proceeding from lofty spheres in Germany, will recognise an almost unrivalled genius for seizing and reproducing the modes of thought characteristic of the people in different nations. And in the very fine narrative poem called *East and West* they will equally appreciate the power of an imagination capable of translating the undying spirit of Chivalry into the modern thought and language proper to the Western and Eastern minds. The country owes a large debt of gratitude to Mr. Kipling for reviving in English poetry the spirit of manly action and imperial enthusiasm as a corrective of the miserable pessimism which is the canker of modern society.

Still Mr. Kipling's method of Poetical Conception and Expression has its limitations, which may be defined by saying that it shows an imperfect appreciation of the difference between the Life of Verse and the Life of Poetry. His work, if I may borrow the convenient jargon of the time, is that of an Impressionist; and Metrical Impressionism bears the same relation to Poetry as Journalism to Literature. The life which he seeks to embody in his poetry is derived from observations of the actual world of sense and experience rather than from the world of universal ideas. Take his conception of Romance for example. He blames his contemporaries for not seeing that there is Romance in the working of an express train. But this is to use the word Romance in a private sense, without reference to its universal historical meaning, and to ignore that craving for the

Ideal and the Supernatural which is a fundamental instinct of the human mind. Again, in a poem called the *Story of Ung*, he seems to place the difference between the artist and those whom the artist seeks to please in the artist's superior powers of observation and exact imitation; he thinks that the artist sees and imitates something in actual nature which others do not see; whereas the real superiority of the painter or the poet, if we measure by the work of the highest excellence, lies, as I have already urged, in the ability to find expression for imaginative ideas of nature floating unexpressed in the general mind.

Mr. Kipling has, quite logically, no belief in any kind of criticism; and his ideas on the subject of Art are put forward in a sketch of a critic in the Neolithic Age, which contains a parable :—

> A rival of Solutré told the tribe my style was outré:
> 'Neath a hammer forged of dolomite he fell;
> And I left my views on art, barbed and tanged, below the heart
> Of a mammothistic etcher at Grenelle.
>
> Then I stripped them, scalp from skull, and my hunting dogs fed full,
> And their teeth I threaded neatly on a thong;
> And I wiped my mouth and said: "It is well that they are dead;
> For I know my work is right and theirs is wrong."
>
> But my Totem saw the shame; from his ridge-pot shrine he came,
> And he told me in a vision of the night,
> "There are nine and sixty ways of constructing tribal lays,
> And every single one of them is right."

That is excellent and amusing verse; but the parable and its moral are untrue, both historically and scientifically. For in the early tribal stage of society the poetical view of Nature is universal; criticism does not exist; the poet puts readily into verse the poetical thoughts shared by all his countrymen. It is when society advances, when men begin to distinguish the thoughts that should be expressed in prose from the thoughts that are proper for verse, that criticism seeks to discover the rules of right and wrong. The sphere of the Universal and Ideal is contracted by the mind itself, and the task of high genius lies in finding out the themes that are fitted for poetry, and in clothing them with the form of expression adapted to their true nature. Of the nine and sixty ways of constructing *civil* lays only the great classical poets of every country know how to invent the way which will continue to give pleasure to the imagination; and, therefore, as I have said many times, it is in the works of the great classical poets alone that the law of poetry is to be looked for.

The failure to recognise the validity of this law is the weak point in Mr. Kipling's poetry. He is not careful in the selection of his themes; he does not reflect on the nature of the Universal; like Ung in his own poem, he has something of a contempt for the ideas of his audience. Consequently he often fails in point of expression. Satisfied with his own individual perceptions, he thinks only of embodying them in a swift and fluent form of verse, without considering how they will strike the judgment of the reader; hence his thoughts often lack distinction, and he takes no trouble to choose out of his vast vocabulary of popular words those which are really adapted for the purposes of poetry. Experience has recently read him a lesson as to the nature of the Universal in poetry which he will doubtless lay to heart. He desired very rightly to do honour to the Canadians for the imperial aim of their proposed financial legislation, and he thought to please them by a set of verses, in which he called Canada "Our Lady of Snows." But he did not altogether please them. The Canadians, with a just critical instinct, perceived that the title of the poem was not poetically true. It was, in fact, an affectation borrowed from those abstract musical modes of diction sanctioned by the example of Mr. Swinburne, not having any sound foundation in Nature, and lacking the simple dignity which the occasion demanded.

Let me now put before you, as succinctly as I can, the whole question in the form which the course of our argument has caused it to assume. The most marked characteristic in the contemporary art and literature of every country in Europe, is the pursuit of Novelty; by which word I mean not the freshness, character, and individuality, which are essential to every work of genius, but the determination to discover absolutely new *matter* for artistic treatment, and the deliberate rejection of those first principles of taste which the greatest artists have traditionally obeyed. In the art of Poetry, for example, the one with which we are immediately concerned, the modern artist, in

L

opposition to ancient practice, either ignores the necessity of finding his groundwork in the selection and conception of a subject common to himself and his audience, or insists on his right of treating his subject without regard to the public taste and experience. Every one can see for himself that this is the way in which an essentially modern dramatist like Ibsen constructs his plays. If for the moment we extend, with Aristotle, the word Poetry so as to include fictions in prose, we observe that, in the most characteristic form of the Russian or French novel, the aim of the writer, almost invariably, is to manipulate *a priori* ideas so as to illustrate a moral of his own making—a structural method which is opposed to the tradition of story-telling from the days of Boccaccio downwards.

Analysis of motive, not ideal representation of action, is, in fact, the first principle of contemporary epic and dramatic composition. Analysis has penetrated even the lyrical mode of poetical expression, causing the poet to look for themes mainly in personal sentiments and opinions, which are as often as not the fruits of pessimist philosophy. Corresponding with this revolution in the sphere of poetical conception, there has been a complete departure from traditional development in the modes of poetical expression. The modern versifier looks for words, phrases, and rhythmical movements, as far removed as possible from the prevailing popular idiom ; and in pursuit of his end he confuses the hitherto well-defined boundaries between poetry, on the one hand, and painting and music on the other, assimilating his practice wherever he can to the methods adopted by the professors of those sister arts.

The question is whether these strongly outlined features are the signs of Life or Decadence in Poetry. The new School of Poetry and its admirers say that they are the manifestation of an exuberant energy, and that the art has before it a boundless future of growth and productiveness. On the other hand, the men of science, represented by Herr Nordau, maintain that the fashionable novelties of the day are the signs of Poetical Decadence. But this conclusion they arrive at from other than æsthetic premises. In Herr Nordau's judgment the Decadence of Art is only a necessary phase of the general decay of modern society; he holds that the action of Imagination is febrile, affected, and unmanly, because society, exhausted by the wear and tear of city life, has become hysterical, nervous, and corrupt. Poetical Decadence is part and parcel of Social Degeneration, and is, therefore, to be judged on the crudest pathological principles.

Against this fatalist method of judgment, equally unscientific in its procedure and depressing in its conclusions, it is necessary to protest. I agree with Herr Nordau in thinking that the tendencies of modern Poetry, Painting, and Music are indicative of artistic Decadence rather than artistic Invention, since they are substantially identical with the characteristics that have always presented themselves in historic periods of artistic and social decline. But it would be unworthy of those who are conscious of moral freedom to believe that the process of decay in such periods has followed an iron law of destiny, or that we are to-day the victims of an imaginative disease which it is beyond our power to remedy. The causes of Poetical Decadence are partly individual, in so far as they proceed from the errors of the artist, partly social, in so far as they depend upon the condition of the public taste; in both cases they are moral, not physical, and are therefore under our own control.

In the individual artist decline of power proceeds from a self-conscious analysis which cuts off the mind from the great universal sources of Inspiration, and leads it to feed upon itself, or to look for the fountains of life in the local and transitory interests of the moment. Artistic vanity of this kind obtrudes itself in all stages of society. Homer furnishes us with an example of it many centuries before the Christian era. You may remember the lines in which, in his own inimitable incidental way, he describes how Thamyris lost the gift of poetry: "The Muses," says he, "meeting Thamyris the Thracian as he went up from Œchalia from the house of Eurytus the Œchalian, made him cease from singing. For he made in his boasts as though he would prevail, even though the Muses, daughters of ægis-bearing Zeus, should sing against him. But they, being provoked to anger, made him blind, and took away from him divine song and made him forget his minstrelsy." Thamyris was self-conscious; he was a follower of Art for Art's sake; enamoured of his own thoughts, his own skill, he failed to understand that all genuine inspiration comes to the mind unconsciously, as we have seen that it came to Scott when he was meditating *The Lay of the Last Minstrel*. Homer and Milton, on the other hand, show themselves reverently aware of this truth when they call on the Heavenly Muse to raise their genius to the height of their arguments, and submit themselves obediently to the external laws of their art.

Self-conscious vanity in the nineteenth century is described by a great writer who was himself as responsible as any man for the propagation of the deadly principle of Imaginative Analysis : " Trop souvent à Paris," says Balzac, " dans le désir d'arriver plus promptement que par la voie naturelle à cette célébrité qui pour eux est la fortune, les artistes empruntent les ailes de la circonstance, ils iroient se grandir en se faisant les hommes d'une chose, en devenant les souteneurs d'une système, et ils espèrent changer une coterie en public. Tel est républicain, tel autre est Saint-Simonien, tel est aristocrate, tel catholique, tel juste milieu, tel moyen âge, ou allemand, par parti pris. Mais si l'opinion ne donne pas le talent, elle le gâte toujours, témoin le pauvre garçon vous venez de voir. L'opinion d'un artiste doit être la foi dans les œuvres, et son seul moyen de succès le travail, quand la nature lui a donné le feu sacré."[1] When authors so dissimilar as Homer and Balzac agree in ascribing the decay of art to exaggerated self-consciousness, the impassioned followers of Novelty would do well to pause and consider in what direction they are hurrying with so much enthusiasm.

[1] *Les comédiens sans le savoir.*

The second cause of the Decadence of Poetry is social, namely, the want of cultivation and refinement in the public taste. Under the rule of the Middle Classes—so different in this respect from the aristocracy of the eighteenth century—the principle *De gustibus non est disputandum* has received, in the sphere of Art, as much encouragement as the principle *Laisser Faire* in the sphere of Politics and Economics. Philosophic authority is cited in favour of this sublime indifference, which arises, in fact, from sheer insensibility. "The Art," says Addison, "is to conform to the Taste, not the Taste to the Art." A true saying, but one that needs to be understood. As the end of art is to produce pleasure, poets and all other artists must take into account alike the constitution of the human mind and the circumstances of the society which it is their business to please. Shakespeare would not have been the greatest of dramatists if he had simply attempted to embody his own æsthetic and moral conceptions, without considering what was expected of him in the structure of his plays, even by "the groundlings." Raphael and Titian were great painters because they reflected, not only on what was beautiful in itself, but on the relation of the beautiful to altar-pieces and other architectural conditions in the religious life of their time. So much submission to the social order on the part of the artist is necessary, if the Universal in art is to be manifested to the world with individual colour, life, and character.

But in allowing this I am far from assenting to the proposition that the idea of the Universal, the enduring law of life in Art, is to be found in uneducated public taste. Popular taste has, no doubt, a foundation in Nature. The majority, judging by instinct, often agree among themselves, and make their opinion irresistibly felt, as is shown by the judgments of the spectators in the theatre, or by the popularity of a novel, and in these judgments there is generally some truth. But the unrefined instinct of the multitude is, as a rule, in favour of what is obvious and superficial: impatient of reflection, it is attracted by the loud colours and the commonplace sentiment which readily strike the senses or the affections. Observe the popular songs in the Music Halls, the pictorial advertisements on the hoardings, the books on the railway stall, the lists in the circulating libraries; from these may be divined the level to which the public taste is capable of rising by its own untrained perception. That which is natural in such taste is also vulgar; and if vulgar Nature is to be the standard of Art, nothing but a versatile mediocrity of invention is any longer possible. Let Art conform to Taste in this sense of the word; let the imagination of the people be identified with the imagination of the majority of the moment; let Money be the standard by which all things are to be measured; and it follows logically that every kind of art must transform itself into some species of journalism, and that what is traditionally known as Fine Art must fall into hopeless decay.

I decline, however, to identify the transient impressions of what is called Public Opinion with the settled Conscience of the People, or to believe that this Conscience is so deadened and materialised as to be unable to apprehend the law upon which the life of Poetry and all fine art depends. Let me remind you of the definition with which we started on this inquiry. "Poetry is the art of producing pleasure for the imagination by imitating human actions, thoughts, and passions in metrical language." "The art of producing pleasure for the imagination." What pleasure? whose imagination? Not pleasure for the mere collection of individuals living in England, the majority of whom, to use the words of Aristotle, are necessarily "without any idea of the noble and truly pleasant, of which they have never tasted." Not pleasure intended to gratify the refined curiosity of the sect or the coterie, or even adapted to the separate perceptions and inclinations of the aristocracy, the Middle Classes, and the Democratic Classes; but pleasure which can be felt by what is best in the English People as a whole, when it throws its imagination back to its own infancy, and travels along the course of the traditions of its art and literature; pleasure such as has been produced by one generation of great poets after another whose work still moves in the reader wonder and delight.

Again, what is meant by *Imitation* in Poetry? Not the prosaic transcript of external things. Not even that imaginative representation of things which may be produced by an analysis of the poet's own consciousness. Self-consciousness must no doubt enter in some degree into all modern artistic conceptions; we cannot escape from it; it is the inevitable attendant of the advance of society in knowledge and civilisation. But if Poetry is to survive—I will go further and say if the civilisation of England is to survive—we must recognise, as the true sphere of imitation, a region of consciousness above and beyond our own; the source of life which Matthew Arnold was thinking of when he speaks of "right reason," "our better self," "the firm intelligible law of things"; and which Mr. Kipling's soldier heroes dimly but undoubtingly apprehend, when they exalt in their peculiar idiom the virtues of discipline, obedience, and order. The poet must imitate the Universal. It is only when he starts from the basis of an universal Idea—whether this be the inspiration of Faith or the tradition of Authority—that he acquires the power to *create;* that is, to reproduce in an ideal form the image of external Nature.

See how this truth is illustrated in the work of the two greatest creators in English Poetry, Shakespeare and Milton. Shakespeare is supreme among poets, because he was the least hampered by the distractions of self-consciousness, or at any rate had his own self-consciousness most under control; accepting alike every species of established order in the world about him, he was able to sympathise with whatever was Catholic and Chivalric, National and Historic, Scholastic and Humane, in English Society, to conceive a multitude of characters at once natural and ideal, and to breathe dramatic life and reality into a hundred imaginary situations that had been for ages floating vaguely in the tales of *trouvères* and annalists. Milton, rising above the sphere of self-consciousness, conquered for himself a large region of ideal freedom by blending in his mind universal, though opposing, conceptions, derived from the dogmas of the Christian Religion, the imagery of mediæval Romance, and all the art, culture, and civic wisdom of Pagan Antiquity.

Inspiration by the Universal, then, must be regarded as the essential source of Life in Poetry. This has been the main contention of the series of lectures I have now concluded. I have shown by reference to the works of the greatest poets how the universal idea is conceived in the imagination; how it demands for itself expression by means of metre as distinct from prose; how when the sense of the Universal wanes in society the art of Poetry also dwindles and declines. But there remains a side of the question which I have only touched superficially. Though the suggestion of universal ideas to the poet proceeds from unconscious inspiration, the right treatment of the Universal is the function of Taste. At this point, in fact, *self-consciousness* necessarily comes into operation. Theoretically we are all ready to acknowledge that the end of every kind of poetry is "to hold the mirror up to Nature," that is, to express the undefined idea of what is naturally beautiful, sublime, or pathetic; the difficulty is to present this common idea to our own generation; "to show the very age and body of the time, his form and pressure."

To put the problem in the shape of a question, How is the poet to subject the liberties of genius to the laws of cultivated taste? For though, in the late stage of society at which we have arrived, each man retains in his own imagination fragments and glimpses of the great ideal view of Nature which in its infancy our society shared collectively, this has been so individualised by the natural growth of civilisation, and so obscured by the intervention of transient fashions of thought, that anything like consent in matters of art and taste seems to be almost impossible. I imagine that Tennyson, perhaps the most skilful poetical *artist* of the century, completely deceived himself when he declared that he sang "but as the linnet sings." The modern poet has to decide in the first place whether the ideas that present themselves to his imagination are genuine inspirations or only Idols of the Fancy; then to discover the form best suited to embody his conception; to estimate the value of different ideas relatively to the composition as a whole; to select some, to reject others, to arrange what remain; to find the right word for the expression of the thought, and the right position of the word in the verse. All these perplexing conditions make the composition of poetry as different as possible from the song of a bird; Art as well as Nature has to be consulted; and if poetic conception is to issue in a permanent form of poetic expression, the poet must be a man not only of the highest invention but of the finest judgment.

Such being the case, it appears to me that it will be both natural and useful to supplement this inquiry into the conditions of Life in Poetry by an investigation of the nature of Law in Taste. I propose during the remainder of my tenure of this Chair to consider that subject in a fresh series of lectures, in which I shall attempt to show the universality of the instinct which has prompted men in civilised communities to express in verse their idea of Nature, and also the causes which have so modified man's idea of the Universal in Nature as to give a peculiar character and individuality to the poetry of every nation; when I have completed this survey I shall seek to draw from it some practical conclusions as to the possibility of directing the course of liberal education in England, and particularly in the Universities, with a view to influencing the national taste.

PART III

LAW IN TASTE

I

INTRODUCTORY

In most of the departments of Life or Knowledge, Englishmen have earned the character of yielding a ready obedience to the claims of Law and Order. We are strict in requiring submission to the prescriptions of Moral Law. We know that our civil liberties depend on our loyal observance of the Common Law of the land. We perceive the necessity of subordinating the freedom of individual fancy to the severe laws of Physical Science. But there is a very extensive region of the understanding within which each of us is inclined to claim for himself an absolute exemption from law; we do not admit that there is any obligation on the individual to examine, school, and regulate his perceptions in matters of Art and Taste. "There has never been in England," says Augustus Schlegel, "an academical school of taste; in art, as in life, every man there gives his voice for what best pleases him, or what is most suitable to his own individual nature." And so far have we carried this liberty that criticism, or the would-be exposition of æsthetic law, has fallen among us into something like disrepute. " The critics," said Lord Beaconsfield, making an epigram which he knew would be popular, " are the men who have failed."

How far is this tendency in the English mind reasonable? It is undoubtedly grounded on two fundamental instincts in the constitution of our nature, our determination to abide by the results of experience, and our love of what is practical. Englishmen are sceptical in all matters that cannot be brought to the test of actual experience, and it is this national characteristic which has given rise on one side to the inductive philosophy of Bacon, Locke, and Newton, and on the other to the speculative school of David Hume, which maintains that no system of order is discoverable transcending the immediate perceptions of sense. Within the domain of philosophy we are right to follow logic to its legitimate conclusions. But reasoning which is valid for the philosopher may for the average mind simply provide an excuse for avoiding the primary duties of thought. We are obliged to recognise not only the fact that from the days of Aristotle men in every generation, and in every civilised society, have occupied themselves with attempts to discover the fundamental laws of Fine Art, but also that, by the very constitution of the human mind, each man is a critic. When we read a work of fiction, or look at a picture or a statue, if we reflect at all, we go through some process of reasoning and comparison which justifies our mind in remaining in a state of pleasure or dissatisfaction. Moreover, we find that this process of reasoning is not an operation peculiar to ourselves, but something that can be compared with and measured by the experience of our neighbours. Evidently, then, our immediate æsthetic perceptions are capable of analysis, and there is at least a possibility, that the common perceptions of any society of men about objects of art may be derived from some absolute system of Law and Order in Nature itself.

Again, it is argued that, even if the laws of taste were discoverable, they would be of no practical use, either to the artist who creates, or to the world which judges of the artist's work. This is an argument which finds a kind of ally in the disposition of the philosopher. For example, a distinguished member of this University, Mr. Bernard Bosanquet, the author of a very valuable *History of Æsthetic*, which may be studied with the greatest advantage by all who wish to follow me in this course of lectures, says: "Æsthetic theory is a branch of philosophy, and exists for the sake of knowledge, and not as a guide to practice." Now that is surely not quite true. Aristotle, the first of æsthetic theorists, was no doubt interested in discovering the laws of fine art, mainly as part of the system of Nature, but no sooner had he defined the fundamental laws of poetry than he proceeded to apply them, as we see from the rules he lays down for the composition of "the perfect tragedy." In the same way Mr. Ruskin in our own time began his *Modern Painters* with an investigation of general principles, and after satisfying himself as to the nature of these, he brought many painters and poets to his bar of judgment, causing thereby a great revolution in the sphere of taste.

The truth is, that art forms so large a part of the enjoyment of life, that the study of its principles cannot be carried on altogether in the sublime and indifferent region of philosophy. The fears, the hopes, the ambitions of men mingle themselves inseparably with the serene practice of art, often, indeed, stirring up something of that eager and acrid emotion which accompanies the conflict of politics in a free country; so that though it be true, as Schlegel says, that " in England every man gives his voice for what best pleases him, or what is most suitable to his own nature," yet it is equally true that every man of spirit is anxious to see his own artistic opinion prevail, and, just as in politics, will use all the machinery at his disposal to make it prevail. To the constant clashing of myriads of individual tastes, advocated without method, and with all the heat of party spirit, is to be attributed the unhappy reputation which has gathered round the name of the English critic.

My object in the course of lectures which I propose to deliver is to consider the question of Law in Taste in a practical temper, to examine what its nature is, where it is to be looked for, how it is to be applied, and to what extent it can be made the subject of mental training and discipline. I am anxious to remove the question alike from the region of metaphysics and the atmosphere of party, and I therefore ask my hearers to condescend to enter upon the inquiry in the most elementary manner, banishing, as far as possible, all technical and philosophical terms, and making use only of such arguments as can be popularly understood.

Now the Law of Taste must be determined by the end of Fine Art, and let me say at once that when I speak of Fine Art, I am satisfied with the distinction which Aristotle draws between the useful and the imitative Arts; between those which have a practical end in use or profit, and those whose end is pleasure; between those which seek to make Nature their servant, and those which are satisfied with imitating her; the latter alone—namely Poetry, Sculpture, Painting, Music, and to a certain extent Architecture—being entitled to the name of the Fine Arts. The end of Fine Art may therefore be regarded from two sides: one being the object of Imitation which the artist proposes to himself; the other the effect which the imitation itself produces on the mind. First, as to the object of imitation. I use the word "imitation" partly because it has been consecrated by long usage in all discussions about Fine Art, and partly because it is, on the whole, the most general and philosophic term applicable to the subject, since it is obvious that, in one sense or another, all the fine arts involve a representation either of external objects or of the facts of human nature. This is the case even with Music. Music, indeed, appeared to the Greeks to be the most imitative of all the arts, because it was the most direct outward manifestation, in a rhythmical form, of the passions and emotions of men. We ourselves regard it in a different light, and find it difficult to associate with Music the idea of imitation except when it is accompanied with words. Nevertheless, the titles assigned by great modern masters to their compositions show that, to a certain extent at all events, human ideas and experiences are intended to be expressed by a combination of harmonious sounds; witness Mendelssohn's Songs without Words, Beethoven's Pastoral Symphony, and the different kinds of marches and requiems of other composers.

The first region in which we may look for the existence of Law in Art is, therefore, the merely correct imitation of external things, as they are conveyed to the mind through the senses. Each of the Fine Arts has certain elementary laws of imitation which the artist is bound to obey; for example, the painter's work must conform to the laws of perspective, and the proper distribution of light and shade; the musical composer must understand the due distribution of keys and rhythms; the poet must be acquainted with the conditions under which words can be harmoniously arranged in metre; and the man who would qualify himself to be a critic in any one of these arts must have the same amount of theoretical knowledge as the artist.

But this principle of the correct imitation of

Nature carries us but a very little way in our investigations of the Law of Taste; because it is evident that Nature and Art work with different materials, and express themselves in different forms. To imitate Nature correctly in any of the Arts is not to copy the exact appearances of things. The sculptor or painter does not attempt to imitate Nature by creating men in flesh and blood, but by representing them in marble and colour; the poet, in so far as he is a poet, will not reproduce on the stage the tragedies of life as they are met with in the police courts and reported in the newspapers; he shows to the spectators the actions and characters of men in situations of his own contriving. Every artist, in fact, puts into his imitation of external things something that is not to be found in the particular aspect of Nature. What that something is has been a matter of dispute from the earliest days of criticism. Some of the ancients called it τὸ καλόν, others τὸ βέλτιον; some of the moderns define it as the Beautiful, others as the Characteristic: this much at least is agreed upon, that the end of Fine Art is to produce an appearance of organic life in the sphere of the Ideal resembling something that exists in the sphere of the Real.

From this it follows very clearly that the end of Fine Art is not accomplished when the artist has put into form the ideal object which he has proposed to himself. For the object of imitation is, by the hypothesis, something external to the mind, and if the work of the artist be alone looked to, we cannot be sure that it is not an image of a monster, or chimera, or some other form of unreal existence. The artist himself may be like Horace's mad gentleman at Argos, who sat in the empty theatre pleasing himself with the idea that he was witnessing the progress of a drama on the stage. We want some test and verification of the ideal life presented to us by Art; and it is on this account that we have to look for the end of Fine Art in the effect which the imitation produces on the mind; in other words, we may decide that, quite apart from all questions as to the nature of the Beautiful or the Characteristic, the end of Fine Art is to produce æsthetic pleasure. When the pleasure felt is universal, when it is felt, that is to say, alike by the skilled critic and by the world which judges from instinct, then, and not till then, can it be said that life has been organised and created in the sphere of the Ideal, and the objective aim of Art certainly realised.

It is true that philosophers deny the necessity of considering pleasure as an essential portion of the law of Fine Art. Mr. Bosanquet who regards the investigation of the law of Beauty as the proper subject of æsthetic science, and who defines Beauty as "the characteristic, in as far as expressed for sense perception or imagination," says: "If, indeed, we were attempting a psychological determination of the feeling that attends or constitutes the peculiar enjoyment known as the enjoyment of beauty, we should probably have to deal with a term not mentioned in the definition above proposed — the term pleasure. But in attempting to analyse what it is that distinguishes perceptions or imaginations productive of this enjoyment from others which are not so productive, it appears to me that we should commit a serious error if we were to limit 'expressiveness' or 'characterisation' either by beauty, which is the term to be defined, or by pleasantness which is a quality not naturally coextensive with the term to be defined."

It may, indeed, be possible for the philosopher, whose mind dwells familiarly among abstract terms, so to isolate his perceptions that the ideas conveyed by the words, the Beautiful, the Sublime, the Ugly, may come to have a kind of objective existence; that he may feel himself able to note the laws of their nature, and to deduce from these the principles and limits of Fine Art. But even the philosopher must, in the first instance, have based his ideas on his observation of concrete things, which he includes under the words "beautiful," "sublime," and "ugly," and it is certain that he could not have detached these primary perceptions from the feelings of pleasure or pain with which they were accompanied. In the ultimate search, therefore, it seems certain that the laws of taste may be more confidently looked for in the affections of the mind, which it is possible to analyse with some precision, than in the nature of an external Order, which may indeed have an absolute existence, but which can only be known to us by its operation on, and its relation to, the organs of perception.

If this be so, however, another question of great difficulty and complexity at once arises. What is the nature of this imaginative pleasure which is so inseparably associated with the productions of Fine Art? Is it to be regarded as an end in itself, perfectly free and independent of all moral considerations? Or does it, like the pleasures of sense, fall within the scope and jurisdiction of the moral law? Must it be held the peculiar property of the individual, which may be enjoyed by him without any sense of responsibility to his neighbours? Or have his neighbours, who share the common perception, a right to pronounce judgment on these enjoyments of the individual, in so far as they constitute an element in the life and well-being of society?

Such are the questions which arise immediately we begin to reflect on the nature of Law in Taste; and in the midst of the multitudinous ocean of sentiments and opinions on which we are tossed, it is surely well for each man to look for the steadfast guidance of the stars; to form in his mind some settled principles by which he may test the value of the various works of art which are produced for his pleasure. I propose, therefore, in my present lecture to ask, in the first place, whether Æsthetic Philosophy, as such, and apart from artistic practice, can reveal to us any immutable truths about the two ends of Fine Art, Ideal Imitation and Imaginative Pleasure; and if not, whether there is any other method that we can pursue to discover the Law of Taste. For this purpose it will be convenient to give a very brief historical sketch, determined by well-known landmarks, of what Philosophy has said upon the two points I have mentioned.

Roughly speaking, the history of æsthetic criticism has run through five periods: the Greek civic period; the Alexandrian and Roman period; the Mediæval period; the period of the Renaissance; and the Modern period following the French Revolution. To take first what has been said in each period about Ideal Imitation. The first to approach the subject was Plato, who appropriated the word Imitation as it was popularly used by his contemporaries, and decided that, as the artist merely copied that surface of Nature which was three degrees removed from the truth of things, he must, as a teacher of falsehood, be banished from the Ideal Republic. Aristotle, continuing the use of Plato's terms, treated the question both more practically and more profoundly. He regarded Art as a rival creator with Nature, holding that the function of Art was to observe Nature's intentions in creation, and to express, in a matter and form distinct from that of Nature, a higher conception of the ends she had in view. Reasoning from these philosophical principles he laid down in his *Poetics*, as a practical critic, certain definite rules with regard to poetical composition, notably as to the construction of the perfect tragedy and the character of the ideal hero.

So far Philosophy had treated Art from a social and political point of view. Plato and Aristotle had been educated in the midst of ideas derived from the traditions of Greek political freedom, and all their criticism of Fine Art was inspired by their conceptions of the duties and capacities of the individual as a member of the State. But in the Alexandrian-Roman period the point of view of the æsthetic philosopher began to alter: the ideas of men grew cosmopolitan; their æsthetic reasoning became more theoretical and abstract. Within this period we find, for example, the philosopher Plotinus grounding himself on Plato in his speculations about the Beautiful; but, so far from condemning the artist's imitation of Nature, he approves of it as helping men to conceive an image of Divine Good. Thus he says of sculpture: "Phidias did not create his Zeus after any perceived pattern, but made him such as he would be if Zeus deigned to appear to mortal eyes." In this period too appears the æsthetic treatise assigned to Longinus, Περὶ ὕψους, or *The Sublime*, from which we see that the imagination of the artist is now allowed to travel beyond the imitation of what is regularly and symmetrically beautiful, and in which we get the first glimpse of the later controversy about the place of the "Ugly" in art. Moreover, there is a growing perception of the interrelation of the different Fine Arts as the vehicles of Imitation. Cicero, for example, says: "In fact, all the arts which relate to humanity have a certain common bond, and are united by a kind of family relationship;" while Plutarch, making the idea more specific, quotes the saying of Simonides that "Poetry is speaking painting, and painting dumb poetry." Finally, we have critical treatises like Horace's *Ars Poetica*, in which, as in the *Poetics* of Aristotle, there is a certain amount of reasoning from general principles, and a certain number of practical rules of composition.

From the Alexandrian-Roman we pass to the Mediæval Period, in which we witness the full effects on Art of the philosophical reasoning of Plato and Plotinus. The result of the Platonic and Neo-Platonic tradition joined to the teaching of the Catholic Church is, as regards Art, and especially the Art of Poetry— Allegory. Things that are seen are used by the poet as symbols and shadows of truths invisible. Dante, for example, says of Allegory: "Thus it is fitting to speak to your wit, seeing that it is only from a sensible object that it can apprehend what it afterwards makes worthy of the understanding. Wherefore the Scripture condescends to your intelligence and attributes feet and hands to God, while it understands something else; and Holy Church represents to you in human likeness Gabriel and Michael, and the other who restored Tobias to health."

The period known as the Renaissance brought the artist back from symbolism to the direct imitation of Nature, and advanced the authority of Aristotle, as an æsthetic philosopher, above that of Plato. This epoch is marked by several widespread controversies concerning the nature of Imitation in Fine Art, all more or less derived from legacies of thought and criticism bequeathed by the Greeks and Romans. In the seventeenth century Corneille, in three famous essays based on a misinterpretation of the *Poetics* of Aristotle, defined the duties of the dramatist in composition. The rules that he laid down were accepted with certain modifications as the law of the French stage, which was finally declared in the celebrated essay prefixed by Voltaire to his *Semiramis*, where he speaks of Shakespeare as a "drunken savage." Partly provoked by Voltaire's arrogance, and partly following national instinct, Lessing, in his *Hamburgische Dramaturgie*, attacked the first principles of the French drama, opposing to them a sounder interpretation of Aristotle's *Poetics*, and a more intelligent appreciation of the art of Shakespeare. Meantime, a parallel discussion, originated by the *Polymetis* of Spence, one of the early holders of this Chair of Poetry, had arisen concerning the relationship between Poetry and Painting. It took its rise from the saying of Simonides to which I have before alluded, and gradually developed into the theories of Mengs and Winckelmann, based on the study of Greek sculpture. This debate culminated in Lessing's essay, *Laocoon*, in which that great critic defined, more precisely than any previous writer, the different functions of Imitation discharged by Poetry and Painting. Almost at the same time philosophical inquiries into these or similar questions were made by Hogarth in his *Analysis of Beauty*, by Burke in his essay on *The Sublime and Beautiful*, and by Sir Joshua Reynolds in his *Discourses*, treating of the Grand and Characteristic styles in Painting, and of the first principles of that art.

Last of all we come to our own period, which may be truthfully called the Revolutionary Period, since it begins with the epoch of the French Revolution. The *primum mobile* of taste in this era is the philosophy of Kant, who started the great fundamental question, How to reconcile the world of sense and phenomena with the world of ideal Order existing in the mind. It would be impossible for me, in the brief time at my disposal, to condense into an intelligible shape the complex and difficult reasoning of Kant on the subject of Beauty and Fine Art. Suffice it to say, he himself concludes that the result of all theorising on such matters must remain purely subjective.

But if that be so, how can the artist be any longer sure that he has a firm groundwork in his imitation of external things, or that he will be able to convey to the imagination of others the organic conception which exists in his own? This was a question to which Schiller and Goethe, whose ambition it was to found a literature in Germany on philosophical principles, felt themselves bound to provide a theoretical answer. Each did so in his own way. Schiller, accepting the doctrine of Kant and Fichte, that the individual mind is the centre of the universe, nevertheless maintained that, for the artist, Beauty may have an external existence. The individual artist, he reasoned, has the capacity of clearly noting and reflecting on the semblances of things in his own mind; he has also within him the power of imitation, or, as Schiller called it, " the play-impulse," in other words, the desire of reconstructing the likenesses of external things in concrete images according to his own ideas of Order; out of these primary innate powers springs the organism of Fine Art. Goethe, on the other hand, who disliked metaphysics, based his æsthetic reasoning on his own perception of the falsehood of the classical conventionalism which had invaded all the arts in the eighteenth century, and maintained that the cause of art was the desire of the soul to imitate the idea of the Characteristic which it notes in the objects of external Nature. He seems to have obtained his generalised idea of the Characteristic partly from the distinct and contrasted types of ideal life embodied in Greek and German architecture, and partly from the observations of Winckelmann and Lessing on the inner significance of Greek sculpture and painting.

Not long after Goethe had originated the idea of the Characteristic, Augustus Schlegel gave it outline and emphasis in his *Lectures on Dramatic Poetry*, by drawing a sharp line of distinction between the Classic and Romantic spirit, and between the different methods of imitation pursued by the poets in ancient and modern times. Next, starting from the basis of the ideas and terms rendered familiar by the writings of Goethe and Schlegel, Schelling provided a philosophical framework for the suggestion furnished by Schiller. He worked up, as it were, through the purely subjective crust of Kant's philosophic principles to a kind of objective point in which he supposed the unconscious spirit of life in the world to meet with the conscious spirit of the individual mind, the result being the perception of Beauty and artistic Creation. This he called the Absolute. Hegel carried the idea a step further. He combined Schelling's conception of the unconscious spirit of life in the world with Schlegel's critical distinctions between Ancient and Modern, Classical and Romantic Art, in such a way that the unconscious life of the world was represented by him as progressing from point to point, like stages in a journey, each of which was reflected in the conscious mind of man through successive phases of Art. Every stage of civilisation in the world has found, in fact, according to Hegel, a central representation in one of the Arts, and each of the arts again has passed through three phases of imitation, called respectively the Symbolic, the Classic, and the Romantic. With Hegel whatever has been fruitful in the German analysis of the nature of Ideal Imitation comes to an end. It is needless to say that the interest aroused by these discussions has by no means been confined to the sphere of philosophy, but has for good or ill reacted on the course of art itself. The speculative theories of Germany led to the war between the Classicists and Romanticists in France after the restoration of the Bourbons, and prepared the way for the Preraphaelite movement in England after the first Reform Bill.

Now if we turn back to the other side of the question, and ask what the philosophy of the world has said about law in taste with regard to the effect which Fine Art produces in the mind, we see, in the first place, that the common wisdom of the Greeks held the purpose of Fine Art to be didactic and educational; the function of Poetry at least being to provide instruction sweetened by pleasure. Strabo, for example, condemning the opinion of Eratosthenes that "the aim of the poet is always to charm the mind, not to instruct," says, "that poetry is a kind of elementary philosophy which introduces us early to life, and gives us pleasurable instruction in reference to character, emotion, action." To Plato this instinctive conception of his countrymen appeared false and vulgar. On the one side, his own course of speculation led him to think that the artist occupied himself with the imitation only of the deceptive and fleeting shows of things; on the other he had a contempt for pleasure as an end in life, rating what he held to be the highest kind of pleasures only fifth in his scale of goods. Speaking of the pleasure produced by tragic poetry, as if Poetry were the sister of an Art like Cookery, he asks ironically: "To what does their solemn sister, the wondrous Muse of Tragedy, devote herself? Is all her aim and desire only to give pleasure to the spectators, or does she fight against and refuse to speak of their pleasant vices, and willingly proclaim in word and song truths welcome and unwelcome? Which is her character?" To this the interlocutor with Socrates has to reply: "There can be no doubt that Tragedy has her face turned towards pleasure and gratification;" whereupon Socrates proceeds with a further question: "And is not that the sort of thing which we were just now describing as flattery?" Plato therefore, who banished poets from his Republic because they were the imitators of Falsehood, would also have banished them on the ground that they were, as he supposed, purveyors of immoral Pleasure. His attitude towards Fine Art resembles that of the English Puritans.

The intellectual position of Aristotle is entirely different. He says distinctly that the end of Poetry, as of all fine art, is to produce a pleasurable effect in the mind. When Plato objects against Homer that he produces imaginative pleasure by stories of the gods which are untrue and immoral, Aristotle is content to reply that these stories, being current among the people, lie at the root of that art of Poetry which is the source of ideal pleasure. By arguing in this way against the moral philosopher, Aristotle separates himself to a certain extent from the popular Greek tradition, which assigned to Poetry a moral and didactic function; he no longer regards the pleasure arising out of poetry as something directly associated with instruction, but as æsthetic enjoyment, a thing which is to be examined according to the laws of its own nature. Nevertheless, he is far from excluding the operation of moral law from the domain of æsthetic pleasure. Moral considerations enter into his definition of Tragedy. "Tragedy," he says, "is an imitation of an action and of life, of happiness and misery; and happiness and misery consist in action, the end of human life being a mode of action, not a quality." There is moral feeling—even though the metaphor on which they are based may be material—in the celebrated words which describe tragedy as "effecting through pity and fear the purgation of those emotions." And there is a distinct application of moral law in the *veto* placed by Aristotle on such a representation in tragedy of gratuitous wickedness, as is given by Euripides in the character of Menelaus in the *Orestes*.

To some modern writers Aristotle has appeared inconsistent in limiting the liberties of æsthetic enjoyment by the intervention of moral law. Mr. Bosanquet observes: "The emphasis which he rightly laid on utterance and intelligence did not lead him to the idea that the delight of these factors of art was no mere psychical accident, but was the manifestation of joy in self-expression, the ultimate root and ground of æsthetic pleasure; and, therefore, when we are asked whether Aristotle recognised æsthetic as apart from real interest (either moral or hedonistic), we are thrown into perplexity." For my own part, I think that this difficulty may readily be cleared up. Aristotle did not, like modern philosophers, consider man in a mere individual human capacity; he regarded him as a "political being," and only cared to contemplate him in a state of society. Hence all his speculations about him are tacitly limited by some practical assumption; he measures virtue in the abstract by its manifestation in the wise and prudent man (ὁ φρόνιμος); and the same kind of test is applied to discriminate the varieties of æsthetic enjoyment. The end of Fine Art is to produce pleasure in the imagination, but the standard of such pleasure is the impression made on the mind of the accomplished and cultivated member of society (ὁ χαρίεις), which may be regarded as the rule of what ought to be, in this department of human nature. Such a man will not require the elementary " pleasurable instruction " spoken of by Strabo; he will indulge his imagination in every kind of enjoyment that gives play to his healthy instincts; but he will repress with sternness those spiritual solicitings which tend to the corruption of his own nature and the enervation of society.

To me, indeed, it seems that Aristotle, in thus associating Art with Morality, is far more profound and consistent than the modern German philosophers who attempt to exclude all moral considerations from what they call the Science of Æsthetics, and who analyse man merely as an isolated sentient being. Kant, indeed, the father of all modern German philosophy, occupies a logical position in the matter. If I understand him rightly in his *Critique of the Power of Judgment*, he holds that those only are perfectly free perceptions of Beauty which are accompanied in the mind with a sensation of pleasure, without any perception of dependence or relation; and that these perceptions cannot be classed under any rational conception or associated with a moral end. But if this be so, the analysis of æsthetic pleasure ought to be limited to the purely physical feelings that are associated with beautiful sights and sounds, such as the example which Kant gives of our pleasure in the beauty of a flower; and hence the consistent followers of Kant have endeavoured to develop his æsthetic philosophy by an investigation of the permanent physical conditions which accompany sensations of mental pleasure, inquiring, for example, what geometrical figures are most pleasant to the eye; how far the pleasures of the ear arise from the import of single notes in music or from measured intervals of sound; and what are the elementary meanings of the association of colours. From questions of this kind all moral considerations are, of course, properly excluded. But obviously the pleasure produced in the imagination by works of Fine Art, and especially Poetry, cannot be examined in this way, and Kant, who maintained that all Beauty capable of presenting an ideal was—as he expressed it—not free but "dependent," would not have considered Poetry as falling within the purely æsthetic sphere.

Hegel and his followers, on the contrary, are like Kant, anxious to exclude moral judgment from the æsthetic sphere, but are at the same time resolved to include poetry within the domain of æsthetic philosophy, and Mr. Bosanquet criticises Kant's position as follows: "If beauty is regarded as subservient to morality, or is judged by the standard of specifically moral ideas, it is beyond a doubt unfree or dependent. But if the content of life and reason is taken into beauty, and perceived not as the expression of morality, but as the utterance in another form of that reasonableness which is also to be found in morality, then we first destroy the restriction of ideal beauty to man—for there is reasonableness in all nature—and we secondly break down the extraordinary paradox that the highest beauty is not free. That beauty which is the largest and deepest revelation of spiritual power is not the most dependent but the freest beauty, because it implies no purpose whatever excepting that which constitutes its own inmost nature, the expression of reason in sensuous form." If it were not presumptuous for a professor of Poetry to criticise a philosopher on his own ground, I should venture to remark that the argument that Beauty and Morality are only forms of reasonable life, and that the former may therefore be included in the sphere of philosophic analysis, is a somewhat extraordinary *petitio principii*.

When we survey the long history of æsthetic inquiry can we say that Philosophy, apart from artistic practice, has thrown any light upon the laws of taste? To this question we must answer, in the first place, that a very large portion of æsthetic philosophy, as being concerned solely with abstract knowledge, has no bearing on our purposes. What we are in search of is some settled principle or principles which shall help us, in appreciating the merits of a work of art, to determine whether the artist has adopted a right method of ideal imitation, and whether our judgment of his work, as measured by the feeling of pleasure or pain in our mind, rests upon a basis of reason. We are in no way helped to a decision on such points when Hegel tells us that "beauty is the presentation of truth to sense and fancy," or when Hartmann, who is supposed by some to have said the last word on the subject, affirms that "beauty is the life of love apprehending its own ground and purpose." One German philosopher after another may suggest a scientific classification of the Fine Arts, but not one of these will help us to decide, in a particular instance, when the poet, in his conception and execution, is passing beyond the limits of his own art into that of the painter, or when the musician is encroaching upon the territory of the poet.

It is said, however, that Philosophy is bound to determine the absolute place of Art in the scheme of Nature, before we can formulate the laws which ought to regulate the work of the artist; and no doubt artists in late periods of production have based their work on abstract systems of reasoning, as Wagner, for example, in music, and the English Preraphaelites in poetry and painting. But experience teaches us to look with scepticism on the absolute principles which æsthetic philosophy claims to have a right to apply to the practice of art. They are the product of a science which, according to Hartmann, its latest exponent, professes to date only from the last decade of the eighteenth century, which has been investigated almost exclusively in Germany, and which thinks scorn of all the critical inquiries of the older Gentile world, including the *Poetics* of Aristotle. There is no trace in it of that progress from point to point of discovery which marks the course of physical science. Everything is at sixes and sevens; the followers of Hegel are at war with the followers of Schopenhauer; the terms which are employed in the classification of the Arts—Symbolic, Classical, Romantic—are not of universal significance, but are the legacy of a chance literary tradition. As to what æsthetic philosophy has discovered concerning the relationship of the arts to each other, the conclusion of Hartmann, who is the last comer in the field, is thus characterised by Mr. Bosanquet: "The whole passage, which I have quoted because it puts Hartmann's view conveniently together and shows the outrageous results of the extreme Wagnerian influence (I do not say of Wagner's own theoretical writings, with which I am not acquainted), could hardly have been written by any man with a true feeling for any branch of art."

These last words—words, be it remembered, of the Historian of Æsthetic Philosophy—suggest a new consideration. The critical rules of the philosopher are of no use to the greatest artists. All great Art precedes criticism. Homer and the Greek tragedians produced their work without reference to the philosophic principles afterwards discovered in it by Aristotle. On the other hand, no great tragic writer ever composed a drama according to the ideal recipe proposed in the *Poetics*. Criticism was practically unknown in England in the time of Shakespeare, who constructed his plays according to his own sense of fitness, limited only by the external conditions then regulating dramatic production. There is nothing to indicate that Wagner's theoretical principles, apart from his practice, will extend the area of operatic music. When Millais advanced in the practical knowledge of his art he abandoned the principles of the Pre-raphaelites on which he had founded his earliest work.

Now, if great works of art are produced without any conscious application of philosophic principles, ought we not, in searching for the law of taste, to look away from the abstractions of philosophy to the concrete productions of art? We know from the enduring feeling of pleasure accompanying the work of the great artist that the method he has taken in producing his work must have been right. We have no such opportunity of verifying the reasoning of the great philosopher. The philosopher comes with his analysis, claiming the whole field of Nature as his dominion. By examining poems, and statues, and pictures, he raises and seeks to solve vast questions of the greatest interest—as to what is the essence of Beauty; how the Ugly is related to the Beautiful; how the various Arts are related to each other—and, arguing from his metaphysical conclusions, he often ventures to prescribe to the artist practical rules of composition. But does any one believe that if a late Greek dramatist had composed a tragedy on the pattern suggested by Aristotle, he would have been able to awaken the same kind of pleasure as had been felt in the sublime irregularity of the *Agamemnon* and the *Prometheus* of Æschylus? Obviously, then, the philosopher must have left some essential condition of life out of his analysis. Meantime the artist has doubtless been unconsciously face to face with many of the abstract problems suggested by the philosopher, but when he comes, for example, to consider how the harmony of his composition is to be reconciled with the introduction of ugly or discordant elements, behold, the difficulty vanishes in the effect. *Solvitur ambulando.*

There is but one Absolute and Divine Source of ideal Beauty, but the rays that proceed from it are modified in their passage through the mind, and are thence reflected in a thousand different forms according to the varying genius of those who strive to imitate it. Chinese, Hindu, Assyrian, Egyptian, Greek, and the modern nations of Europe, have all embodied in the Fine Arts their ideas of what is spiritual and unseen. To reduce their opposite conceptions to a central law of taste would be impossible, nor do I believe that there is real evidence of progress and development from one type of Fine Art to another. We are entitled to graduate the artistic merit of different races, just as we discriminate the races themselves in the scale of intellect, but practically the ideal art of each of them may be said to proceed from within, and to contain in itself its peculiar law of taste. In other words, the law of taste in each nation consists in the development of its own genius or character, in conformity with its sense of natural Beauty.

How, then, may we proceed by inductive methods to investigate the law of Character in national Art? First, from the outside, by observing in each nation the growth of its powers of ideal Imitation. The purpose of all the Fine Arts is eminently social; and the truly great artist in any society derives his fame from his power to give expression to the common perception of what is noble and beautiful. These perceptions are always clearest and most unclouded in the early stages of a nation's life while it is still unconscious, or only half-conscious, of the greatness of its capacities and its destinies. It is then that the bent of the national genius discloses itself. Faith is firm. The mind receives impressions vividly, and feels no doubt about their truth. The artist selects with unerring judgment characteristic forms of expression, and proceeds in a definite direction from point to point of invention. Again there is in every society which has the gift of ideal imitation a specially fruitful period of productive art. Such was in Greece the period between Homer and the death of Pericles, when all the Fine Arts reached their zenith. Such, too, in the history of Italian painting was the period between Giotto and Raphael. By careful observation of the works of art produced in these periods we may generalise confidently as to the particular bent of Greek and Italian taste.

But the æsthetic character of any society may also be investigated from within, by tracing the natural turn of its criticism, in other words, the declaration of law by those who judge of right and wrong in art from the effect which art produces in the mind. There comes a stage in the life of every nation when it emerges from the state of almost intuitive action into the full consciousness of thought, when its instinctive unwavering perception of the forms of external nature is obscured or distorted by the vast variety of interests which it observes in itself. The growth of commerce, the changes of religion, the revolutions of politics, the conflicting ideals of education, the general march of civilisation, all sweep successively, like advancing tides, over the primal instincts of infantine society. There is something in such progress like the stages described by Wordsworth in the life of the individual:

> The youth, who daily further from the East
> Must travel, still is Nature's priest,
> And by the vision splendid
> Is on his way attended;
> At length the man perceives it die away,
> And fade into the light of common day.

But in the life of nations the vision never entirely dies away. The desire of ideal imitation, the shadow at least of Poetry, remains to the last; but in the late days of national life artistic creation is always accompanied by criticism. The historical period at which Criticism appears varies according to the character of different nations. Sometimes, as in Greece, it arises in the natural order of development, after the great period of instinctive creation has exhausted itself. Sometimes, as in the classical period of French literature, Creation and Criticism seem to go hand in hand. In Germany Criticism preceded the artistic creations of Goethe and Schiller. In England the principles of Criticism have constantly fluctuated according as the character of artistic production has been modified by internal changes of society. But amid all this variety there may be traced a certain unity; and while the progress of art is materially affected by the changes of critical taste, taste itself, in so far as it is the expression of general perception, is determined by that National Character, or ἦθος, which is the original source of art.

Life in Art and Law in Taste are, in fact, the opposite sides of the same proverbial shield. Life in Poetry, as I have already said, is the re-creation in an organic form of the universal ideas or impressions which the mind derives from Nature. Law in Taste is the intuitive perception of the conditions of life which constitute the organic unity of the work of art. Hence Pope, with epigrammatic truth, associates the spheres of Poetry and Criticism:

> In poets as true genius is but rare,
> True taste as seldom is the critic's share.
> Both must alike from Heaven derive their light,
> These born to judge, the others born to write.

That will be the text of the series of lectures I propose to deliver. To deal with so great a subject exhaustively volumes would be required. But I hope, within the time by which my occupation of this Chair is limited, to suggest to you lines of thought which may not be unprofitable. In my next lecture I shall dwell on the idea of unity common to all Art, as illustrated in the *Poetics* of Aristotle, the great representative of Greek character and Greek criticism. In the three following lectures I shall show how this idea of unity reappears in the respective poetry of the French, German, and English nations, and how it is modified in each case by the national character, and by different moral, social, and political conditions. I shall then, in four lectures, take Chaucer, Milton, Pope, Tennyson and Byron as the types of poetical art in different periods of English history, in order to show how each of them preserves in his work that unity and continuity of character which is the great law of taste. My concluding lecture, summing up the results of our inquiry, will be devoted to the practical consideration of the methods which ought to be pursued in liberal education with regard to the training of taste.

II

ARISTOTLE AS A CRITIC

IF ever a man was qualified by genius and circumstances to declare the fundamental laws that govern the production of works of fine art, it was Aristotle. Aristotle was the fitting representative of a race whom Nature had endowed more richly than any people before or since with the power of embodying beautiful conceptions in ideal forms of expression. He lived at an epoch when that race had passed indeed the meridian of its greatness, but was far from having sunk into decrepitude. Born in 384 B.C., within twenty years of the death of Socrates, he died in 322 B.C. within twenty years of the battle of Chæronea. During that period the arts of Poetry, Painting, and Sculpture continued to flourish, so that Aristotle was acquainted not only with the principles observed by great masters in the full maturity of art, but also with the devices to which men naturally resort when the springs of natural invention are beginning to fail. The *Poetics* abound in instructive comparisons between the opposite aims of Polygnotus and Zeuxis in painting, of Sophocles and Euripides in poetry:

inferences are drawn not only from the *Iliad* of Homer but from the *Deliad* of Nichochares; and the contemporary mimes of Sophron and Xenarchus, the tragic novelties of Carcinus, and the metrical experiments of Chæremon, furnish matter for criticism not less interesting than the established practice of the elder poets. Philosophy was fully developed, and Aristotle was already classed among the greatest, if not allowed to be the greatest, of philosophers. He had examined in the *Politics* all the known varieties of civil government; in the *Ethics* the laws of morality; in the *Physics* the laws of external Nature; in the *Metaphysics* the first principles of existence; in the *De Anima* the constitution of the soul in living things. He seems to have approached the subject of Fine Art and Poetry with peculiar interest and enthusiasm. Though the *Poetics* is not an elaborate treatise on technical practice, it is exhaustive in its examination of principle, and the condensed philosophical epigrams, which drop from the writer in a manner elsewhere unusual to him, show how deeply he had thought upon the subject. Every species of poetry which the Greek world had yet produced is considered by him; so that in the *Poetics* we have a study of all the varieties of the art close to the source of nature, and unobscured by those conflicts of nations and languages. of religions and philosophies, which have since confused the human imagination.

What wonder then that Aristotle's treatise on Poetry should have been accepted by a large portion of the world with the reverence due to the utterance of an inspired law-giver? That in France the oracles he was supposed to have delivered on the question of the Dramatic Unities should have been allowed to control the stage practice of the greatest poets? That in Germany, Lessing, the immediate forerunner of Goethe and Schiller, should have avowed his faith that the *Poetics* of Aristotle was as infallible as the *Elements* of Euclid? The wonder rather is, that in England the authority justly belonging to this work should not have been recognised. It is no doubt the case that, from the days of Sidney and Ben Jonson down to the time of the First Reform Bill, a considerable section of the English world of letters have endeavoured to reinforce the advocacy of their own opinions with the supposed doctrines of Aristotle; but, on the other hand, the *Poetics* has never been, like the *Ethics* and *Politics*, prescribed as a systematic part of liberal education in this country; the general tendency has rather been to deny the judicial competency of Aristotle to intervene in any controversy of modern taste.

This disposition is mainly the result of a belief that Aristotle's doctrines are in some way hostile to our darling liberty. To any one who understands the *Poetics* it will be clear that men who reason thus are the victims of a gross superstition; still, it is unquestionable that, either from a misunderstanding of his text or from political and national prejudices, the meaning of the philosopher has, in many passages, been egregiously perverted by his would-be disciples, and in such a way as to bring discredit on his teaching.

If we are rightly to value the *Poetics*, we must separate what is essential in the treatise from what is merely local and accidental; and I shall therefore attempt first to examine the principles on which the reasoning of Aristotle about Fine Art depends, and then to distinguish these from the purely technical rules which have been elevated by critical tradition into such disproportionate importance.

The three main principles underlying Aristotle's criticism are: (1) That the function of Poetry, as of all Fine Art, is imitation, not instruction; (2) That the object of imitation in Poetry is the Universal, not the Particular; and (3) that the test of the justice of poetic imitation is the permanent pleasure produced in society by the work, not merely the pleasure felt by the artist in creating it. With regard to the first of these propositions, Aristotle found the term Imitation established in popular usage; the Greeks had perceived instinctively that the first aim of every artist was to imitate an object. It was for this very reason that Plato objected to art itself as immoral; since he supposed it to be the aim of the poet and painter to copy what was essentially false, as being only an imperfect resemblance of true Being. Aristotle, with profounder insight into the nature of human instinct, accepted the popular term, and explained the origin of Poetry as follows: "Poetry in general seems to have sprung from two causes, each of them lying deep in our nature. First, the instinct of imitation is implanted in man from childhood, one difference between him and other animals being that he is the most imitative of living creatures; and through imitation he learns his earliest lessons; and no less universal is the pleasure felt in things imitated."

I venture to think that Aristotle is less successful in his explanation of the cause of this universal instinct. He says: "The cause of this again is, that to learn gives the liveliest pleasure not only to philosophers but to men in general, whose capacity, however, of learning is more limited. Thus the reason why men enjoy seeing a likeness is that, in contemplating it, they find themselves learning or inferring, and saying perhaps, 'Ah, that is he!' For if you happen not to have seen the original, the pleasure will be due not to the imitation as such, but to the execution, the colouring, or some such other cause." The objection to this reasoning is, in the first place, that it seems to run counter to Aristotle's general position in the *Poetics*, which is, that Art is not directly didactic; and secondly, that the very fact of our being pleased with the recognition of a likeness proves that we have already acquired a knowledge of the original.

I imagine that our pleasure in Fine Art arises primarily from imitation itself, because we thereby feel both in ourselves and in the artist a certain sense of divine power, which brings us into closer relation with the Creator of things. Many of the Greeks, as I have said, regarded Poetry as a kind of elementary branch of philosophic education, but Aristotle did not agree with this opinion, which is indeed confuted by the constitution and history of man. A single illustration of the matter will be sufficient for our purpose. Shakespeare's *Tempest* evidently aims at producing pleasure simply by means of imitation; it is in no sense of the word didactic. Ben Jonson, in the Prologue to *Every Man in His Humour*, finds fault with the play for its want of moral aim; and, in the Prologue to *Every Man out of His Humour*, he defines what he considers should be the didactic end of the drama:

> Who is so patient of the impious world
> That he can check his spirit, or rein his tongue?
> Or who hath such a dead unfeeling sense
> That heaven's horrid thunder cannot wake?
> To see the earth cracked with the weight of sin,
> Hell gaping under us, and o'er our heads
> Black ravenous ruin with her sail-stretched wing
> Ready to sink us down and cover us,—
> Who can behold such prodigies as these
> And have his lips sealed up? Not I; my soul
> Was never ground into such oily colours,
> To flatter vice and dark iniquity:
> But with an armed and resolved hand,
> I'll strip the ragged follies of the time
> Naked as to the birth.

Now the answer to Jonson's protest is that, three centuries having since gone by, for one man that laboriously studies his dramatic satires, powerful as they are, ten thousand read with delight such a creation as *The Tempest*. Hence it may be inferred that in none of the professedly didactic poems of the world, such as the *De Rerum Natura*, the *Georgics*, and the *Essay on Man*, does the virtue lie in the philosophy, but rather in the purely imaginative ideas which the skill of the poet enables him to group about his central philosophical conception.

"The cause of this again"—as Aristotle would say—is involved in the second great fundamental principle of the *Poetics*, namely, that Poetry is an imitation of the Universal, not of the Particular. At first sight there is to us, as to the Greeks, something strange in a proposition like this; for if the end of Fine Art be imitation, close fidelity to the original would seem to be the first essential in an artist's work. But immediately we begin to think, we see that the artist is not a copyist of Nature, but a rival creator with her, going to work in a different way and with a different end. Nature works with materials apprehended by sense and experience— flesh, blood, spirit, and the like: the artist works with ideas and imitates ideas; and thus, though his work is a likeness of something in Nature, yet the likeness exists only in his own mind and in the mind of those whom he hopes to please. To put the truth in a concrete form: Aristotle says, in one place, that the dramatist deals with character, passion, and action. Action, passion, and character are objects to be observed in nature, and the poet must produce a likeness of them; but Aristotle says, in another place, that the dramatist will proceed after the manner of a good portrait painter, who is in the habit of making his portrait somewhat more beautiful than the original. What I suppose he means is, that the inferior portrait painter will indeed be able to reproduce the outward lines and colours that exist in the face and form of the person before him, but will not be able to represent the life and character of the man himself. These are manifested in the expression; the good painter, seizing this, will divine the unseen source from which it springs, and will be able to heighten what he actually observes in such a way as to express more beautifully the intention of Nature. He will thus be able to convey through the likeness of an individual an universal idea of character. On the same principle, in the higher walks of painting, we see that, when Raphael represents St. Paul preaching on Mars' Hill, he does not pay attention to what the Apostle says about himself, that his "bodily presence was weak and his speech contemptible," but paints him with the commanding figure and gesture which is felt to be appropriate to the greatness of the message he is delivering.

What, then, is this Universal in Poetry, if in Painting its presence may be detected in the strictest kind of artistic imitation that exists, namely, the art of the portrait-painter? Two passages from the *Poetics* may be cited as peculiarly illustrative of Aristotle's meaning. One is that in which he contrasts Poetry with History: "It is evident from what has been said that it is not the function of the poet to relate what has happened, but what may happen, what is possible according to the law of probability or necessity. The poet and the historian differ not by writing in verse or in prose. The work of Herodotus might be put into verse, and it would still be a species of history. Poetry, therefore, is a more philosophical and a higher thing than history; for poetry tends to express the universal, history the particular. By the universal I mean how a person of given character will on occasion speak or act, according to the law of probability or necessity; and it is this universality at which poetry aims in the names she attaches to the personages. The particular is, for example, what Alcibiades did or suffered. In comedy this is already apparent; for here the poet first constructs the plot on the lines of probability, and then inserts characteristic names—unlike the lampooners who write about particular individuals. But tragedians still keep to real names, the reason being that what is possible is credible; what has not happened we do not at once feel to be possible, but what has happened is manifestly possible, otherwise it would not have happened."

The other passage occurs in the 25th chapter where Aristotle is defending Homer against objectors. He says: "In general the impossible must be justified [in poetry] by reference to artistic requirements, or to the higher reality, or to received opinion. With respect to the requirements of art a probable impossibility is to be preferred to a thing improbable and yet possible. Again, it may be impossible that there should be men such as Zeuxis painted. 'Yes,' we may say, ' but the impossible is the higher thing; for the ideal type must surpass the reality.' To justify the irrational we appeal to what is commonly said to be. In addition to which we urge that the irrational sometimes does not violate reason ; just as it is probable that a thing may happen contrary to probability."

In these profound and penetrating, though unsystematised, observations are contained all the essential principles necessary to the production of a work of Fine Art. The aim of Fine Art is to create an appearance of organic nature in the world of ideas; and the Universal is the ideal space which the imagination must secure for itself in order to create with perfect freedom. The highest work of Art is that which, while presenting the most lively image of Nature, least hampers the imagination by suggesting a comparison of itself with particular things. Thus, in Greek tragedy, the dramatist first obtained for himself a secure base of poetic probability by choosing his fable from the accepted legends of his race. As Aristotle says, the things he represented were said to have happened; how they happened was a matter for full liberty of representation within the limits of the probable; and it was therefore open to the poet to introduce into his work the element of τὸ βέλτιον, or the ideal, by means of music, scenery, uncommon language, raising the stature of the actors above the mortal standard, and other devices. Shakespeare, up to a certain point, works exactly on the same lines as the Greeks; that is to say, he finds the required likeness to external nature in the incidents of some well-known story, into which he projects all the vitality of his own experience; he provides the ideal atmosphere of his tragedies in the vagueness and uncertainty of the time and place of the action, and in the lofty, metaphorical, and unreal character of the language used by the actors. Where he differs from the Greeks is in the closeness with which, in certain parts of his action, he imitates particular nature, as in the Grave-diggers' scene in *Hamlet* or the reasoning of the Fool in *Lear;* a device which, harmonising with the character of the composition as a whole, not only furnishes the most agreeable contrasts, but insensibly enhances the feeling of reality and probability in the more ideal parts of the representation.

Though the nature of the Universal can best be understood by reference to the heroic styles of Poetry, whether epic or dramatic, yet its presence is equally necessary in those works of fine art in which the imitation deals with the more ordinary characters, actions, and passions of men, the adopted vehicle of expression being prose. Aristotle admits the Mimes of Sophron and Xenarchus, which were written in prose, into the sphere of poetic imitation; and in the same way the nature of the Universal in art may be illustrated from such works as *Don Quixote* and the Waverley Novels. We observe, for example, the Universal in the trial scene in *The Heart of Midlothian*. In many respects this is an imitation of things as they immediately appear to the senses; the story being based on the incidents of everyday life, the locality being an ordinary Court of Justice, the diction of the actors a close reproduction of the dialect of the people. And yet the extraordinary effect of nature which the scene produces in the mind is not the result of an accurate study of particulars. In the generalisation of character, in the selection of incidents, in the contrast of emotions, the fiction is so artfully raised above the level of experience, that the imagination moves in an ideal world. Helen Walker, the heroine of the story as it happened in reality, did not, we feel very sure, speak with the poetry that pervades the whole character of Jeanie Deans; Effie Deans is invested with an attractiveness not likely to have been possessed by her original; if the father of the prisoner fainted during the actual trial, the episode would not have been accompanied with all the picturesque and pathetic circumstances imagined by the novelist. In every direction there is room for the development of τὸ βέλτιον, Aristotle's indispensable element of the ideal.

Observe this again in a yet more limited sphere, the set of circumstances represented in Miss Austen's *Pride and Prejudice*. Everything in this novel—time, place, action, diction, costume—reminds us of our daily life; and yet under this commonplace surface a great artist has revealed a most dramatic conflict of universal human emotions. To have imagined a being, manly, honourable, generous, but so eaten up with the pride of birth and rank that he has brought himself, on conscientious principles, to separate a friend from a young woman with whom he is in love, on account of her undesirable connections; to bring him, by the irony of events, to fall in love with the sister of her whom he has injured, a person possessing all the fascinations of grace, frankness, and high spirit, supplying by the lightning rapidity of her wit and intuition her want of knowledge and experience; to exhibit the conflict between the man's pride and his passion; to cause his pride, when it can no longer resist, to revenge itself for its defeat by an offensive proposal of marriage; to paint, in language of the exactest propriety, the maidenliness and severity with which the heroine rejects the suit, and the humiliation, the astonishment, the indignation of the hero; finally, to describe the gradual process by which the fine nature of the man, recognising the justice of his sentence, purges itself of its master vice and makes a generous return for the indignity done to it—never was there a more admirable δέσις, or complication of plot, in any Greek comedy; never a more well-conceived περιπέτεια, or reversal of the action; never a more satisfactory λύσις, or *dénouement* of the moral situation. Justly may we transfer to the creator of so perfect a work the compliment which was, perhaps with some exaggeration, paid to Menander: "Oh Nature and Jane Austen, which of you has copied from the other?"

You will observe that the essential characteristic of the Universal, according to Aristotle, is to represent "what is possible according to the law of probability or necessity." Herein lies the great distinction between Fine Art and Philosophy. Both of them seek to express Truth, but truth of a different kind, and expressed by different means. Philosophy expresses Truths of Fact, Fine Art

Truths of Idea: Philosophy proceeds by means of analysis, Fine Art by means of imitation: Philosophy seeks to arrive at the causes of things as they are, Fine Art to create an image of things pleasing to the mind. As society advances in refinement, there is a constant tendency among artists to encroach on the sphere of philosophy; and this practice receives some encouragement from the language of Aristotle himself, who says that "poetry is a more philosophical and a higher thing than history." But it is clear that Aristotle did not mean by this to imply that the method of poetry was the same as the method of philosophy, for he says, in another place, that the poet bases his work on what is, logically speaking, a fallacy; that is to say, the poet asks the reader to grant him, as the groundwork of his ideal creation, a hypothesis of things that have at the time no actual existence.

This is indeed the method of all great dramatic and epic poets and of the masters of romantic fiction, but it is not that of certain other great writers, such as Ben Jonson and Balzac, who may be called the Realists of Art, and whose work, as being the product of robust genius, is of high intellectual interest. Ben Jonson and Balzac endeavour to arrive at the Universal by observing the facts they see before them, extracting from them some general motive of moral conduct or some principle of social action, and then reconstructing the result of their analysis in an ideal form. But I do not think any one would venture to assert that their creations are as probable and life-like as those of the other poets I have mentioned. They are at once too abstract and too particular. Ben Jonson, for example, observed with unrivalled accuracy the various humours, follies, and vices of the society that revolved round the Court of Elizabeth and James I.; he sought to perpetuate them in an ideal form. But to us his persons seem almost as abstract as those of the old Moralities, and even in his own day he was obliged to label them with names like Morose, Puntarvolo, Pennyboy, Truewit, which, like the comic masks of the Greeks, might in some degree indicate to the audience the nature of the character intended. On the other hand, in his *Alchemist*, it is almost painful to observe the vast amount of learning he has employed in idealising a form of imposture which has long ceased to interest society.

The case is not very different with Balzac. In Balzac we find always the idea of the Universal; the Seven Deadly Sins make their presence felt in every page of *La Comédie Humaine;* but they are so overlaid with a multiplicity of sordid detail, copied directly from real life, that we are almost justified in doubting whether the sins themselves have not vanished with the obsolete society of Louis Philippe. Both Jonson and Balzac, moreover, disregard another principle of Aristotle's, namely, that the drama (and of course in the same way the novel) should not dwell overmuch on the representation of evil. If good on the whole did not preponderate over evil, human society could not exist; yet, in such representations of life as *Père Goriot* or *La Cousine Bette*, the interest of the reader is almost entirely absorbed in the contemplation of what is mean and bad. Perhaps it will be said that evil is, on the whole, paramount in such a drama as *King Lear;* but here the characters are raised so high above the ordinary level, and the action is thrown into so remote a past, that the scenes of horror and wickedness in which the play abounds do not press too strongly upon our sense of reality, while the representation of evil is mitigated by the idea of religion and retributive justice :

>   This shows you are above,
> You heavenly justicers, that these our crimes
> Do speedily avenge !

And :

> The gods are just, and of our pleasant vices
> Do make us plagues to scourge us.

Throughout *King Lear* we feel that Tragedy is, according to Aristotle's definition, through pity and terror effecting a purgation of these emotions ; it is not so in *La Comédie Humaine.*

I almost shudder when I think what Aristotle would have said about the conception, formed by some of our modern Realists, of the law of poetic probability, that is to say, of the method by which Fine Art makes fictitious personages behave and speak in the sphere of ideal action as we feel that they ought. For example, an ingenious writer promises to tell me a story of life in the time of the Indian Mutiny, and I look forward to being transported out of myself into scenes of heroic adventure, devotion, and self-sacrifice, in a period which has now for all Englishmen begun to invest itself with the purple atmosphere of Romance. But I have not been long introduced to the ideal actors in the tale, before I find myself mixing familiarly with John Nicholson, or Hodson of Hodson's Horse, or Herbert Edwardes, and obliged to follow a narrative of the siege of Delhi, related with all the minuteness of a Kinglake or a Gardiner. And as I listen to the discourse of this or that great historical personage, enlivened with the " said he," or " said she " of the novelist, I wake out of my dream of imagination, and ask with an inevitable scepticism, " Did they ? "

Again, another famous story-teller undertakes to show me what should be the ideal character of " The Christian " in the nineteenth century. I suppose that 1 am about to travel into that poetical region of the *Pilgrim's Progress* which I can so readily realise in imagination, and visions arise before me of the Land of Beulah, and the Delectable Mountains, and Vanity Fair, and the House Beautiful. Nor, indeed, are the action or the actors of the story much more closely related to the course of real life than the adventures of Mercy, or Pliable, or Greatheart, or Mr. Worldly-Wiseman ; so that something of a moral shock is felt in the imagination when such very abstract persons appear before us in Roman collars and high-heeled shoes, delivering their souls in the comic songs of the Music Hall and the dialect of the slums. If only the author had known what Aristotle says about the representation of character : —" The fourth necessary point is consistency ; for, though the subject of the imitation, the person who suggested the type, may be inconsistent, still he must be consistently inconsistent"—if only the novelist, I say, had been aware of this principle of Fine Art, he would hardly have attempted to blend the style of Bunyan with the style of M. Zola.

Let us try again. I lately studied with great interest an experiment made by an eminent French novelist, whose name is favourably known in this University, M. Paul Bourget, to modernise the story of Hamlet. It may be conjectured that M. Bourget, if he had lived in ancient times, would have sympathised with the contemporary critics, mentioned by Aristotle, who found fault with Homer for making the Greeks stand still while Achilles chased Hector round the walls of Troy. Perhaps he thought that a character like Hamlet would hardly have been the product of the dark ages; or that those ages were not likely to have possessed Universities; or to have reasoned philosophically on the principles of the drama. At any rate he set himself to correct these historic improbabilities, by presenting the extremely modern character of Hamlet in a modern setting.

Up to a certain point he had before him perfectly plain sailing. Nothing was easier than to arrange the Confessions of a sentimental young Frenchman, corresponding, to a certain extent, with the soliloquies of Hamlet; to make the hero relate how almost his earliest recollection was the discovery of the murdered body of his father; how he vowed to discover and slay the assassin; how his mother, a kind of French

Mrs. Copperfield, married again; how he himself was sent to a Lycée, in which his brooding suspicion began to settle in the right quarter.

But here M. Bourget's difficulties began. The ghost of Hamlet's father is an essential part of the machinery of the play; but a ghost would not readily assimilate with the atmosphere of a French novel; he must therefore be replaced. The ingenious author replaces him with—a maiden aunt, a sister of the hero's father, into whose confiding ears (of course in strict accordance with the law of probability) the deceased husband has poured, through a series of letters, his fears and jealousies as to the state of his wife's affections. On her deathbed the maiden aunt signifies by gestures to her nephew that she wishes these letters to be destroyed without being read. He promises to destroy them, but nevertheless reads them, an action which causes him, in his Confessions, profuse self-reproaches. "O my prophetic soul,—my stepfather!"

Our modern Hamlet has now confirmed his suspicions with the discovery of a motive, but, being Hamlet, he is still far from having made up his mind to act. Shakespeare's hero was able to advance upon the information of the ghost:

<blockquote>
The play's the thing
Wherein I'll catch the conscience of the king.
</blockquote>

But as a play like the one in *Hamlet* could hardly be acted in a modern French drawing-room, the avenging son can only try to frighten his stepfather by dark innuendoes, showing that he is aware of his guilt, and hinting that an old *juge d'instruction* has his eye upon him. Devices of this kind naturally fail to shake the marble composure of the guilty man, and since the author cannot avail himself of Rosencrantz and Guildenstern, or the voyage to England, or the fencing-match, he is obliged to work out his *dénouement* by one of those never-failing hypotheses which Gaboriau leads us to suppose are the usual instruments of the French police, involving, on this occasion, the existence of a black-mailing brother of the stepfather and some more compromising letters.

Now, at the end of such a story, has not every one a critical right to ask, Is this really the way in which crime is committed, discovered, and punished in the nineteenth century? On the other hand, is there anything in Shakespeare's treatment of the legendary story of Hamlet that shocks our sense of poetic probability? And if the answer to the latter question be No! does it not then follow that every man who would compose a work of Fine Art must live in the atmosphere of τὸ βέλτιον, or the Higher Reality?

The third great fundamental principle of Aristotle's criticism is, that the test of all true Imitation is the enduring pleasure it produces in the mind of society, not simply the pleasure which the artist feels in creation. I believe I am right in saying that Pleasure nowhere enters into Aristotle's definition of Fine Art; and yet it is no less certain that, throughout the *Poetics,* the pleasure produced for mankind in general is assumed as the moving cause of all Poetic creation. This is apparent from sentences like these: " Every one feels a natural pleasure in things imitated:" "The drama is superior to the epic because it affords the most vivid combination of pleasures:" "The poet is guided in what he writes by the wishes of his audience; the pleasure, however, hence derived" (that is, from the happy endings of tragedies) "is not the true tragic pleasure."

And this reasoning is just. For man being, as Aristotle says, φύσει πολιτικὸν ζῷον, created for the purposes of society, the poet or painter is not to be regarded as an isolated lunatic, but as the representative of his kind. Were it otherwise, the man who produced a series of monsters, like those described by Horace at the beginning of the *Ars Poetica*, might insist, without fear of contradiction, that he was the author of beautiful works of art. Or again, as indeed often happens, the co-operation of a number of clever people to impose their own taste on society might be taken as the determining standard of artistic beauty and truth. But, indeed, the standard lies not in the will of the artist, but in the constitution of human nature. Doubtless the artist has alone the power of expressing the unseen truth which many feel; the great artist, the fine artist, therefore, is he who is able to create an image of what is universally felt; who knows equally well what are the resources and what the limits of his art; what means he possesses to snatch from nature her mysterious secrets; and how to resist those temptations of his own mind that are always ready to betray him into ambitious error.

The artist who, though he may, in a sense, be a man of genius, has not attained to the region of fine art, will, on the contrary, insist on enforcing his own will in creation against the instincts and intuitions of society. That I may not appear to dogmatise, let me attempt to apply the law of Aristotle to the two great opposing factions of modern painters—the Naturalists and the Impressionists. Both of these, bitterly antagonistic to each other, are equally contemptuous of the claim of the normally constituted spectator to form a judgment of his own on the general effect of a picture. Yet what says Aristotle? "A beautiful object, whether it be a picture of a living organism or any whole composed of parts, must not only have an orderly arrangement of parts, but must also be of a certain magnitude, for beauty depends on magnitude and order." This is only another way of saying that, if a man attempt to portray a beautiful object, without regard to these necessary rules, he will fail to produce a pleasurable effect on the mind.

The Naturalists who seek to reduce painting to the level of photography, adhere so strictly to the imitation of the particular in Nature, that they seek to copy every hair on a caterpillar, every leaf on a tree. This is not what the human imagination requires: "An exceedingly small object," says Aristotle, "cannot be beautiful, for the view of it is confused, the object being seen in an almost imperceptible moment of time." At the opposite extreme the Impressionists endeavour to introduce into painting the principle of Music. I met the other day with the following very eloquent description by Mr. Whistler of the harmonies produced in Nature by the approach of Night: " When the evening mist clothes the riverside with poetry as with a veil, and the poor buildings lose themselves in the dim sky, and the tall chimneys become campanili, and the warehouses are palaces in the night, and the whole city hangs in the heavens, and fairyland is before us—then the wayfarer hastens home; the working-man and the cultivated one, the wise man and the one of pleasure, cease to understand as they have ceased to see, and Nature, who for once has sung in tune, sings her exquisite song to the artist alone, her son and her master, her son in that he loves her, her master in that he knows her. To him her secrets are unfolded, to him her lessons have become gradually clear. He looks at the flower, not with the enlarging lens that he may gather facts for the botanist, but with the light of one who sees, in her choice selection of brilliant tones and delicate tints, suggestions of future harmonies."

Every one must admit that this is a very delicate analysis in words of an imaginative impression on the mind; but the question for the painter is, How can the vast and vague image of a city at night, conveyed to the soul of the artist through his eye, be reproduced to the eye and soul of the spectator by means of form and colour? We are in the region of τὸ ἄπειρον, the Infinite. "No object of vast size," says Aristotle, "can be beautiful, for as the eye cannot take it all in at once, the unity and sense of the whole is lost for the spectator; as, for instance, if there were a picture a thousand miles long." That is the truth of the matter. All Fine Art requires unity of conception: there is a Poetry in Painting, a wide and varied sphere : the principle of τὸ βέλτιον may be variously expressed in the general truths of light and colour and landscape, as they are in the art of Cuyp, and Rembrandt, and Gainsborough, and Turner, and Constable : but everywhere there is a limit; and the test of the justice of the ideal imitation is the feeling of completeness and of serene and harmonious pleasure awakened in the mind of the beholder.

I think I have said enough to show that the greatness of Aristotle as a critic is the result of his knowledge of the laws of human nature, which are the foundation of every organic creation of art. No critic has ever equalled him in his profound analysis of the constitution and the operations of the mind of man; no critic has so felicitously illustrated the soundness of his abstract principles by concrete illustrations, drawn from the practice of great artists. I have left myself but little space to dwell on what I venture to think the weak points in the criticism of the *Poetics;* nor, indeed, would it be worth while to do so, were it not that, by some caprice of destiny, it is just the more fallacious of Aristotle's doctrines that have most influenced the course of artistic taste.

His critical method is, it seems to me, attended by two disadvantages. One of these arises out of the excess of his own genius; he exaggerates the functions of logical analysis in Fine Art. So long as he restricts his unrivalled powers of observation and induction to the operations of nature and the positive practice of great artists, his reasoning is incomparable; but his good angel leaves him when, confiding in his logic, he presses on into the territory of invention and dares to lay down rules for the poets. We see him at his best in his definition of Greek Tragedy: " Tragedy is an imitation of an action that is serious, complete, and of a certain magnitude; in language embellished with each kind of artistic ornament, the several kinds being found in separate parts of the play; in the form of action, not of narrative; through pity and fear effecting the proper purgation of these emotions." Every word of this is original, profound, true; and not less admirable is his employment of logic in his 25th chapter to defend the practice of Homer against prosaic critics.

Compare, however, with passages like these his employment of the same method in his exhaustive enumeration of the different kinds of Recognition possible in Tragedy—how superficial and trivial are the results of his analysis! Or see him striving to define what must be the structure of a Perfect Tragedy, by proving that it ought not to be this, that, or something else : " A perfect tragedy should, as we have seen, be arranged not on the simple but on the complex plan. It should, moreover, imitate actions which excite pity and fear, this being the distinctive mark of tragic imitation. It follows plainly, in the first place, that the change of fortune presented must not be the spectacle of a virtuous man brought from prosperity to adversity; for this moves neither pity nor fear; it simply shocks us. Nor, again, that of a bad man passing from adversity to prosperity; for nothing can be more alien to the spirit of tragedy; it possesses no single tragic quality; it neither satisfies the moral sense nor calls forth pity or fear. Nor, again, should the downfall of the utter villain be exhibited. A plot of this kind would doubtless satisfy the moral sense, but it would inspire neither pity nor fear; for pity is aroused by unmerited misfortune, fear by the misfortune of a man like ourselves. Such an event, therefore, will be neither pitiful nor terrible. There remains, then, the character between these two extremes—that of a man who is not eminently good and just, yet whose misfortune is brought about not by vice or depravity but by some error or frailty. He must be one who is highly renowned and prosperous—a personage like Œdipus, Thyestes, or other illustrious men of such families."

When we examine this attempt to limit the procedure of the poet, we find that it breaks down in all directions. In the first place, the enumeration of the possibilities of tragedy is not exhaustive, for not only does it plainly omit to conceive the structure of a play like *Macbeth*, but it does not even take into account the tragic composition of such a play as the *Agamemnon*. Again, the premises of the reasoning are not always true: for example, as Professor Butcher very justly points out, it is not true to say

"The spectacle of a virtuous person brought from prosperity to adversity moves neither pity nor fear;" otherwise the *Antigone* would not be a good tragedy. And once more Aristotle is inconsistent with himself, for whereas he has said elsewhere that " unity of plot does not consist in the unity of the hero," he now makes everything tragic in a tragedy depend on the character of the hero rather than on the nature of the action as a whole.

The other weak side in the criticism of Aristotle is a certain defect of poetic sensibility or intuition, probably arising out of the circumstances of his time. We are always aware in the *Poetics* of the presence of the Genius of Prose, which makes us feel that the social temperature must have affected both the creative instinct of the artist and the judgment of the critic: it is difficult, for instance, to believe that such hopelessly matter of fact objections against Homer as those which Aristotle notices would have been possible in the generation of Æschylus, or even in that of Aristophanes. Poetic invention indeed was by no means dead, but it had passed out of the region of Inspiration, and was becoming more and more mechanical amid the processes of conscious art. Though Aristotle allows that poetry is a thing inspired, he writes throughout his treatise as if all its effects could be attained by analysis, and the examples with which he supports his reasoning show that he shared the preferences of his age.

When he speaks of Comedy he is always thinking in anticipation of the prosaic principles of the

New Comedy: the old and poetic comedy of Aristophanes he practically ignores. In tragedy, though his ideal seems to be the *Œdipus Rex*, and though he frequently compares Euripides disadvantageously with Sophocles, yet it is evident that the practice of Euripides is what he himself best understood. Æschylus, on the other hand, he rarely mentions; and the reasons for this order of preference may be divined from his view of the relative importance of the different parts of Greek tragedy. The parent source of the Greek drama was undoubtedly the Chorus, both as being the vehicle of expression for the religious feeling on which the idea of tragedy depended, and also as the primal institution out of which the whole structure of the play was gradually evolved. Hence the predominance of the Chorus in the tragedies of Æschylus, and hence too, in consequence of the cooling of religious feeling in society, the trivial position it came to occupy in the plays of Euripides. Aristotle regards the Chorus merely as one of the six parts of which every Tragedy consists, and all that he thinks it worth while to say about it is, that "Song holds the chief place among the embellishments."

On the other hand, Aristotle places the whole life of tragedy in the plot. "The plot," he says, "is the first principle, and as it were the soul of a tragedy." This is quite in accordance with the ideas of Euripides, Agathon, and their followers, who endeavoured to replenish the sinking springs of inspiration with all the contrivances of artistic ingenuity.

But it is surely not true. The plot of a play is the external framework which holds together the poetic organisation; it is, if you will, the backbone of tragedy, but it would be wrong to say that the soul of the *Eumenides* or the *Prometheus Vinctus* or of *Macbeth* lay in the outward form of those works. The soul of any tragedy lies in the conception of the poet, in the intensity with which he imagines the reality of a dramatic situation, and breathes life and being into the materials from which he creates. Out of the essential unity of the poetic conception the plot is evolved by degrees; but in embryo the tragedy was in existence already; all the plots of the really great tragedies of the world are founded on legendary stories; and looking at the matter from the opposite side, though Aristotle praises Agathon, who began the practice of inventing his own tragic plots, yet since none of this poet's plays have come down to us, it may be not unfairly inferred that they wanted the life and soul that produces immortal pleasure.

It is indeed evident that, in the *Poetics*, Aristotle attempts to lay down two kinds of critical law of very different reach and value, one of which stands to the other much in the same relation as International Law to Municipal Law. He declares, in the first place, not expressly but by implication, the first principles of the Law of Unity, which, being based on the constitution of human nature, is itself the foundation of all Fine Art. In doing this, he confronts the poet or painter as the representative of the rights of society. He says to the artist in effect: "Such and such are the laws of the human mind; in your compositions you are bound to obey them. It is of course open to you to disregard these limits, and to seek to overleap them; it is even possible that, if you do so, you may, by ingenious and novel contrivances, succeed in producing momentary pleasure; but you will not be able to arouse that enduring and universal pleasure which I assume to be the aim of your ambition: hence you will not have created a work of Fine Art."

So far, well. But Aristotle goes beyond this: he attempts from the Law of Unity to deduce a number of technical bylaws, and to impose on taste what we may call an Act of Poetical Uniformity. Here he is plainly proceeding *ultra vires;* he is invading the liberties of the poet, attempting, by means of logical analysis, to restrict the prerogatives of genius; and hence his critical edicts cease to possess universal authority. He failed to fathom all the conditions necessary for poetical creation even in his own age; much less could his analysis exhaust the springs of inspiration in the times that were to come.

Yet so binding is the force of logic, so vast the intellectual power of Aristotle, that his followers, through many generations of the world's history, endeavoured to emphasise whatever was most faulty in his criticism. The deep and universal truths on which his reasoning was founded lay beneath the surface; his technical rulings were explicit; and these the Italian, French, and a few even of the German critics after the Renaissance—some from a natural preference for Absolute Authority, others because they confounded the laws of taste with those of mathematics—sought to stereotype into a critical code. Without reflecting that Aristotle was only speaking as a Greek to Greeks, and drawing his inferences from a comparatively limited range of observation, the Castelvetros, the Voltaires, the Prussian Fredericks, accepted his local and particular rules as so many infallible Vatican decrees. They misconstrued the text of the *Poetics*; they deduced from the most casual remarks of the philosopher principles of poetical orthodoxy of which he never dreamed; they invented binding dogmas about the dramatic unities, and the limits of tragic action and character: in short, while they entirely neglected his doctrine of the Law of Unity in Art, they disgusted all lovers of rational liberty by seeking to enforce with pains and penalties his Act of Poetical Uniformity.

Time has cured many of these aberrations. Modern scholars, particularly English and German scholars, have devoted themselves with admirable patience and industry to the elucidation of Aristotle's critical treatise. Among these we his countrymen have every reason to be proud of Professor Butcher's edition of the *Poetics*. In this, perhaps for the first time, the general principles of Aristotle's philosophy have been made to illustrate his æsthetic opinions; and the essential and universal elements in his criticism have been detached from what is merely local and accidental with such beautiful lucidity, that there is now no reason why the *Poetics* should not be read by a Headmaster with the cleverer boys in any of our great Public Schools. All that Aristotle says about Imitation, the Universal, Poetic Truth, and the Law of Ideal Probability, is made to emerge in distinct relief like the clear outlines of Greek sculpture. And these are eternal truths. No man who has not an intuitive or an acquired knowledge of what Aristotle means by these principles can understand the necessary conditions of a work of Fine Art. Armed with this knowledge, on the other hand, he may penetrate the organic ideas in the work of Homer and Sophocles; he may confirm the truth of Aristotle's critical principles by observing how exactly his ideas have been followed by those who were separated from him by generations of time and diversities of religion and language; he may apply them to test the value of the artistic novelties which are presented for contemporary judgment. Perhaps in this gradual course of education he may rid himself of some of the scepticism implied in such a maxim as *De gustibus non est disputandum*. For human nature is the same in all ages, and, in the common consent of mankind about what is really great and beautiful in art, we find a sure intimation of the unity of the soul and a pledge of its immortality.

III

THE IDEA OF LAW IN FRENCH POETRY

FINE art, as I have already attempted to show, is the imitation, by the poets, painters, sculptors, and musicians of any people, of the idea of the Universal in Nature. This idea springs out of the character of the race, the course of its history, the common perceptions of its men of genius. As the life of a nation develops, the practice of its various artists instinctively falls in with the growth of society, advances with it to maturity, and languishes in its decline. Sometimes, as in ancient Greece, the history of art seems to manifest itself with almost as much certainty and regularity as the life of a flower, or a tree, or a human body. The Greek poet discovered by a kind of spontaneous instinct how to express the idea of greatness in his race in the divine simplicity of hexameter verse; the Greek musician learned at a very early stage how to imitate human passions in dance and song. With the remarkable development of civic life that followed the Persian invasion the Greek architect and sculptor co-operated to embody in marble the loftiest ideas of religion. Instinctively, in the same age, the dramatist combined, from the epic minstrelsy and the religious hymn, a mode of imitation fitted to express the profounder ideas of society about life and nature. With rare and delicate taste, Æschylus and his two great successors made the drama, in its progressive development, a mirror for all the changes of moral and religious feeling that transformed the Athenian mind between the battle of Marathon and the Sicilian Expedition. And when, after the battle of Chæronea, the Greek enthusiasm for liberty and the old Hellenic belief in the Gods died away together, the loss of imaginative energy in society reflected itself in the purely prosaic imitation of the New Comedy. In all directions the law of Greek art was embodied in the works of great artists, and, as I said in my last lecture, Aristotle's best criticism in the *Poetics* is not new legislation, but the declaration of the law of Nature already existing in art.

Had it been the destiny of Aristotle to declare the æsthetic law of any modern European nation, his task would have been far more difficult. In no Christian society has the artist shown the same spontaneous faculty for imitating Nature as in Greece. Many obstacles stand between Nature and the imagination of the modern artist. To begin with, he has been cut off from the fountainhead of his primæval instincts by the conversion of his ancestors to Christianity. Moreover, the nation in modern Europe is not constituted simply, as in the small Greek states, but is vast and complex, composed of antagonistic classes, each with its own perceptions and ideals, which often baffle the attempt of the artist to divine the ideas common to the whole society. Lastly, the modern imagination and judgment are bewildered by the presence of surviving models of Hellenic art, which constantly oppose themselves to the ideas derived from Christian education. Nevertheless, a historic examination of art will hardly leave room for doubt, that the varieties of ideal imitation in the different countries of Europe have been as much the product of national character, as was the case in the City States of Greece; and I propose in this lecture to illustrate, as clearly as I can in the time at my disposal, how national forces have combined to give a dominant bias to the genius of French poetry.

Experience shows how closely the master qualities of the French character still correspond with Cæsar's description of them. The assimilation of Visigothic and Frankish elements have not materially altered in the Gaul either the brilliant and fickle temperament, vividly coloured by transient emotions, the rapid logical perception of things, or the sense of artistic form and proportion common to all races that have felt the influence of the Latin mind. As this national character expands in the course of French history, there passes before the imagination a long drama of something like civil war between two mutually irreconcileable factions — the bourgeoisie and the feudal aristocracy. The landmarks of the struggle stand forth prominently; the long agonising conflict of the early ages between the Crown, as the representative of civil law and order, and the great vassals, as the representatives of feudal privilege ; the victory of the Crown, allied with the bourgeoisie, under Louis XI. ; the religious wars between Catholics and Huguenots ; the accession of Henry IV. and the elimination of the Huguenots as a political power; the wars of the Fronde and the annihilation of the political power of the feudal aristocracy ; the absorption of all the powers of the State by the Crown in the reign of Louis XIV. ; the decay of the Monarchy in the eighteenth century; the French Revolution.

As illustrating the working of the Law of National Character in literature, nothing can be more remarkable than the vivid reflection of this course of political development in the various stages of French poetry. There, in the very infancy of society, may be observed the trenchant antithesis between the genius of the two opposing classes in the contrasted styles of the Provençal lyric and the *fabliau* of the Trouvère ; the one the poetical vehicle of the inhabitants of the Castle, the other of the inhabitants of the town. We see the two types brought into deliberately satiric contrast in the famous *Romance of the Rose*, in the latter part of which the bourgeois John de Meung mocks at the ideals of his chivalric predecessor William de Lorris. The alliance between the Court and the bourgeoisie is symbolised in the poems of Marot, who set himself to refine the character of the old French poetry to suit the more fastidious taste of Francis I. On the other hand, the poetry of Ronsard, the representative, with the Pleiad, of the party of the aristocracy, reflects in a new form the old tendency of the castled nobility to mark out for themselves a manner of conception and expression sharply separated from that of the vulgar. Ronsard's movement, in spite of his real genius, is seen from the first to be against the inevitable tendency of things, and is therefore doomed to failure; and in the same way D'Aubigné's Huguenot ideals, unable to make head against the Catholic tendency in the French nation, find utterance, like a lonely " Vox Clamantis," in the lofty strains of *Les Tragiques*. Henry IV. ascends the throne; and with Malherbe, as the dictator of poetical taste, the victory of the Monarchical over the feudal principle in French politics, the victory of reason over imagination in French poetry, is practically decided.

If, turning from this general historic view, we ask how these two parties respectively manifested their character in French literature, it is clear, in the first place, that the qualities in the French nation which the aristocracy communicated to the language were of the feminine order, both in their virtue and their defect. How remarkable is the long array of brilliant women who have left a name in French literature— The Countess of Champagne, Christine de Pisan, The Marquise de Rambouillet, Madame du Sablé, Madame de Sévigné! How powerful an influence on the course of refined taste was exercised by the Cours d'Amour, the Hôtel Rambouillet, the Salons of the Précieuses!

From the noble ladies of France, and the men who, according to the laws of chivalry, declared themselves their servants, the French idiom acquired that exquisite vein of irony and innuendo which made French conversation for so long the standard of manners in European society, and French prose the finest instrument of criticism, letter-writing, and diplomacy. But the masculine qualities of imagination are conspicuous by their absence. What the French aristocracy wanted in their literary style was substance, sincerity, a sense of the reality of things. Weigh the names of their representative men, Charles of Orleans, Ronsard, Voiture, Chapelain, St. Amant, against such names as Rabelais, La Fontaine, Molière, and Voltaire, representatives of the bourgeoisie; observe the triviality of matter in the lyrics of the Troubadours, in the poetry written for the Hôtel Rambouillet, in the romance of the *Grand Cyrus;* and you will see the defeat of the French aristocracy in the conflict of History explained in the conflict of Ideas.

The bourgeois element in French poetry is of an evidently opposite kind. It has none of the romance, delicacy, or spiritual imagination, which distinguish the work of the chivalric party; its qualities are, above all, good sense, shrewd observation, keen logic, a penetrating appreciation of hypocrisy and unreality, an unerring sense of the ridiculous, an Epicurean enjoyment of life. Deprive this bourgeois genius of its native tendency to vulgarity, by putting it under the patronage of the Court, give it subjects for imitation suitable to its knowledge and powers, find it an instrument of expression analogous to its favourite *fabliau*; and the flower of the French imagination will in time unfold itself in the Comedies of Molière and the Fables of La Fontaine. It is in the works of these two writers, perhaps above all others, that we may observe the operation of what it is not improper to call the idea of Natural Law in French Poetry.

Molière has been severely censured by the more austere critics of France as a careless and slovenly writer. He is blamed for want of polish in his style, for his incorrect selection of metaphors, for his audacious plagiarisms; and all these reproaches he has to some extent justly incurred. But his defects are almost the inevitable accompaniment of his splendid qualities as a comic creator. Molière imitated the ridiculous in Nature wherever he found it. When he thought that Spanish or Italian phrases, or the vulgarisms of French idiom, were expressive of character, he used them without any regard to the delicate nerves of the French Academy. With as little hesitation he drew on the inventions of the classic and Italian dramatists or the *fabliaux* of Boccaccio, if they furnished him with convenient plots for framing his observation of what was deserving of ridicule in his own society. But all his creations are eminently original. Nowhere else than in France could such universal types of human nature as M. Jourdain, Tartufe, and Alceste have been conceived and embodied. No one but Molière could have observed with such nice precision, and have expressed in dialogue so sparkling and lifelike, the essence of absurdity in the manners of *Les Précieuses* or *Les Femmes Savantes*. As a mirror for such universal truths of Nature the refined literary language of the Academy, and the conventional standard of manners in the Hôtel Rambouillet, were equally inadequate. Molière in his Comedies doubtless leans to farce; but he does so because the old popular French farces furnished him with the ideal atmosphere required to give poetical truth to the observed realities of Nature. Nor do his bourgeois instincts carry him into excess. His seemingly buffoon extravagance of conception and spontaneous exuberance of expression were kept within due limits by the sense that his plays were to be performed before the most fastidious of monarchs, who would never have tolerated the exhibition of vulgarity beyond what was necessary for the purposes of art. Hence, in spite of its negligence, the composition and language of Molière are in the highest sense well-bred, harmonious, and classic.

Exactly analogous to the dramatic practice of Molière is the literary practice of La Fontaine, except that, as the poems of the latter were intended to be read, no one has ever blamed him for incorrectness of style. La Fontaine makes no more effort than Molière to raise himself into a consciously ideal atmosphere. He cares no more than Molière did for the praise of absolute originality; his fables, like the plots of Molière, are borrowed from the inventions of predecessors, fabulists such as Phædrus, Babrius, Horace, and a hundred others. But through all this borrowing and adaptation, the unmistakable character of the old French *fabliau*, and the individuality of La Fontaine, make themselves felt. His verses breathe the easy Epicurean air characteristic of his class. His peasants and citizens are types of the men and women whom he saw in the farms and markets; his beasts use the average human language of prudence and good sense. In the flow of his verse we listen to the natural idiom of the conversation of his time. Nevertheless, the ideal atmosphere, required for the imitation of the Universal, is never absent from his creations, and knowing as he did that he was writing for refined society, his poetry, with all its apparent ease, is in reality the result of the most careful selection of words and harmonies.

The dominant bias of French taste, however, discloses itself not merely in works in which the artist is felt to be dealing with materials akin to his own nature, but in the abstract reasoning by which men of genius have endeavoured to regulate practice in the higher spheres of poetic invention. For example, the French idea of law in art is strikingly exhibited in the approved rules of composition for the tragic drama. Unlike the dramas of Athens and of England, the tradition of the theatre in France is not of popular origin, but is the late creation of a few great poets, accommodating their practice to the taste of comparatively refined audiences. There was, indeed, a time when the itinerant stage of the Middle Ages found a welcome among the French, as among the

English people, but these exhibitions had so dwindled during the miserable period of the Hundred Years' War, that, at the close of the sixteenth century, one company of actors, in the Hôtel Bourgogne, was sufficient to satisfy the dramatic requirements of the whole country. When the taste for the stage began to revive the poet was free to invent for himself, and he naturally turned for his models to the tragedies of Seneca, never meant for acting, in which an abstract situation is worked out by means of rhetorical harangues and sharply pointed dialogue. The form thus adopted proved so acceptable to French taste, that, in spite of the efforts of Voltaire and Diderot, it kept possession of the stage for nearly 200 years.

Having thus grounded the practice of the drama on the authority of Seneca, the French poets proceeded to regulate it by the supposed theory of Aristotle. Corneille was the first to define the law of the stage in his *Discourse on the Three Unities of Action, Time, and Place.* He assumed that the external form of the Greek drama was something immutable; that Aristotle had defined its changeless rules in the *Poetics;* and that these rules had been faithfully observed in his own tragedies. Now the only unity on which Aristotle really insists is Unity of Action; and in his *Discourse* Corneille plainly shows that he does not know what Aristotle meant by Unity of Action. Unity of Action in the *Poetics* means simply the representation on the stage of a fictitious story, with a proportioned beginning, middle, and end, involving a display of human passion, character, and misfortune, in such a form as to appear probable and lifelike to the spectators.

Shakespeare and the Greek poets perfectly understood the working of this fundamental law. So vividly does Shakespeare conceive his ideal situations as a whole, that he even realises in his imagination the state of the climate and temperature, as when Hamlet says to Horatio: "The air bites shrewdly; it is very cold;" or when Duncan praises the amenity of Macbeth's Castle:

> This guest of summer,
> The temple-haunting martlet, does approve,
> By his loved mansionry, that the heaven's breath
> Smells wooingly here: no jutty, friese,
> Buttress, nor coign of vantage, but this bird
> Hath made his pendent bed and procreant cradle:
> Where they most breed and haunt, I have observed,
> The air is delicate.

So, again, in *As You Like It*, when Oliver asks the way to Rosalind's cottage, with what particular details the poet brings the scene before us!—

> Good morrow, fair ones: pray you, if you know,
> Where in the purlieus of this forest stands
> A sheep-cote fenced about with olive trees?

To which Celia replies:

> West of this place, down in the neighbour bottom:
> The rank of osiers by the murmuring stream
> Left on your right hand brings you to the place.

The fact is, that both the Greek and English dramatists were the natural successors of the minstrels

—the former of Homer and the cyclic poets, the latter of the mediæval *trouvères*—and their imaginations were accustomed to live in the ideal action of the story-tellers. Now for a story in itself Corneille cared nothing. What he meant by unity of action was the unity of abstract idea in a drama. He understood very well the nature of the stage effects required to produce emotion in an audience; and he constructed his plays logically and scientifically with a view to securing these effects. I imagine that the way in which he composed a tragedy was something like this: First he searched for a situation in which he might exhibit a conflict between the will and the passions; then, when he had found the subject, he filled in the situation with the characters, and determined their relations to each other in successive scenes; after that, he thought out the emotions and sentiments proper to each scene; lastly, he coloured the whole of the dialogue with impassioned rhetoric and epigrammatic points.

Composing on this principle, Corneille was able to exclude from the structure of his drama every external incident that was not necessary to the evolution of his abstract idea, but he was far from attaining unity of action. He strove to imitate, as far as possible, the outward form of Greek tragedy, and took note of Aristotle's saying, that it is not necessary to represent on the stage the whole of a recorded action. But he did not observe that the reason of this was that, in the Athenian theatre, the audience were all familiar with the whole story represented, and so were able to supply from their imagination the necessary gaps in the action. But this is not the case in *The Cid*. Corneille, in this play, merely selects from the story of the Spanish hero such episodes as he deemed necessary for the treatment of his own idea. We are plunged at the opening of the play *in medias res*. We do not know, except from the table of *dramatis personae*, who Don Rodrigue and Chimène are; who Don Diegue and Don Gomes are, or what were the events which led to the quarrel causing the complication of the whole drama. The dramatic situation resembles a chess-board after the game has been developed according to one of the conventional openings. The love of Rodrigue for Chimène is held in check by Rodrigue's filial obligation to avenge the insult offered to *his* father; the love of Chimène for Rodrigue is checked by the duty imposed on her to avenge the death of *her* father; the dramatic interest depends on the solution of the psychological puzzle.

It is extremely interesting and instructive to observe how carefully Corneille applies the Law of the Three Unities to a tragedy thought out on this completely abstract principle. He wished to make the play appear logical to the audience *on the stage;* he did not care about making it appear real to *the universal imagination*. Accordingly, he pleads apologetically, in his *Discourse on the Three Unities*, that he has not departed from the rule of Unity of Place further than he was absolutely obliged by the nature of his subject. And as to the Unity of Time, since the action of the play is restricted by the supposed law to twenty-four hours, the dramatist is obliged by the course of events to make Don Rodrigue first kill Don Gomes, then conquer the Moors, then come back to fight a second duel with Don Sanche; and that he may do all this within the prescribed time limits, his father, Don Diegue, opposes the desire of the king to give *The Cid* an interval for rest and refreshment, observing that it is nothing for a man of his son's heroic valour to come from a battle to a duel without making a pause!

And yet, though Corneille is so anxious to satisfy the demands of a dramatic law which has no existence in truth or nature, he sees no improbability in representing Chimène making long speeches to her lady-in-waiting in order to show the audience the state of her mind in the struggle between her inclination and her duty; no improbability in bringing Don Rodrigue to his mistress, after he has killed her father, to entreat her to plunge the same sword into his own heart; no improbability in causing the king to decide that Chimène's plea for vengeance against the man who has killed her father shall be satisfied by a duel between Rodrigue and Chimène's selected champion, the prize of victory being the hand of Chimène herself; no improbability in leading us to suppose, at the close of the play, that Chimène marries her father's slayer and lives happily for ever after! Such improbabilities could never have been conceived by any poet who understood the meaning of Aristotle's principle of Unity of Action in the imitation of Nature; but they proved no obstacle to the appreciation of the tragedy by an audience which accepted the artificial hypothesis with which the poet started, and mainly desired to have their own love of antithesis and rhetoric satisfied in a dramatic form of representation.

Far be it from me, as an Englishman, to speak with disrespect of the great dramatists of France. Viewed in their relation to the taste of French society, plays like *Horace, Cinna, Phèdre,* and *Athalie* seem to be marvels of dramatic skill and invention. My argument is that a society like that of France was incapable of conceiving tragic action like that found in the plays of Æschylus and Shakespeare. The action of the poetic drama in Greece and England was a reflection of widespread popular energy, of freedom of thought, speech, and deed, of national greatness and patriotism, exalted by an inward sense of power and by the defeat of such foreign enemies as Xerxes and Philip II. No such inspiring air of liberty stirred the imagination of France in the seventeenth century. With what feelings would Louis XIV., retaining in his memory his youthful experiences of the Frondist wars, have witnessed on the stage the sufferings of legitimate kings, deprived, as in *Richard II.* and *Macbeth,* of their thrones and lives by the usurpation of ambitious subjects? How would his monarchical pride have revolted against such a spectacle as King Lear, stripped of his last shred of authority, the sport of the elements, the companion in adversity of fools and madmen! What would the Jesuits have said to the daring doubts and speculations of Hamlet's conscience ? Absolutism and centralisation called for another order of dramatic exhibition in France. Driven from her free range in external Nature, the Muse of Tragedy retired into the recesses of the human soul, whose inner conflicts she might represent without rousing the political suspicion of king or cardinal. Yet even here she was haunted by the phantoms of her own self-consciousness. The overpowering sense of the authority of Aristotle, the anticipation of the verdict of the associated critics of the Academy, the oppressive idea of a dramatic standard formed by ancient models of unrivalled excellence, all these influences co-operated to make the French dramatist voluntarily fetter himself in his imitation of nature. The Law of the Three Unities is an illustration of the tendency in the French character, as developed by the history of France, to repress the liberties of imagination by the analysis of Logic.

As the French law of the stage is defined by Corneille in his *Discourse on the Unities,* so the law of French literary taste is expounded by Boileau in the *Art Poétique.* Critics are apt to undervalue poems of the class of Horace's *Ars Poetica* and Pope's *Essay on Criticism,* because they regard them as abstract treatises on taste, containing cold and commonplace maxims of composition; whereas their real interest and importance lie in the fact that they are declarations of law by a victorious literary party. The *Ars Poetica* and the *Epistle to Augustus* were manifestoes of the Hellenising party in Roman literature, directed against those who favoured the rude facility of poets like Lucilius and Plautus. The *Essay on Criticism* is an argument in verse against the taste represented by the Metaphysical Poets of the seventeenth century in England. More suggestive than either of these poems, because more relentless and uncompromising, the *Art Poétique* stands out prominently as the final declaration of Law, by the literary representatives of the French bourgeoisie, in alliance with the Crown on the one hand, and with the Classical Humanists on the other, against the aristocratic literary party represented in the coteries of the *Précieuses*. The artistic value of the apparently abstract rules formulated in the poem consists in their oblique way of reflecting on the practice of the Scudérys, St. Amant, and Pradon. The *Art Poétique* is the formulated expression of the law of French poetry, first recognised nearly a century before in the verses of Malherbe, whose praises Boileau so enthusiastically sounds. "Lastly," he says, "came Malherbe, the first in France to give an example of just cadence in verse, to show the power of a word in its right place, and to restrict the Muse to the laws of duty. Restored by this wise writer, our language no longer offered any rude shock to the refined ear. Stanzas learned how to close gracefully; one verse no longer ventured to overlap another. Everything approves the justice of his laws, and this faithful guide still serves as a model to the authors of our time. Walk in his steps; love his purity; imitate the clearness of his happy style."

What, then, was the ideal which Boileau, by his reasoning and illustrations, set before the French poet? The expression of Truth, Reason, Logic. The aim was not wanting in life and vigour. Genius, says the critic, at the opening of the *Art Poétique*, is indispensable, but the medium in which genius must work is good sense. "Tout doit tendre au bon sens." And again, "Good sense must prevail even in song." Hardly so deeply laid as the foundation of Horace, "Scribendi recte sapere est et principium et fons," the rule implies that the standard of the correct imitation of nature is the lucid perception and logic of the bourgeois mind, aided by the refined manners of the court. "Étudiez la cour, connaissez-vous la ville." Above all, whatever subject is chosen, the poet must go to its essence, and not be satisfied till he has found the exact and perfect form of words required for the expression of the thought. Not a word about Beauty, Liberty, Imagination, Fancy. In every phrase we hear the voice of the stern proscriber, the Sulla of poetry, on the watch to put on the list for massacre some dangerous partisan of the Hôtel Rambouillet, who has managed to escape critical notice.

Boileau was well aware that Poetry could not dispense with the aristocratic element in language; and being at war with the principle favoured by the social aristocracy, he sought to fill the void in his critical system by allying himself with the literary aristocracy of the Renaissance, and exalting the authority of the Greek and Roman classics. The principle was excellent so long as it meant no more than self-criticism by the highest standard of antiquity. But Boileau was almost inevitably carried into error by his logic. He regarded all the types of verse composition met with in the history of French literature as immutable moulds of thought; and he fancied that the classic propriety of each could be determined by settled rules. "Every poem," he says, "shines with its proper beauty. The rondeau, Gallic by birth, has the artlessness of nature, the ballad, strictly subject to its old maxims, often owes a lustre to the caprice of its rhymes. The madrigal, more simple and more noble in its style, breathes gentleness, tenderness, and love." Thus, in opposition to his own and Horace's teaching, that the form of poetry must necessarily adapt itself to the thought, he speaks as if poetry lay in stereotyped forms of versification. In spite of his foundation of sound reasoning, he came insensibly to identify the imitation of Nature, under the guidance of good sense, with the mere external imitation of Greek and Roman poets.

Two examples will show the inconsistencies into which his logic betrayed him. Among the various types of poetry which he found himself obliged to define was the Eclogue. According to the dictates of good sense this form of poem must, he says, avoid the two extremes of pompous elevation on the one hand, and of rustic meanness on the other. An easy abstract rule; but what does it practically mean? "Between these two excesses," says Boileau, "the path is difficult. In order to find it, follow Theocritus and Virgil. Let their feeling compositions, dictated by the Graces, never quit your hands; turn them over by night and day. They alone in their learned verse will be able to teach you by what art an author may without meanness lower his style; how to sing of Flora and the fields, of Pomona and the woods; how to animate two shepherds to contend on the flute, to celebrate the allurements of love's pleasures; to transform Narcissus into a flower; to cover Daphne with bark; and by what art at times the eclogue invests the country and the woods with consular dignity." Would a poet who in Louis XIV.'s time acted obediently on these instructions have been imitating Nature according to the law of Good Sense?

Again, Boileau found himself much perplexed how to apply the principle of Good Sense to his idea of an epic poem. The epic, he says, sustains itself by faith and lives by fiction; therefore you cannot dispense in a poem of this kind with the machinery of pagan mythology. Hence it is impossible to write a Christian epic. "In vain," he says, alluding to the attempts in this direction of poets in the anti-classic camp; "in vain do our deluded authors, banishing from their verse these traditional ornaments, strive to make God, the saints, and the prophets act like the deities sprung out of the poets' imagination, take the reader into Hell at every step, and introduce him to Ashtaroth, Beelzebub, and Lucifer alone. The awful mysteries of the Christian faith are incapable of gay and brilliant ornament. On every side the Gospel presents to the mind the spectacle only of Repentance and Judgment, and the inexcusable mixture of fiction gives to its truths an air of fable. What an object to offer to the eye, the devil blaspheming against heaven—the devil, whose aim it is to abase the glory of your Hero, and who often disputes the victory with God!"

True enough in its application to the feeble invention of Scudéry and his companions, a criticism like this only proves that the French were incapable of producing a great epic poem. It does not prove that there was anything fundamentally wrong in the conception of *Paradise Lost*. And the same rigid restrictive logic characterises all Boileau's devices with regard to diction and versification—the exclusive use of the Alexandrine, the cæsura always in the middle of the line, the avoidance of the *hiatus* and the "enjambement," the choice of words to harmonise exactly with the movement of the rhythm,—all which are only the final declaration by the Academic dictator of the laws first promulgated by Malherbe. For the time the victory of Boileau and the ideas of the cultivated bourgeoisie over the party of mediæval Romance was complete. Nor was it a mere transient fashion of taste. For about one hundred and fifty years the Law of Classicism, as defined in the *Art Poétique*, exerted an irresistible authority. In spite alike of the half-hearted efforts of Voltaire to enlarge the liberties of dramatic action, and of the experiments of Diderot in sentimental comedy, the classic style, founded on the Law of the Three Unities, reigned supreme upon the French stage through the eighteenth century. But it was a party triumph, a Pyrrhic victory, won by the vigour of a certain element in society, and liable to be reversed when the class from which the movement sprang lost its vitality. Undermined by the growth of natural science, by the philosophy of the encyclopædists, and by the sentimentalism of Rousseau, the imposing structure of French classicism fell almost at the first discharge of artillery brought against it by the Romantic party after the restoration of the Bourbons.

It is not to be denied that it deserved its fate. But at the same time it would be well for us Englishmen to examine very carefully the true lesson to be learned from the triumph of French Romanticism. The Law of Classic Taste in France could not have remained paramount for so long a period; its authority could not have been instinctively recognised by so many great creative intellects, or so clearly defined by a succession of able critics, if it had not represented something real and positive in the constitution of the French character. And looking at the matter historically, when we see that the idea of the manner in which Nature ought to be imitated in Poetry, as expressed in the *Art Poétique*, is actually embodied in the poems of La Fontaine and Molière, and that the idea of the structure and versification proper to the drama is the same in the tragedies of Racine and Voltaire as in the criticism of Boileau, then candid minds will allow that, however narrow may have been the sphere of imitation, and however restricted the perception of harmony, both adapted themselves to an irresistible tendency of things in the development of French society. The great error of the Romanticists was that they ignored the existence of this historic law. As a revolt in the sphere of art and imagination their movement was fully justified, and nothing would have been easier for them than to show that a law of taste, which might have been suitable for the times of Louis XIV., was quite unsuitable for the times of Charles X.

What the Romanticists wanted, however, was not a revolt but a Revolution. The rules, distinctions, practices, and traditions, which had been the result of so much ingenious thought and labour, were to be swept away, and Poetry was to find for herself a basis in first principles, supposed to be entirely modern. What were they? The manifesto of the victorious Romanticists is to be found in the Preface to Victor Hugo's *Cromwell*, which founds its reasoning on this colossal generalisation : " To sum up the facts we have just observed, Poetry has three Ages, each of which corresponds with an epoch of society : Ode, Epic, Drama. Primitive times are lyric, ancient times are epic, modern times are dramatic. The Ode sings eternity; the Epic solemnises history; the Drama paints life. The character of the first kind of poetry is *naïveté;* the character of the second simplicity ; the character of the third truth. The rhapsodists mark the transition of the lyric poets to the epic poets, as the romance-writers from the epic poets to the dramatic poets. Historians arise in the second epoch; chroniclers and critics in the third. The personages of the Ode are Colossi : Adam, Cain, Noah ; those of the Epic are giants : Achilles, Atreus, Orestes ; those of the Drama are men : Hamlet, Macbeth, Othello. The Ode derives its life from the ideal, the Epic from the grandiose, the Drama from the real. In a word, this threefold Poetry springs from three great sources—the Bible, Homer, Shakespeare."

The upshot of this reasoning is, that the end of the modern or romantic drama is to paint real character, and Victor Hugo tells us very naïvely how this was done in the case of *Cromwell*. He had for a long time accepted the portrait of the regicide, painted by Bossuet, as true to life; but, happening to come across an old document of the seventeenth century, he discovered that the portrait did not resemble the original. The idea must therefore be corrected, and the proper place for correcting it was the Drama. Accordingly he read a vast number of books, from which he generalised the character of the man and his times, chose a dramatic moment in the life of his hero which would enable him to exhibit his real motives to the reader, surrounded him with more than sixty other *dramatis personae*, and finally completed the portrait of the character in a play which extended itself to about 12,000 lines. It seems, indeed, to have struck Victor Hugo that there was something paradoxical in the fact that a composition founded on æsthetic principles, in an epoch of the world in which the drama was the natural vehicle of imaginative thought, could not possibly be acted, and he made a half promise that, at some future time, he would adapt *Cromwell* for the stage. I am not aware, however, that he ever reduced his ideas to practice.

But what Victor Hugo did not perceive was that, while he professed to be sweeping away all French dramatic tradition, while he imagined himself to be imitating Shakespeare, and to be creating in a spirit of unfettered liberty, he was showing a complete ignorance of the principle on which Shakespeare's plays are constructed, and was unconsciously following, though with a variation, the stage principles of his predecessors. As I have already said, Shakespeare's method of dramatic creations, like that of the Greeks, is to reduce what was originally a well-known epic story into such a form as will please the imagination of spectators in a theatre; the method of the French playwright is to analyse an idea in his own mind and then to reproduce it in a dramatic shape. It matters not that the idea which Hugo analysed was that of a single man's character, while that which Corneille analysed was a psychological situation; that, in *The Cid*, the spectacle to be contemplated is a conflict between Love and Honour, and, in *Cromwell*, the conflict of motives in the mind of a regicide; in both cases the imaginative process is the same, the logical combination of abstract ideas; in both cases the artistic result is fundamentally the same, a play depending for its effect on rhetorical speeches and epigrammatic points. This is the method of Seneca, not the method of Shakespeare.

Examine, again, the motto of another great standard-bearer of Romanticism, Théophile Gautier. His principle, "Art for Art's sake," seems to promise the artist unlimited liberty in imitating Nature, pro-

LECT. III THE IDEA OF LAW IN FRENCH POETRY

vided he is possessed of adequate skill. When illustrated by Gautier's own practice, however, his maxim evidently implies a determination to identify the methods of poetry with the methods of painting. Gautier endeavoured to imitate Nature in words, exactly in the same way as the painter imitated her in form and colour. Now, in my lecture on "Poetical Decadence" I fully admitted that the art of poetry included an element analogous to the art of painting, as may be plainly seen in the descriptions and similes of great poets like Homer, Virgil, Milton, Spenser, and Ariosto. Nor do I deny that Gautier's poetry abounds in admirable pictorial *tours de force*, such as the humorous picture, in his *Émaux et Camées*, of Winter as an old violinist. "With red nose and pale face, and with a desk of icicles, he executes his theme in the quartet of the Seasons. He sings with an uncertain voice old-world quavering airs: his frozen foot warms itself while it marks the time. And like Handel, whose wig lost its powder when he shivered, he makes the white sprinkling of snow fly from the nape of his neck."

But to confine the function of poetry, as Gautier did, to word-painting is surely, in the first place, to form a meagre conception of the art, and in the second place, this supposed invention of the Romanticists is really nothing more than an application of the old classic law of Boileau, that the poet is bound to find for his verse the word exactly corresponding with the image in his mind. Turn to the *Lutrin*, and Boileau's picture of the Treasurer of La Chapelle in bed will furnish you with a brilliant sample of the word-painting which was Gautier's whole poetical stock-in-trade: "In the dark retirement of a deep alcove is piled a costly feather-bed. Four pompous curtains in a double circle defend it from the light of day. There, amid the calm and peaceful silence, reigns over the swan-down a happy indolence, and there the prelate, fortified by breakfast, and sleeping a light sleep, waited for dinner. Youth in full flower beams in his countenance; his chin descends by two storeys on to his breast, and his body, thick-set in its short stature, makes the bed groan beneath its lazy weight."

Do not the instances I have given furnish in themselves an answer to the reasoning of the Romanticists? Had these children of the Revolution possessed real self-knowledge they would have perceived that their most successful work was conceived in accordance with the old classical law, and they would have aimed only at such an amplification of that law as would give free play to their own gifts and genius. Unfortunately they were animated by a spirit not of comprehension but exclusion. The party of the Romanticists had gained the upper hand, and they were determined to proscribe and massacre the party of the Classicists as ruthlessly as the Classicists of the seventeenth century had proscribed and massacred the party of the *Précieuses*. Romanticism under Louis XIV. and under Louis Philippe was equally the protest of a faction against the inevitable tendency of things; but in the one case it was the struggle of a social caste against the principle of Absolutism, in the other of a literary coterie against the principle of Equality. Just as Mdlle. de Rambouillet and her friends sought to separate themselves from the vulgar world by the nicety of their manners and language, so did Théophile Gautier and his followers seek to shock the instincts of the bourgeoisie by their red waistcoats and outrageous verses. "For us," says Gautier, in his account of the Romantic movement, "the world divided itself into 'Flamboyants' and 'Neutral Tints,' the one the object of our love, the other of our aversion. We wanted life, light, movement; audacity of thought and execution, a return to the fair period of the Renaissance and true antiquity; we rejected the tame colouring, the thin and dry design, the compositions resembling groups of dwarfs, that the Empire had bequeathed to the Restoration."

To the foreign critic it seems that, as in French politics the centralising principle has overpowered local liberty, so in French art the native tendency is for logic to prevail over imagination. Whatever literary party has been dominant in the taste of French society has sought to establish its supremacy by imaginative Analysis. The result has been to develop in the art of our neighbours great beauty of abstract Form, a splendid capacity of lucid expression, but more and more to turn away the creative impulse of the artist from the imitation of universal ideas of life and action. In the rival theories and practice of the modern French Naturalists and Impressionists I seem to detect, under a changed form, the old party struggle between the Classicists and the Romanticists. In one direction, I see the disciples of Gustave Flaubert, by a new application of the precepts of Boileau, employing all the resources of precise and artistic language to decorate the sordid commonplace of bourgeois life; in another, M. Anatole France, as the successor of Renan, arresting the transient impressions of his own mind in a succession of delicate phrases, which would have been the delight of the Hôtel Rambouillet. But, in both directions, Analysis undermines the conscience with the suggestion of subjects and ideas which lie at the very foundation of the Family and the State.

Must these things be? Is it impossible for the French novelist to contemplate Man under any aspect except that which involves some relation to his neighbour's wife? impossible for him to transport the imagination into the world of ideal action? Perhaps it may be answered, that all the energies of the nation are concentrated in Paris, where lies its brain, and that Analysis alone can penetrate to the principle of life underlying the wild excitement of the Parisian Bourse, the gossip of the Parisian journal, the intrigues of the Parisian drawing-room. But Paris is not France: the poetry of the people, its historic soul and character, lies elsewhere. Turn away from the dissolving scene of life in the capital, with its superficial reflection of vulgar materialism, to the bypaths of rural France, where Nature pursues her ancient round in the midst of silent labour and elemental pieties. Pause in imagination, for example, in the valley of the Loire, as that noble river flows peacefully amidst historic battle-grounds; through walled towns, where every stone seems to recall some national memory—Orleans, Tours, Angers; through fields in which, here and there, peasants may still be seen, as Millet saw them, listening with bent heads to the voice of the Angelus; under gray châteaux, which, perhaps no longer tenanted by the descendants of their former lords, look down, at fixed seasons, on popular festivals celebrated around them since the Middle Ages—will any man of taste and imagination, viewing scenes like these in the light not of romance but of history, and thinking of all the movement and animation of the present in its relation to the past, venture to say that Molière and La Fontaine would have found nothing worthy of imitation in the France of this century? Would they not have been able to show us in an ideal form, though it were but in comedy, how much of the historic character of their country has survived the conflict of thirty generations; how many of the primæval springs of national life combine to preserve the unity of French society; to what extent the ancient religion is still a moving power in the hearts of the people? Let it be granted that it is no longer the drama or the poem, but the novel, which is the vehicle of imaginative expression. Yet the novel also can be made the mirror of the ideal imitation of Nature, and the novelist who is able to give a reflection of the true morals and manners of France in the classic language inherited from Pascal and Mme. de Sévigné, will command an European audience as wide and appreciative as in the days of Louis Quatorze.

IV

THE IDEA OF LAW IN GERMAN POETRY

THE same inevitable forces out of which arose the character of French Poetry are seen to be working, though under very different circumstances, to determine the character of German Poetry; and it is this law, or idea of law, in Germany which I propose to make the subject of my present lecture. First of all, let us consider precisely the nature of the facts with which we have to deal. It cannot be said that Germany has expressed the idea of the Universal, either in the creative departments of Poetry or in the plastic Arts, with as much character as Italy, England, France, or even Spain. The Germans have produced no romantic epic of universal European fame, like the *Orlando Furioso*, no classic epic that can be named with *Paradise Lost;* no romance like *Don Quixote;* no tragic drama comparable, I do not say with the tragedies of Shakespeare, but even with those of Corneille and Racine; no comic drama approaching within visible distance of that of Molière. In painting, two German names alone are household words, Holbein and Albert Dürer. To compensate for these deficiencies, the Germans are supreme in Music: Handel, Mozart, and Beethoven form a triumvirate whom the united musicians of the rest of Europe would challenge in vain. From Germany have come the great men of contemplation in Religion, Philosophy, and Criticism—Luther, Kant, Lessing. And in lyric poetry —that department of the art which is most akin to Music—their compositions (I am thinking of the ballads of Schiller and Uhland, of *Faust*, and of Heine's Songs) have roused emotions in the hearts of men untouched by the lyric poetry of any other nation, with the possible exception of the poetry of Byron.

I think that these facts are precisely the results that might be expected to follow from the genius of the German character, and the course of German history. German genius, at least as manifested outwardly up to quite modern times, has been rather contemplative than practical. The German has—or had two generations ago—the same strange contrasts in his character as are noted by Tacitus: the love of arms, joined with the tendency to domestic indolence; the passion for intellectual liberty, accompanying the neglect of the arts of society; energy in war, followed by reverie in peace. In peace, says the practical Roman historian, "ipsi hebent, mira naturae diversitate, cum idem sic ament inertiam et oderint quietem." Something of this contradictory combination of qualities is visible in the characters of many of the greatest Germans; they are content that their bodies shall never travel out of sight of their own hearth-smoke, if their souls have freedom to soar through the Infinite. Luther, shaking the world from his monastery, with his doctrine of Justification by Faith; Kant, revolutionising philosophy in his little provincial town, beyond whose walls he rarely stirred; both were true Germans. And hence it seems to me quite natural that, when the Germans strive to express their idea of the Universal in the sphere of creative imagination, they should turn with the readiest sympathy to that one of the Fine Arts which at once exerts the widest sway over the pure emotions, and is least under the direction of Reason, least subject to the limitations of plastic form; in other words, the German genius has closer affinities with the Art of Music than with the Arts of Poetry and Painting.

If, however, we look at the creative departments of Poetry, as actually developed in Germany, we shall see how faithfully the practice of the poets reflects the ideas of action proper to the history of the German people. The political history of Germany is the exact antithesis of the history of France, for while the prominent feature of French history is an excessive centralisation leading to Absolutism, the character of German history is an excess of Individualism resulting in Anarchy. Until recently the Germans had no political ideal of united action which could be reduced to practice. At a time when Spain, France, and England were all nations with clearly defined interests and policies, Germany was a loose aggregation of States, in which the old feudal, semi-tribal order was still predominant; the Emperor being its impotent head, and against that head all the other members, each in conflict with the other, being in rebellion—the Princes at war with their Sovereign, the Cities and Knights with the Princes, the Peasantry with the Knights and the Cities. From the midst of this caldron of chaos rose the Reformation, and from the Reformation the Thirty Years' War, with its political and spiritual divisions of Catholic against Protestant, and its fruits of desolation, poverty, despair. When the wars were over, each petty exhausted state settled down within its own limits, and began to cultivate civil arts in its own way, having cut itself off from the mediæval ideals of the Christian Republic, without having been able to assimilate the ideals of the modern Nation.

Such was the state of politics in Germany at the time when the foundations of modern German literature were laid. The most characteristic period of German Poetry is the century between the Seven Years' War and the French Revolution of 1848; and during that period the most common complaint of German writers of genius is the want of great central ideas of action to form a basis of national art. Goethe, in his *Dichtung und Wahrheit*, describes the prevailing condition of things in the middle of the eighteenth century: " Because in peace patriotism really consists only in this, that every one sweeps his own doorstep, minds his own business, learns his own lesson, that it may go well with his house, so did the feeling for Fatherland excited by Klopstock find no object on which it could exercise itself." Germany was full of men of imagination; they were all anxious to write great epics and great dramas; unfortunately they had to make their poetical bricks without straw, having neither characteristic ideas of political unity, nor any continuous tradition of rude art out of which they might consciously develop more perfect forms. Hence each poet was forced to think out the first principles of composition for himself; and one of the characteristics of German poetry is, that, in the higher walks of the Art, Criticism precedes Creation.

Now if we apply the twofold Law of Fine Art to Klopstock's *Messiah*, the most celebrated epic that Germany has produced, we shall see how its form was affected by the imaginative conditions I have just described. The matter may be best illustrated by the method of comparison, and Klopstock's idea of poetical law be inferred by contrasting the mode of composition followed in the *Messiah* with that of *Paradise Lost*. Both Milton and Klopstock agree in the selection of a subject of universal interest; in both of them the matter which is the foundation of their conception is derived from the Bible. But Milton has obtained for himself perfect freedom of poetical creation by laying his action in the prehistoric period described in the first chapters of Genesis, whereby he is enabled to treat the story of the Fall in the epic form consecrated by the usage of such great poets as Homer and Virgil. He has shown equal judgment in limiting the action of *Paradise Regained* to the single episode of the Temptation, which he can treat in epic style without any departure from Scripture authority. Klopstock, on the other hand, has formed no central conception of the action which he proposes to relate. He begins his epic with the events immediately preceding the Crucifixion, but he transports his action, as he pleases, from the sphere of the real to the supernatural, embellishing it with episodes of angels and demons which have no basis in the Scripture narrative. This attempt to fuse what is historical with what is purely poetical betrays a fatal want of judgment in view of the nature of the subject, and would never have been made if Klopstock, before beginning to write, had realised the truth of what Aristotle says as to the difference between Poetry and History.

Observe again the remarkable contrast in the vehicles of language which Milton and Klopstock respectively employ for the expression of their ideas. The English of Milton is a fusion of the Saxon and Latin elements in our tongue, the one stream bearing on its face all the spiritual character derived from its Teutonic source, the other coloured with the rich hues of traditional Latin civilisation and philosophy. The language of Klopstock is that pure German which he himself thus describes: "Let no living tongue venture to enter the lists with the German. As it was in the oldest times when Tacitus describes it, so it still remains, solitary, unmixed, incomparable." A true description, however boastful, but not one that recommends the German language as the vehicle for a subject into which have flowed all the ideas of the late Alexandrian philosophy, the mediæval science of the Schoolmen, the civil conceptions of Roman Law, and the mystical theology of the Jewish Talmud. A similar difference is visible in the metrical form of the two poems. The blank verse of Milton is essentially a national metre, refined with the highest art from the usage of three earlier generations of English poets; the metre of the *Messiah* is an exotic imitation of the classic hexameter, invented by Klopstock, and having no root in the German language. In these essential respects, therefore, the *Messiah* must be pronounced to want the *national character* required to make a first-class German epic poem.

Again, let us apply the two-fold law of Fine Art to the German drama. What is meant by the Universal in dramatic poetry is a situation of general interest, such as we find in *Macbeth* or the *Œdipus Rex*; characters animated by motives common to humanity; love, jealousy, revenge, as we see them exhibited in men like Othello and Orestes; sentiments of general human application, "To be, or not to be," or "The quality of mercy is not strained," etc. etc. In order that the dramatist may produce these universal effects, it is practically necessary, first, that the subject or idea of the action shall be common both to his audience and to himself, and, secondly, that the form or character of his drama shall have been the product of long stage experience, as was the case both in Athens under Pericles and in England under Elizabeth. Now neither of these conditions was satisfied when Lessing founded the modern German drama in the eighteenth century; Germany had then neither a national idea of action, nor a national dramatic tradition. Lessing himself says in his *Hamburgische Dramaturgie*: " Out on the good-natured idea to procure for the Germans a national theatre, when we Germans are not yet a nation! I do not speak of our political constitution but of our social character. It might almost be said that this consists in not desiring to have an individual one. We are still the sworn copyists of all that is foreign; especially are we still the obedient admirers of the never enough to be admired French."

In spite of these unfavourable circumstances, three men of eminent genius—Lessing, Schiller, and Goethe —determined to lay the foundations of a national theatre. How did they set to work? Lessing, as he confesses, formed his dramatic conceptions in the spirit not of a poet but of a critic. He based his idea of the Universal on the *Poetics* of Aristotle, of which he says: " I do not hesitate to acknowledge (even if I should therefore be laughed to scorn in these enlightened times) that I consider this work as infallible as the *Elements* of Euclid." His first impulse towards dramatic creation was accordingly to prove that the French dramatists did not rightly understand Aristotle's meaning in the *Poetics*, and then to build his own theatrical edifice on what he conceived to be Aristotle's first principles. But this procedure was a violation of the Law of Character in Fine Art, for, as I have said in my lecture on Aristotle, the rules for composition in the *Poetics* were generalised only from Greek examples, and in many respects were not applicable to the circumstances which necessarily determined the form of the modern drama. True, Lessing had no traditional forms on which to model his creations, because the mediæval drama had died out without having developed any German stage. But the forms which he himself evolved *à priori* from his critical imagination were devoid of national life and character. This is particularly noticeable in what is perhaps his greatest dramatic effort, *Emilia Galotti*. His aim in this tragedy was to exhibit, in a dramatic form, the moral effects of corrupt aristocratic manners such as then prevailed in the Courts of the German princes. He thought that he might effect his aim by allegorising the story of *Appius and Virginia*, for he hoped that the fame of that legend would enlist on his behalf the sympathies of his audience. But he never considered whether the action of a father stabbing his daughter to preserve her chastity was characteristic of modern manners, or in accordance with what Aristotle calls the law of ideal probability. Though Corneille as a critic is not to be compared with Lessing, he shows himself in *Horace* to have a more practical understanding of the fundamental laws of the drama, for he takes care in that play not to offend against the appearance of probability, by modernising the facts of the story, while at the same time he flatters the prejudices of his audience, by pretending that the Romans felt and spoke like Frenchmen.

Schiller's dramas have far more life than Lessing's, because he wrote as a poet, not primarily as a critic, and so breathed his own genius and ardour into his ideal creations; but he had as little conception as Lessing of the essential law of the stage. Hear what he says in his preface to the *Robbers:* "This play is to be regarded merely as a dramatic narrative, in which, for the purpose of working out the innermost operations of the soul, advantage has been taken of the dramatic method, without otherwise conforming to the stringent rules of theatrical composition, or seeking the dubious advantage of stage adaptation." In other words, Schiller wrote for the reflective reader, not for spectators in the theatre absorbed by the ideal reality of action; with him the audience is left out of account. And what is true of his *Robbers* is more or less true of all his plays; seek for the element of poetry in them, and you will find it to be rather lyrical than dramatic; the best passages in *Don Carlos, Wallenstein,* and even *William Tell,* are those in which he pours out his own emotions, not those in which it is necessary for him to carry the audience out of themselves into the action and passion of the imaginary situation.

As for the plays of Goethe, with the exception of *Faust,* of which I shall speak presently, they breathe the spirit of sculpture, the most remote of all the arts from the genius of action. Heine describes them with cruel justice; he likens them to the statues of the gods in the Louvre, "with their white expressionless eyes, a mysterious melancholy in their stony smiles." "How strange," he continues, "that these antique statues should remind me of the Goethian creations, which are likewise so perfect, so beautiful, so motionless! and which also seem oppressed with a dumb grieving that their rigidity and coldness separate them from our present warm, restless life, that they cannot speak and rejoice with us, and that they are not human beings, but unhappy mixtures of divinity and stone." No more in the drama than in the epic did the Germans find that ideal matter and form which needed to blend congenially with their imaginations before it could assume the character of Fine Art.

How different is the case with German lyric poetry! The German song-writers began to be celebrated in the last quarter of the eighteenth century, just at the period when the mind of Europe was agitated with the apprehended approach of a great change in the structure of society, the more mysteriously alarming that its nature could not be divined. All felt it, but most of all the Germans. Cut off from the outlets of expression in political life, the ardent minds of Germany sought with the more vehemence to give utterance to this universal feeling in the sphere of imagination and emotion. In the German language they had an instrument admirably adapted to their purpose. As Klopstock said of it, it had remained since the days of Tacitus "solitary, unmixed, incomparable." With its ancient inflections, its homely words, its abstract terms, its extraordinary powers of compounding itself, this venerable parent language was capable of touching primitive chords of emotion in all who possessed a strain of Teutonic blood—that is to say, in every nation north of the

Alps. But it was not possible to strike out at one heat the essential character of national art, and German philosophers, as well as German poets, made many experiments before they hit upon the true form. The failure of the Holy Roman Empire to produce any working ideal of life and action had left the German mind in a position of contemplative isolation, and with a strong tendency to regard all human affairs from a cosmopolitan point of view. Such an abstract mode of conception was foreign to the genius of Fine Art, which deals either with concrete images or positive emotions, and will not come to the artist at the bidding of analytical philosophy.

Hence the critical advice of Herder, a truly representative German, to his young countrymen in the eighteenth century was barren and futile. Herder said: "National literature is of little importance; the age of world literature is at hand, and every one ought to work in order to accelerate the coming of the new era. What we want is a poetry in harmony with the voices of the peoples and with the whole heart of mankind. Our studies must be cosmopolitan, and must include the popular poetry of the Hebrews, the Arabs, the Franks, Germans, Italians, Spaniards, and even the songs and ballads of half-savage races." That is the opinion of a man who understands the necessity of expressing the Universal in poetry, but who has not the least conception of the meaning of the characteristic. It is needless to say that nothing in the shape of Poetry ever came in Germany, or could come anywhere, out of such a horrible witches' cauldron as Herder proposed to mix.

Not less contrary to the true law of character in art was the attempt made by the patriotic party in Germany to express in the lyric poetry of their native language ideas of a civil or political order. If ideas of this kind be embodied in lyric verse, the style adopted must be lofty and severe, but of what was needed for such a style the Germans, with their want of political training, had no conception. How far they were from attaining it may be imagined from a comparison of Gray's *Elegy in a Country Churchyard* with Frederick Schubart's once famous poem, *Die Fürstengruft,* or *The Vault of the Princes.* Both poets have here selected a subject of universal interest, and both seek to draw out its essential character by a series of contrasted images. Gray hits the mark. How solemn and heroic is the march of the verse in which he represents the compensations in the respective lots of prince and peasant that make them equal in the grave!

> Th' applause of listening senates to command,
> The threats of pain and ruin to despise,
> To scatter plenty o'er a smiling land,
> And read their history in a nation's eyes,
>
> Their lot forbade: nor circumscribed alone
> Their growing virtues, but their crimes confined,
> Forbade to wade through slaughter to a throne,
> And shut the gates of mercy on mankind;
>
> The struggling pangs of conscious truth to hide,
> To quench the blushes of ingenuous shame,
> Or heap the shrines of luxury and pride
> With incense kindled at the Muse's flame.

Schubart's poem, on the contrary, is a rhetorical invective against the princes of Germany, whom he reproaches as the tyrants of their race. It proceeds to its climax by a succession of contrasts, glaring, violent, theatrical, though not wanting in force and power, describing the coffins of the princes rotting in the glimmering light of the vault, with silver shields hanging over them, and grinning skulls, emblems of vanity. There is no flesh now—so the poet reflects—on the hands which once, by a stroke of the pen, consigned good and wise men to prison; the stars and orders shine like comets on the breasts of skeletons. The ear can hear no more the voice of flattery or lascivious music, or the cry of hounds and horses, with which they sought to still the voice of conscience. Let the hoarse croak of the raven be far from the vault, and every rural sound, as well as the voice of mourning, lest they should awake those who in their day were deaf to the prayers of the peasant whose fields they ravaged, and to the sobs of children and the sighs of soldiers, made orphans and cripples in their wars.

In a poem like this we feel the characteristic imagination of the German people endeavouring in an uncongenial subject—for the presence of death demands solemnity and humbleness—to express its sense of the infinite, the terrible, the grotesque, the spectral, without ever arriving at the desired effect. A nearer approach to perfection is made by Bürger, whose imitations of the old ballad style woke an answering chord in the imagination of Walter Scott, and helped to hasten the romantic revival in England. In his *Leonora,* Bürger expressed the wild unrest of the European imagination during the revolutionary epoch in a highly characteristic manner, by associating it with the images of demons and spectres still surviving among the people of Germany.

It was not, however, till Goethe produced *Faust* that the German lyric poets discovered the form of art qualified to give expression to the universal revolutionary emotion. In *Faust* everything is as it should be in art. The varied characters of Faust himself, Mephistopheles, and Gretchen, together form the full complement of spiritual human feeling which manifested itself in an outward form during the epoch of the French Revolution; the picturesque scenes of local life which are scattered through the drama — Auerbach's wine-cellar, the Brocken, the town fountain, the cathedral — are all necessary to the general effect; the little touches of sentiment—Gretchen's song of the King of Thule, the flower divination, the peasants' holiday enjoyment—if one of these had been away, the poem would have lacked something of its complete perfection.

And yet the form of *Faust* is not essentially dramatic but lyrical; it could never be satisfactorily acted on the stage like a play of Shakespeare; in its theatrical aspect it is only suitable for opera. Why then has it achieved its undisputed place as one of the great representative poems of the world? The answer is because, while its form is exactly suited to the universal nature of the subject, the character of that form is specifically German. *Faust* is German in its subject. The legend of Faustus grew up in Germany itself during the sixteenth century, and had therefore for generations been in the minds of the people. Goethe assimilated it, brooded over it during his youth, and poured into this mould all his own individual characteristics, as well as the national characteristics of his race. Again *Faust* is German in its dramatic form. Faust himself, with his vast intellectual energy and his sense of *ennui*, represents the philosophic mind of Europe in the eighteenth century, but, above all, the mind of Germany, deprived of the opportunities of action, and recalling the description of Tacitus: " Ipsi hebent: idem homines inertiam amant, quietem oderunt." Mephistopheles is but the reflection of the ironic, scoffing spirit which is the natural product of such a soil in the cultivated portion of society; Gretchen, on the other hand, with her simple domestic instincts and her trusting piety, typifies the unsophisticated elements in the German people. Finally, *Faust* is German in its style: there is in it none of that uneasy artificial sense of experiment which we find in earlier German poets of the eighteenth century; the versification is easy and flowing, suited alike to the nature of the subject and to the genius of the language.

It is precisely these qualities that give colour and character to the songs of Heinrich Heine, Goethe's lineal successor in German poetry. I believe that it was Thiers who described Heine as the wittiest *Frenchman* since Voltaire, one of those epigrams in which the superficial cleverness is a symptom of internal falsehood. Heine no doubt imitated Voltaire in the raillery with which he assailed established beliefs and institutions; but his raillery is quite devoid of the logical analysis which characterises the work of the author of *Candide*. It would be equally true to say that Heine was the wittiest *Englishman* since Byron, whom he also imitates in his combination of the cynical with the pathetic; but Heine's irony is not less remote from Byron's aristocratic scorn than from Voltaire's philosophic mockery.

Heine was a representative German, though no doubt the hatred of the Jew for the country, with all its institutions and rulers, that oppressed the Jewish race, was also strongly developed in his character. In one of his most characteristic songs he imagines a girl in a foreign land struck with compassion for him and inquiring who he is. He answers:

> I am a German poet,
>   In the German land well known;
> When men count the best names in it,
>   They will count with these my own.
>
> And what I feel, little maiden,
>   Men feel in the German land;
> When they reckon its fiercest sorrows,
>   My sorrows with those will stand.

What were the German sorrows? Heine unites in himself the characters of Faust, Mephistopheles, and Gretchen, despair, scoffing, tenderness; and he expresses the agony caused by this conflict of emotions under the image of the lover who has lost his love.

The image he employs is both universal and nationally characteristic; universal in its ordinary application, as well as in giving utterance to the yearning of the human heart for the infinite—

> The desire of the moth for the star,
> Of the night for the morrow,
> The devotion to something afar
> From the sphere of our sorrow—

characteristic in its expression of the sense of vanity in the German mind, caused by the contrast between their own energy in metaphysical speculation and their impotence in political action. But of the essential elements in his poetry I venture to say that the least congenial to his imagination was the scoffing wit of Mephistopheles, and that the chief ingredient in his art was the domestic tenderness of Gretchen.

We may see this from the prevailing features in Heine's lyrical style. Matthew Arnold and other critics have spoken with just appreciation of the perfection of Heine's lyrical form, but it is worth while to note more precisely the essential character of that form. Its character lies, I think, in the use of images, which are at once perfect in expression, and which yet suggest something beyond what is expressed, of metrical words which set in motion an infinite train of thoughts and emotions. Let me attempt by a single example, which will speak for itself, to show you what I mean. Here is a very inadequate rendering in English of a little poem complete in three stanzas about the three Kings of Cologne:

> The three holy Kings from the Eastland came;
>   Each asks wherever he passes,
> "Which way is the way to Bethlehem,
>   My lovely lads and lasses?"
>
> The young and the old, they could not say;
>   The Kings fared onward featly,
> And followed a golden star alway,
>   That shone full high and sweetly.
>
> The star over Joseph's house abode;
>   They passed 'neath the roof-tree lowly;
> The Baby cried, the Oxen lowed;
>   Then sang those three Kings holy.

Imagine Voltaire, or indeed any one but a German, writing anything like that. It strikes exactly the same note as Goethe's "There was a King of Thule" in *Faust*. And this note was possible to the German poet, and to no other, because the German people were nearer than any other nation to the Middle Ages, because, with their Christianity, they had retained in their imagination something of their old primeval beliefs about Nature, and because their pure unmixed language was qualified to give expression to this ancient unconscious association of ideas. To a certain extent their poetic faculty was shared by other branches of the Teutonic and Celtic races, and Wordsworth notices the mysterious effect in his stanza describing the unconscious song of the Highland Maiden:

> Will no one tell me what she sings?
>   Perhaps the mournful numbers flow
> For old forgotten, far-off things,
>   And battles long ago.

But as the folk-lore of Germany is far richer and wilder than that of England, in proportion as it has kept clearer of the stream of Hellenic civilisation, so is it better adapted, by the simple domesticity of its imagery, to touch what may be called the universal Gothic heart of modern Europe.

It is in this spiritual elfin region that Goethe and Heine find the largest freedom for their imagination. In their verse we listen to mysterious voices from the pine-trees rustling outside the windows of the lonely cottage in the mountains, or to strange primeval colloquies between plants and animals; the white gleam of the Siren's body is perceived in the whirlpool; small armies of dwarfs and kobolds creep out of the bowels of the earth. Not in the bitter Mephistophelian cynicism with which Heine often thinks it fine, in Byronic fashion, to close his pathetic lyrics, not there do we feel the genuine heart of the poet, but in those self-forgetful reveries, tender and mysterious as the folk-songs of Marguerite, in which he talks in their own language to the peasants of the Harz mountains. Witness that unequalled cottage scene, where the little maiden whispers her beliefs with pleasing trepidation to her lover by the sinking fire :—

> Little folk and tiny people
> Bread and bacon leave us none ;
> Late at night 'tis in the cupboard,
> In the morning it is gone.
>
> Little people to the cream-bowl
> Come by night and take the best ;

And they leave the bowl uncovered,
And the cat laps up the rest.

And the cat's an old witch-woman
Who, at midnight's stormiest hour,
Often in the haunted mountains
Crawls on the old ruined tower.

There in old time stood a castle,
Feasts were held and arms would glance
Knights, and squires, and noble ladies
Used to thread the torchlight dance.

But it chanced a wicked sorceress
Cast her spell on tower and guest;
Now there's nothing left but ruins,
Where the owlets build their nest.

Aunt, who's now in heaven, told me
That the proper word of doom,
At the proper hour of midnight,
Spoken in the proper room,

It will turn those ancient ruins
Into castle halls once more;
Knights, and squires, and noble ladies
Dance as gaily as of yore.

And whoe'er he be that speaks it,
Tower and people at that word,
With the sound of drum and trumpet,
Shall proclaim their youthful lord.

Not only in Goethe and Heine do you hear this note of genuine lyric inspiration. It is of the essence of the poems of Uhland and many another less known singer who has taken the rough diamonds of suggestion from the Volks-Lied and polished them into gems of art. Let me venture to give you one more specimen from the songs of Wilhelm Müller, father of our eminent Professor of Comparative Philology, which will show you, even in the imperfect mirror of our own language, with what exquisite skill the German lyric poets link universal sentiments with images drawn from the traditions of the people. The subject of the poem is Vineta, an old town said by German legend to lie buried beneath the Baltic :

> Often on the evening silence stealing
> From the sea-depths, fathoms, fathoms down,
> Bells sound faintly wondrous tidings pealing
> Of the old-world, ocean-buried, town.
>
> There it stands for ever, ruins hoary,
> Undecaying in their billowy grave;
> From the bulwarks flakes of golden glory
> Rise, and paint the mirror of the wave.
>
> And the fisher who, at red of even,
> Once has seen that vision near the shore,
> Heedless of dark cliff and frowning heaven,
> Haunts the enchanted spot for evermore.
>
> Often from the heart's deep places stealing
> Upward, upward, to the world above,
> Come to me, like far bells faintly pealing,
> Voices of the days of vanished love.
>
> Yes! a faëry world is sunk thereunder,
> From whose hoary ruins still, meseems,
> Visions, full of heaven's own light and wonder,
> Rise, and paint the mirror of my dreams.
>
> And whene'er I hear those faint bells ringing,
> Through the magic waves I sink, ah me!
> Sink, and seem to hear the angels singing,
> In that old-world town beneath the sea.

T

I cannot impress too strongly upon those who hear me that a knowledge of the way in which the law of Fine Art operates will not enable us to produce works of Fine Art. That can be accomplished by Genius alone. But, on the other hand, Genius can achieve nothing of permanent value without obedience to Law; and the knowledge of the operation of Law is of service to Genius because it strengthens the judgment; it shows the artist how he must obey nature in order to command it; it teaches him to judge himself; to recognise the limits within which he can enjoy artistic and individual freedom; to test the quality of his own art by comparing it with what is permanent in the characteristic art of his country.

Hence all that I have attempted to do in this lecture is to estimate the law or character of German Poetry historically. I do not for a moment presume to assert that German Poetry in the future will inevitably move in the same grooves and channels as in the past. Character is modified by circumstances to an almost unlimited extent, and during the present generation the history of Germany has undergone something like a revolution. The idea of German Unity, which floated with incorporeal ghostliness before the men of the eighteenth century, has in our times taken a positive external shape; the German State, the German Empire exists; what we want to know, before we can foresee how far this change in history will modify the character of German art, is just what no foreigner can at present know, namely, whether the structure of German Unity has been imposed upon the nation, by the genius of great rulers, statesmen, and soldiers, or whether it is the natural product of the mind and character of the people. In the former case it may be destroyed, as it has been created, from without; in the latter the ideas of action it excites will be reflected in the sphere of spiritual imagination. We can see that, in the material aspect of things, Germany, as a state, has freed herself from the reproach which, from the days of Tacitus, has clung to her, of being wanting in practical aim. It can no longer be said of her rulers: "Ipsi hebent: inertiam amant, quietem oderunt." The full powers of the State are devoted to perfecting the splendid scientific faculties of the German mind, so as to make it irresistible in the operations of war and the enterprise of commerce, and to render the influence of Germany paramount in the councils of Europe.

But after all, the question as regards Fine Art is, What effect has this great historical change made in the elementary German character, or how far has that character caused the change, because the source of all Poetry, of all ideal creation, is the mind of the People itself? How will the intense passion of the German mind for free thought and speculation reconcile itself with the rule of the military Absolutism, which seems to be the necessary instrument for realising the ambitions of the new German State? And again, in what poetic form will these imperial ideals express themselves without destroying that domestic sensibility and that spirit of romance and reverie which have been in the past the parents of German song and German music?

It is certainly a striking fact that the establishment of the German Empire has not been followed by a period of characteristic creation in German Fine Art, at least in the arts of Painting and Poetry. There have been characteristic movements of art in other nations. The movement of the Poetical Preraphaelites of England, and that of the Poetical Symbolists in France, may not fulfil the requirements of the Universal, but certainly neither of them is wanting in distinct character. Nor is characteristic movement wanting in that one of the Fine Arts in which the Germans specially excel, for a German of remarkable genius has, within our own generation, endeavoured to extend the functions of Music, by making it into a vehicle for the expression of intellectual ideas. Of the wisdom of his aims I do not venture to speak, since the question, whether this particular art is justified in appropriating the principles of another, is one that belongs to the Chair of Music rather than to that of Poetry. But of what is passing in the poetical imagination of the German people, as distinct from the mind of the German State, we know nothing—for in poetry the German soul is at present silent.

I do not wonder that it should be so. To find out the form of Poetry fitted to reflect the conflict of ideas between Feudalism and Socialism, Catholicism and Rationalism, as well as the forces that attract the centrifugal units of German nationality to the Imperial Crown, is a task that requires meditation both long and deep. Yet the problem will doubtless be faced. And when the Muse of Germany speaks again through the genius of a great poet, it is to be expected that her utterances will not simply take the old lyrical form, but that she will also employ those forms of drama or romance which are needed to express universal ideas of life and action. In the sphere of Poetry, as in that of Politics, the Germans will perhaps awake the sleeping Barbarossa.

V

THE IDEA OF LAW IN ENGLISH POETRY

As illustrating the subject of my present lecture, I find a passage in Pope's *Essay on Criticism* which is well deserving of examination. It is this:

> But soon by impious arms from Latium chased
> The banished Muse her ancient boundaries passed.
> Through all the northern world the arts advance,
> But critic learning flourished most in France.
> The rules a nation born to serve obeys,
> And Boileau still in right of Horace sways.
> But we brave Britons foreign laws despised,
> And lived unconquered and uncivilised :
> Fierce for the liberties of art, and bold,
> We still defied the Romans as of old.

In these lines the poet is describing the progress from Italy to the north of Europe of the great movement known as the Classical Renaissance. Considering that the description is in verse, the history in the first six lines is surprisingly accurate. It is, of course, not true that the storming of Rome by the Constable Bourbon, the feat of "impious arms" to which Pope is alluding, was the cause of the spread of the movement northwards; but it is an undoubted fact that soon after that event the effects of the Renaissance begin to show themselves in the poetry of the courts, both of Francis I. and of Henry VIII. Though the sun of Italian poetry was then far declined, the "critic learning" grounded on the supposed authority of Aristotle, and fostered in the Academies of Italy, was very influential in preparing the way for the later Academic criticism of France. Pope is fully justified in saying that the doctrines, ascribed by this tradition of culture to Aristotle, "flourished most in France"; and he is also right in explaining the fact by the tendency in the French character to submit to absolute authority. It is no wonder that, taking the tradition at second hand from the French critics, who themselves echoed the opinions of Scaliger and Castelvetro, imagining too that the science of the Greeks had been transmitted through Horace's *Ars Poetica* to the poetical treatises of Vida and Boileau, he should have believed that the "rules" he looked upon as the source of true culture were derived straight from the imperial head of ancient philosophy.

When, however, he comes to describe the attitude of the English mind towards these "rules," his history becomes superficial and incorrect. At no time was it true, in the broad sense of the word, that English artists "despised foreign laws": on the contrary, one of the most noticeable features in the history, alike of English painting and of English poetry, has been the influence exercised on the course of our artistic development by foreign models. Of the careful study bestowed from the middle of the last century by our painters on the work of the Italian, Dutch, and French masters, I need say nothing. Confining my attention to the history of poetry with which Pope is dealing, it will be sufficient to disprove his assertion by reference, in the infancy of our poetry, to the work of Chaucer, who not only translated the *Roman de la Rose*, but derived much of his philosophy of life from that poem; who also in his *House of Fame* constantly kept in view *The Divine Comedy* of Dante; and who drew the scheme of *The Canterbury Tales* from the *Decameron* of Boccaccio. After Chaucer we pass on to the practice of Wyatt, Surrey, and their followers imitated from Petrarch; after that, on the one hand, to the poetry of Milton, so profoundly influenced by the Italian writers, both in Latin and vernacular verse, and, on the other, to Beaumont and Fletcher, who, under the influence of the style and structure of the Spanish play, altered the whole tradition of the English romantic drama.

Even if we examine Pope's history within the limits to which he intended to confine it, it cannot be said that the English, as a nation, ever set themselves deliberately to oppose the authority of the supposed Aristotelian "rules." On the contrary, the first elaborate treatise of criticism in the English language, Sir Philip Sidney's *Apologie for Poetry*, is confessedly grounded upon them. Half a century before Corneille, Sidney had advocated with ardour the principle of the Unities, as expounded by the critics of Italy; and he censured Spenser for using dialect in his *Shepherd's Calendar*, on the ground that the experiment was an innovation on classical example. Ben Jonson, in the next generation, constantly sneers at his contemporaries for their barbarous neglect of the Unities. Dryden, though he never ventures to deviate from the practice of the English stage into the paths of critical orthodoxy, always speaks with superstitious reverence of the authority of French critical law. And, if any further proof were required to indicate the gathering volume of opinion in this direction, it would be furnished by the drift of thought in Pope's *Essay on Criticism*, and by Addison's dramatic criticisms in the *Spectator*, which vividly reflect the movement of taste in the reign of Queen Anne.

In any case, supposing it had been true that the English had defied the critical tradition of the Humanists, passed on to France from Italy, this would not have proved them to be uncivilised. For, in the first place, the laws in question were not the laws of Aristotle. The rule of the Unities of Time and Place is not to be found in the *Poetics* of that philosopher; the only Unity, on the necessity of which Aristotle insists as a law of dramatic poetry, is Unity of Action. The first mention of the law of Unity of Time is in the commentary of Scaliger on the *Poetics*, published in 1561, where the principle is deduced by mere inference from casual expressions of Aristotle; the law of Unity of Place is in like manner inferred quite arbitrarily and for the first time by Castelvetro, in his edition of the *Poetics*, published in 1571 ; Aristotle nowhere lays down such a rule in his treatise, nor did the Greek dramatists observe it in practice. Corneille was the first dramatist to proclaim his submission to rules dictated to him by the two Italian critics ; he defended his practice by reasoning, but he only succeeded in establishing it, because it fell in with the taste of the logical, and rather prosaic, French genius, which completely misinterpreted Aristotle's use of the term Imitation.

Once more : let us even suppose Aristotle to have been the author of "the rules," as Pope imagined ; this fact would not have obliged English dramatists, on any rational theory of authority, to obey his particular edicts. The Law of the Three Unities could at most have been classed with Aristotle's by-laws, such as his requirements for the form of the perfect tragedy, or for the character of the ideal tragic hero ; and these, as I have before urged, being derived from his observation solely of the practice of the Greek stage, have no application whatever to the form and structure of the drama in other nations, which is based on conceptions of the Universal in Nature in many respects fundamentally different from the ideas of the Greeks.

Had Pope been better acquainted with the meaning of Aristotle, he would have perceived that, provided his countrymen conformed to the philosopher's grand principle of imitating the Universal in Nature, they were quite right to imitate it according to the law imposed upon them by their national character and history. So long as they obeyed in a philosophic spirit their own municipal law of art, they might despise foreign laws without incurring the reproach of insular barbarism. The application of the French "rules" to a play like *Hamlet*, which caused Voltaire to call Shakespeare a drunken savage, shows an ignorance of the methods of art actually employed by the English poet which recoils on the head of the French critic; and though Boileau pronounced dictatorially that it was impossible to write an epic upon a Scripture subject, yet the logical impossibility of the critic was overcome, without any violation of the true laws of Poetry, in Milton's *Paradise Lost*. To attempt to confine the liberties of the poet by any *a priori* system of critical legislation is, as I have said more than once, worse than useless. Genius must be left to find out the law for itself.

Not that this implies that there is no law beyond the will of genius. "Fierce" as the English poets were, and rightly were, for the liberties of wit, the best and most representative of them knew that these liberties must be confined within certain limits and directed to a definite end. The end they had in view was the imitation of the Universal, but the aspect of the Universal that manifests itself to the English artist is modified and coloured by a character peculiar to his own society, so that the poetical forms in which he reflects his ideas are necessarily different from the forms in use among the artists of other nations. It is for the artist to decide in what way he can turn to his purpose the principles, instincts, and institutions, which go to make up national character; how far he may successfully extend his individual liberties within the law can only be determined by the force of his genius. All that the critic can usefully do is to collect the law of art, by observing what are the elements common to the work of a nation's greatest artists, and to note the working of the law of national character in art, by comparing the manner of imitating the Universal prevailing in one nation with that prevailing in another.

It was for this reason that, before attempting to discover what is the predominant idea of law in English Poetry, I examined in previous lectures how the law of national character has manifested itself in the poetry both of France and of Germany. For it is plain that in their elements, the French, German, and English minds have much in common with each other; we all originally spring from one race; we were all converted from heathenism to the Christian religion; we all inherited the institutions of Teutonic chivalry; the English language is made up of words mainly derived from German and French sources. It may, therefore, be concluded that Nature has put us all in the way of taking the same view of the Universal; and that the very divergent views of it, which are, as a matter of fact, disclosed in the art and poetry of the three nations, are due to peculiarities in the character and history of each people.

Comparing the English character then either with the French or the German, the first thing that strikes every inquirer is the great multiplicity of elements which the English exhibits, in contrast with the simplicity of the other two. The German race has remained completely unmixed, and many features, noted in their character by an accurate observer like Tacitus, have survived in it with very little change. Again, much of what Cæsar says of the character of the ancient Gauls is obviously applicable to the character of the modern Frenchman. At first sight this seems somewhat strange, when we remember that the conquering Franks were of pure Teutonic descent; but when we see how completely, in the French language, the German element has been merged in the Romance, it is easy to understand that the genius of the barbarous victors was subdued by the civilisation of the Romanised Celt.

No ancient historian has attempted to analyse the character of the English nation. It is made up of British, Anglo-Saxon, Scandinavian, and Norman elements, each of which has been fused in the organic whole without entirely losing its individual existence. How much influence the British element has exercised on our whole character may be doubted; if we are to judge from language, very little, for the number of Celtic words we use may be easily reckoned. Nor do I think that Matthew Arnold is anything but fanciful when he ascribes certain features in the style of English poetry to the Celtic strain in our blood, though of course

I should be the last to deny the influence of the Celtic genius as one of the sources of mediæval English Romance. The love of constitutional liberty, which is so dominant a feature in the English character, may fairly be ascribed to our German ancestry; but the somewhat sluggish and stationary temper of the Saxons must, after they were once insularised, have sunk into torpor and decay, if it had not been quickened by the life and movement of the adventurous Scandinavian immigrants; on the other hand, the directing genius of the Normans runs in unbroken continuity through the entire history of the English nation.

If we turn our inquiry from race to language, we find the same principle of simplicity in the elements prevailing in German and French as compared with English. I quoted in my last lecture Klopstock's description of the purity of the German language, the structure of which he boasts to have remained unchanged since the days of Arminius. French, on the contrary, exhibits the growth of fresh organic forms out of the structural decay of Latin, and reflects in its history a regular process of transformation and development. English derives its vocabulary both from French and German, showing a curious drama of give and take between the two opposing elements. Physically, the dominant character of the German in our language is indicated by the imposition of the Saxon mode of accentuation on immigrant words. Thus the words *Saturn, beauty, fortune, nature,* in which the accent is now thrown back, according to the Saxon principle, on to the first syllable, were in the time of Chaucer and his contemporaries accentuated, according to the French principle, on what would have been the penultimate syllable of the Latin word *Satùrn, beautèe, fortùne, natùre*. But, by way of compensation, the superior power of the French, in all matters relating to art and culture, manifests itself in the disappearance of the Saxon alliterative verse before the invasion of French metres determined by accent and rhyme.

Passing from the elements of character in themselves to the war of the elements in action, we may observe, in the sphere of politics, how very differently each of the three nations has proceeded in its attempt to reconcile the conflicting principles of which its life is composed. Our primitive ancestors, besides bequeathing to each of us certain universal ideas of the duties of man to God, to the Family, and to the State, handed down also certain common institutions—Monarchy, Aristocracy, and Popular Control—representing various interests and tendencies in society, by means of which it has been our destiny to develop, according to our several circumstances, the course of our national life. The history of France and Germany shows us the spectacle of one or other of these principles growing to such power that, like Aaron's serpent, it swallows up the rest. On the other hand, though the dominant feature in the political history of England is undoubtedly

> Freedom slowly broadening down
> From precedent to precedent,

the growing movement of liberty thus described does not, as Tennyson's verses seem to imply, arise from the inward expansion of a single principle; it is the total result of the conflict between the equally balanced forces of Monarchy, Aristocracy, and Democracy. There is no trace in the history of England of the centralising tendency of things in France, absorbing all the functions and colour of local liberty into an omnivorous Absolutism. There is visible none of the anarchical rivalry of Orders that prevailed in the Holy Roman Empire, reducing the power of the Imperial throne to impotence and inaction. At one time in our history the Monarchical principle was predominant, at another the Aristocratic; forward movement and fresh equilibrium were attained by the People throwing its weight into one scale or the other, as circumstances required. Centuries of conflict, sometimes ending in civil war, were needed to develop the principle of hereditary liberty, contained in such documents as Magna Charta and the Bill of Rights, into the complex fabric of the British Empire. The leading feature in the character of the English Constitution is its power of reconciling contrary impulses of action.

As it has been with us in the external sphere of politics, so it is in the sphere of faith and imagination. From the very early days of our religion we can see that a universal conflict has been proceeding in the mind of Christendom, between the principle of authority, represented by Councils defining the dogmas of the Church, the principle of individual liberty, represented by the constant succession of heresies and schisms, and the naturally opposed principles of Paganism and Revealed Religion. But during the last six centuries the making of organic thought in the great national communities of Europe has been the result of the fusion, in different proportions, of certain antagonistic elements,—Catholicism, Feudalism, Humanism, and Reform,—and each nation has striven to settle the struggle proceeding in its midst in the way most consistent with its own character.

France, in which the principle of kingly authority showed from the first a tendency to be predominant, found little difficulty in reconciling, at least superficially, the principle of Catholicism with the principle of the Renaissance. A Concordat with the Pope enabled Francis I. to repress the inconvenient aspirations of the Gallican Church; and the Pagan splendour of the late painting and sculpture of Italy was welcomed at the Court of a monarch who boasted the title of the Most Christian King. But the spirit of the Reformation never gained a foothold in the French imagination. Though Clement Marot translated the Psalms, and though Rabelais, in the early editions of his Romances, introduced ideas favourable to the Humanist reformers of religion, the general character of Marot's poetry is not devotional, and Rabelais made haste to suppress his liberalism as soon as he found it was disapproved by authority. The genius of D'Aubigné, the greatest of the Huguenot writers of mediæval France, is hardly representative of his nation, and perhaps the only attempt to treat the subject of revealed religion spiritually in French poetry is Boileau's aridly Jansenist Epistle on the Love of God.

Germany, in the sphere of spiritual thought, has been as unreservedly on the side of individual liberty as France on the side of central authority. She it was, above all other countries, who nourished the genius of the Reformation. In the persons of Luther and Kant she led the revolt against what is established both in Religion and Philosophy. But then Germany, owing to the unmitigated feudalism of her institutions, was incapable of assimilating the intellectual movement of the Renaissance at the same time as the great nations of Western Europe. The Classical Revival was essentially civic in its origin, and there was in Germany in the sixteenth century no recognised civic centre round which art and literature could organise themselves to the same extent as in France and England. When the different States of the Empire, at the close of the Thirty Years' War, settled down into exhausted quietude, the Renaissance began to make its influence felt in the Courts of the Princes; but its operation was entirely opposed to the experience of the European nations of the West. Winckelmann, Lessing, and Goethe had no doubt a far clearer insight into the nature of Greek art than the French and Italian critics, who followed the pseudo-Aristotelian tradition, but they viewed it in the abstract, as critics and philosophers, and not in its relation to the life of their own country.

England has marked out for herself a path of Culture between that of France and Germany. The bent of her historical character has been to blend the principles of liberty and authority. She has studied how to accommodate the necessities of innovation with the traditions of old experience. Into our Universities, the cradles of the ancient Scholasticism, we received the teaching of Erasmus and his fellow Humanists, so that when Luther, with all his violent Tertullian-like hatred of Greek poetry and philosophy, poured himself forth in a flood of rebellion against the old *régime*, carrying on the tide of his enthusiasm all that Germanic element in the English nation which, nearly two centuries before, had been stirred by the preaching of Wycliffe, we were saved by the strength of our dykes from the submerging of invaluable elements in our life and history. Yet this did not prevent the spirit of the Reformation from penetrating the inmost recesses of the national character, or from finding vivid forms of expression in the greatest works of English poetry. I need say nothing, for the fact is obvious, of its influence on the composition of *Paradise Lost;* but its presence in the plays of Shakespeare, though more subtly disguised, is equally unmistakable. I do not think that any one can read with attention either *Hamlet, Macbeth,* or *Measure for Measure,* without perceiving how powerful was the conflict in England between the selfish, egotistic, material principle of life, deliberately advocated by such an illustrious representative of the Italian Renaissance as Machiavelli, and the principle of Conscience, which was the prime spiritual cause of the Reformation.

From all this it seems to follow, first, that the

"rules," or "foreign laws," of which Pope speaks with respect in the *Essay on Criticism*, are only one of many elements that have combined to determine the course of our national art and culture; and that, if English poetry, like the poetry of other nations, is a mirror of our national character and history, then the great fundamental law under which the genius of the English poet must act, in order to produce any lasting work, is the knowledge both of what may be called the Balance of Power between the constituent elements of our imagination, and also of the method of fusing these contrary principles into a harmonious whole.

In practice we find this to have been the aim of all the most representative English masters, not alone in the art of poetry but in the art of painting. "The summit of excellence," says Sir Joshua Reynolds in his *Fifth Discourse*, "seems to be an assemblage of contrary qualities, but mixed in such proportion that no one part is found to counteract the others. How hard this is to be attained in every art, those only know who have made the greatest progress in their respective professions." So hard, indeed, is it, that one notices throughout Sir Joshua's teaching a perhaps excessive tendency to insist on the necessity of often suppressing elements of life, valuable in themselves, for the sake of harmonious effect. For example he says : "A statue in which you endeavour to unite stately dignity, youthful elegance, and stern valour, must surely possess none of these to an eminent degree. Hence it appears that there is much difficulty as well as danger in an endeavour to concentrate in a single subject those various powers which, rising from different points, naturally move in different directions." But genius is genius precisely because it knows how to overcome apparently insuperable difficulties. If it had not been for the authority of Sir Joshua, apparently on the other side, I should have ventured to suggest that the particular combination of qualities he supposes was to be found in the statue of the Apollo Belvedere, and I am at least confident that it is well within the reach of poetry, which of all the arts is the one with most capacity for the imitation of contrary qualities in action.

It is not too much to say that in English Poetry the reconciliation of contraries is the character impressed on the works of a long succession of great poets, who have been so conscious of the strife of principles in their own sphere, and of the dominant tendencies in the spirit of their age, that they have each known how to imitate in an ideal form the movement of life in Nature and Society. We see, for example, the principle at work in the *Vision of Piers the Plowman,* in which the poet's powerful but confused attempt to work out an ideal scheme of harmony between Church and State so strikingly anticipates the actual course of events at the Reformation. We see it, too, in the brilliant, vivacious, squabbling, company of Chaucer's pilgrims to the shrine of St. Thomas of Canterbury, the representatives of so many opposing interests and so many distinct orders in society, yet all united by the sense of a common religious duty to be performed, and already so far advanced in the art of self-government as to be willing to compose their quarrels under the general and moderating guidance of the host of The Tabard. The most profound and comprehensive conception of the mingled tragedy and comedy of life ever expressed in poetry is to be found in the dramas of Shakespeare, in whose genius the elements are so mixed that it is difficult to say whether the spirit of the ancient Church, of the Reformation, or of Humanism, is the stronger. The *Satires* of Pope, faithfully reflecting in this respect the genius of the eighteenth century, seem almost to eliminate the mediæval element from the national imagination, in a purely civic development of the principle of the Renaissance; but in Byron and Tennyson the spirit of individual liberty returns on the top of the tide, seeking, under the guise of mediæval forms, to express its revolt against the classic and aristocratic conventions of the eighteenth century, without, however, losing sight of the historic conflict of principles in English Poetry.

In future lectures I shall hope to illustrate the working of this law of national character more fully and particularly from the practice of our most representative poets. Meantime, let me say a few concluding words about the kind of test we ought to apply, to see whether the law is fulfilled in any work of contemporary English poetry that we may be called upon to judge. In the first place, I would repeat what I have said in an earlier lecture, that the presence of the Universal in a work of art cannot always be inferred from the popularity of that work.[1] Tempting no doubt it is to decide in this way, for never was there an age in which Fame travelled with such lightning speed as our own. There is something dazzling and impressive in the sale of tens of thousands of copies of a poem or a romance, nor is it for a moment to be denied that any book which succeeds in pleasing the imagination of so many human beings must possess in itself some striking qualities of art, though not necessarily, or even probably, of fine art. For the people judges by its emotions, sensations, and instincts, not by its reason; and it is almost as impossible to divine the effect which a work of imagination will produce on the popular mind as to forecast the temper in which public opinion will act in the sphere of politics. All that we can be sure of is that the quality in a work of art which fascinates the imagination of the people will be, like the considerations that sway them in politics, simple, obvious, akin to their superficial sentiments, and as unlike as possible to that mysterious struggle of opposite forces, the sum of which eventually determines the national action and character. A novel like *The Sorrows of Werther* will always be, in the beginning, more popular and famous than a poem like *Faust*.

Looking at the matter from the opposite side, while a work of genius will necessarily have in it an element strongly appealing to the universal, and therefore to the popular, imagination, we know by abundant evidence that the kind of imitation

[1] Pages 150-151.

which arrests general attention is not that in which the essential motive thought of a great poet resides. For example, a number of contemporary allusions to *Hamlet* prove beyond question that what most impressed the audience in the Elizabethan theatre was by no means the general plot of the play or the character of the Prince of Denmark, but the appearance of the ghost. It is equally certain, from the title attached to the early acting copies of *King Lear*, that the imaginative pleasure experienced by the spectators arose much less from the sublime representation of the madness of the old king, than from Edgar's realistic assumption of the character of poor Tom of Bedlam.

Equally fallacious is it to look for the character, which is the mark of all Fine Art, in singularity of expression. There is a very strong tendency in our times to adopt this standard of judgment. Whether it be disdain for the judgment of the multitude, or an instinctive perception that singularity is eventually the surest means of attracting the attention of the crowd, every observer must have noticed the growing inclination of men of genius to invent forms which reflect not so much the universal character of the nation, as their own personal peculiarities. At first this studied pursuit of unpopular ends meets with coldness and contempt in the public at large, but it is noted and even approved by the intellectual few, who appreciate more intensely eccentricity in an author, in proportion as they value in themselves the sagacity which enables them to interpret it. By degrees an ever-increasing circle of admirers imposes its own thoughtfulness on the unreflecting public, which, though still unable to understand, is no longer bold enough to ridicule. "Those who come to mock remain to pray." Surrounded by a powerful bodyguard, the once neglected inventor of singularities tramples with impunity on the traditions of art, and the coterie invests with a species of temporary authority an eccentric practice which may have its primary roots in Mannerism and Affectation.

The just mean of a true work of Fine Art lies between Popularity and Singularity; such a work is the expression of Universal truth bearing the stamp of national character. The critic in judging a new poem will do well to ask certain questions about its qualities. First as regards its conception. Does it strike the imagination, in its general effect, as imitating the idea of Nature as a whole? Does it reflect in itself the strife of opposing principles which make up the sum of our civilisation, our Christian faith, our hereditary institutions, the long tradition of European culture? Are these conflicting ideas fused in it in the same way as we see them fused in Chaucer's *Canterbury Tales*, in Shakespeare's *Hamlet*, in Pope's *Essay on Man*, in Gray's *Elegy*, in Tennyson's *In Memoriam*? So too in respect of expression, every English poem, which is really a work of fine art, will combine in itself the universal with the particular. If it is justly conceived, if it holds the mirror truly up to nature, then the expression also will seem natural, the art will be concealed, and the effect left on the mind will be Repose and not Violence or Singularity. Close examination alone will reveal what thought and labour have often been given to arrive at this result; the selection and rejection of ideas; the choice of words characteristic yet not forced; the variation of periods; the combination of harmonies; in a word, all that subtle mixture of elements which gives life and soul and movement to an individual style. And as a style of this kind is generalised by the poet from a wide acquaintance with the practice of the best poets in our literature, so it can be rightly judged only by those who have a knowledge of the historic development of our language. In criticising the language of a modern poet, look in his verse to see if it possesses the hereditary national quality of condensing thought in an epigrammatic form—see if you can find a family likeness in it to lines like these:

> Uneasy lies the head that wears a crown.—SHAKESPEARE.
> They also serve who only stand and wait.—MILTON.
> A man so various that he seemed to be
> Not one, but all mankind's epitome.—DRYDEN.
> Man never is, but always to be, blest.—POPE.
> The paths of glory lead but to the grave.—GRAY.
> Who would be free themselves must strike the blow.—BYRON.

In all these lines the total effect of the idea expressed is simple, natural, universal, and yet the individual character is strongly marked, and the means adopted to produce the effect are very complex. Such a reconciliation of opposing qualities is the universal condition of all Fine Art.

VI

CHAUCER

I SAID in my last lecture that the whole course of English Poetry was a continued illustration of the primary law that the Universal Pleasure, which is the end of Fine Art, proceeds from the harmonious fusion of contrary qualities. To-day I shall try to show that the first example of this great law or characteristic of English metrical composition is to be found in Chaucer, who is therefore rightly regarded as the Father of our Poetry.

I am well aware that, in stating these propositions, I have to face two strong contrary currents of opinion: one the popular belief or prejudice derived from the instinct of Race; the other, the scientific reasoning of critical experts, who judge of all questions of literature mainly by the light of Language. As regards the first of these forces, we live in a democratic age, and a democracy is impressed by the simplicity of phrases, rather than by the science of reasoning. English democracy likes to think that, in the British Constitution and the British Empire, the

Anglo-Saxon element is the only one worth considering; and patriotism welcomes any theory which derives the genius of our Poetry from a purely Anglo-Saxon source. The theory best calculated to flatter this instinct is the theory of the Philologists, that, modern English being the direct offspring of Anglo-Saxon, and Poetry being merely the highest and most beautiful form of language as it exists in any particular age, Cædmon, and not Chaucer, is to be honoured as the founder of English Poetry.

If this view is to be justified, those who maintain it must be able to prove certain positive facts. They must show a continuity in the art of English Poetry from Anglo-Saxon to modern times, attested first by the Saxon birth and lineage of the poets; secondly, by the adoption in the English nation of a mode and system of versification peculiar to the Anglo-Saxon race; thirdly, by the development of a general tradition of Culture derived from purely insular and indigenous sources. I hope to make it clear to you, not only that none of these three things can be proved, but that they are the exact opposite of the truth; that from the time of Chaucer an element of nationality, which is not Anglo-Saxon, is introduced by the very necessity of things into the lineage of our poets; that, in consequence of the innovations of Chaucer, the Anglo-Saxon prosody was superseded by modes of metrical composition of French origin; and that, by the genius of the same poet, the exhausted stream of Anglo-Saxon thought was replenished and invigorated from the fresh fountains of imagination then beginning to stir the mind on the continent of Europe.

To begin with the question of birth and race. Before the Norman Conquest of England all the poets of the country were of course of Saxon descent. We have Cædmon and Cynewulf and the authors, whoever they were, of the fine poems *Judith*, and *The Death of Byrthnoth*, and *The Battle of Brunanburh*. After the Conquest Orm and Layamon continued to write in a language that still preserved something of the ancient Saxon structure. But Chaucer, it is plain, was of a different race. The name of his family—le Chaucier—probably derived, according to Professor Skeat, from their occupation either of hosiers or shoemakers, betokens French affinities; while Verstegan, doubtless relying on some tradition, describes him confidently as being of the Wallon extraction. And if we consider, it seems to be perfectly agreeable to the nature of things that a poet of a third strain, not Saxon, not Norman, but capable of understanding the qualities of both, should have first learned to express the genius of the two opposing races who, under the strong rule of the Norman kings, had fused themselves for ever into a single people. Poetry must reflect in the sphere of imagination whatever is the sovereign principle of action in the national constitution. That predominant force in the days of the elder Plantagenets was certainly not mainly Saxon. The Anglo-Saxon monarchy had fallen a victim to its own internal decay, and the Norman Conquest was due to the inward need, felt by English society, of being reduced to form and order by some force external to itself. For more than two centuries the great Saxon body of the nation suffered the chastening discipline imposed upon it by the powerful brain and the iron will of its Norman rulers.

A striking passage in Hallam's *Middle Ages* vividly describes the position of the Saxons in England after the Norman Conquest: "I would not extenuate the calamities of this great revolution, true though it be that much good was brought out of them, and that we owe no trifling part of what inspires self-esteem to the Norman element of our population and our polity. England passed under the yoke; she endured the arrogance of foreign conquerors; her children, even though their loss in revenue may have been exaggerated, and still it was enormous, became a lower race, not called to the councils of their sovereign, not sharing his trust or his bounty. They were in a far different condition from the provincial Romans after the Conquest of Gaul, even if, which is hardly possible to determine, their actual deprivation of lands should have been less extensive. For not only they did not for several reigns occupy the honourable stations which sometimes fell to the lot of the Roman subject of Clovis or Alaric, but they had a great deal more freedom and importance to lose. Nor had they a protecting church to mitigate barbarous superiority; their bishops were degraded and in exile; the footstep of the invader was at their altars; their monasteries were plundered and their native monks insulted. Rome herself looked with little favour on a church which had preserved some measure of independence. Strange contrast to the triumphant episcopate of the Merovingian kings!"

In these depressed conditions no Saxon poet, unless endowed with unusual flexibility of mind, could have so divested himself of the attributes of his race, as to imitate the manners of his age in the gay temper and with the wide knowledge of the world exhibited in *The Canterbury Tales*. He would have had none of the sympathy or insight required for the production of such finished portraits of the ruling classes as those of Chaucer's Knight, Monk, or Prioress. On the other hand, no Norman poet living in England would have been likely to study the characters of such insignificant members of society as Reves, Millers, and Carpenters, or indeed of the wealthy commercial classes, whose representatives make so considerable a figure in the group of pilgrims. Chaucer, however, being neither Saxon nor Norman, was admirably fitted by his social position to understand the general movement of things. The son of a London vintner, his early observation and criticism of the humours of middle-class life inspired him with the idea of that characteristically English imitation of nature, afterwards carried to such splendid heights by Shakespeare in his Histories, Tragedies, and Tragi-Comedies. As a servant in the house of John of Gaunt, he had an acquaintance not less accurate and profound with all the niceties of artificial taste, by which the conquering nobility sought to distinguish their manners from those of the vulgar;

hence his satirical portraits of courtiers and fine ladies and gentlemen are as finely finished as those of Dryden and Pope in a later age. In the ideal atmosphere of *The Canterbury Tales* the petty distinctions between Saxon and Norman seem to disappear, since both races are measured by the universal standard of humanity and common-sense.

In passing to the second question, namely, how far Chaucer is justly called the Father of English Poetry by virtue of his language and versification, I may remark that I have been myself exposed to strong critical censure for making the assertion, that between the poetry of Cædmon and the poetry of Chaucer there is absolutely no link of connection. I venture to repeat that the proposition is unassailable. I am not, of course, so foolish as to mean that the words which Chaucer used, and which we with further alterations use to-day, are not derived from the vocabulary of Cædmon; the question, however, relates less to words in themselves than to syntax and prosody. If Tennyson is to be regarded as the lineal descendant not only of Chaucer but of Cædmon, then it appears to me that, by parity of reasoning, Victor Hugo must be allowed to trace his poetical pedigree back to Ennius, the poems of Guillaume de Lorris and Jean de Meung being treated as half-way houses on the road. This, of course, would be generally recognised as absurd; yet the scientific principle is precisely the same. The alliterative versification of the Anglo-Saxons, as of all the primitive Teutonic nations, was the product of the language in its synthetic form; and when that original structure fell into decay, the fabric of metrical harmony naturally collapsed at the same time. What the English poets in the fourteenth century had to decide was, whether the ancient Anglo-Saxon metrical forms could be still preserved, with such modifications as were required by the altered conditions of the language; or whether the language required to be recast in new moulds of harmony imposed upon it from without. Both these conflicting ideals had their supporters in the fourteenth century. The most distinguished champion of the Conservatives was Langland, author of *The Vision of William concerning Piers the Plowman*. He was backed in his literary practice by other poets, whose names, doubtless well known in their day, have now perished, and who wrote the poems called *William of Palerne*, and *Sir Gawayne and the Green Knight*. Chaucer was the head of the innovating poets, who wrote in rhyme after the French manner. His system proved victorious; and he has therefore justly been acclaimed by Wyatt, Surrey, Spenser, Dryden, and Wordsworth, as the founder of the art of English Poetry.

On the other hand, as always happens in such cases, the supporters of the defeated party revenged themselves by denouncing Chaucer as the corrupter of the true art of English Poetry; just as Nævius, who tried to maintain at Rome the use of the old Saturnian metre, observes, in his self-made epitaph, with an oblique sneer at Ennius, that the Camenæ would bewail himself as the last who knew how to speak the Latin tongue. Skinner, a philologist of the seventeenth century, who, like his modern descendants, cared much more for antiquities than for literature, speaks of Chaucer in a Latin passage, which may be thus translated : " Through this unwholesome itch for novelty the Flemings, by introducing French words indiscriminately into their country, seriously polluted the purity of the national tongue; and the poet Chaucer set a very bad example by importing whole waggon-loads of words from France into our language, robbing it, adulterated as it was in consequence of the Norman Conquest, of almost all its native grace and beauty." In rather milder language, Verstegan, another philologist, says : " Some few years after came Geoffrey Chaucer, who, writing his poesies in English, is of some called the first illuminator of the English tongue. Of their opinion I am not, though I reverence Chaucer as an excellent poet for his time. He was, indeed, a great mingler of English with French, unto which language (belike for that he was descended of French or rather Wallon race) he carried a great affection."

Here we have a double charge brought against Chaucer : he is said to have destroyed the existing standard of his native tongue, which in itself possessed "grace and beauty," and to have done so by mixing it with an incongruous foreign idiom. That Chaucer imported into the English of his time whole waggon-loads of French words is undeniable; but that he thereby helped to destroy a beautiful and elegant form of existing literature is a mere flourish of rhetoric. The Anglo-Saxon language of course possessed a literary standard both in verse and prose, just as the Anglo-Saxon kingdom before the Conquest enjoyed a political constitution; but, like the latter, it showed no capacity for growth and expansion. Even in the hands of Layamon, writing about one hundred and fifty years after the Conquest, the structure of the alliterative measure, preserved by many generations of minstrels, is seen to have fallen into complete decay; while, though Saxon prose, under the direction of Alfred, had proved itself an admirable instrument of translation, it was never used for any form of original composition more inspiring than chronicles and homilies. It possessed, therefore, no quality capable of arresting either the internal change which was rapidly transforming the structure of the popular speech, or the political tendency to discourage in the schools the use of the Saxon grammar. Higden, the antiquary, says in the reign of Edward III.: "The impairing of the birth tongue is by cause of two things: one is for that children in school, against the usage and manner of all other nations, be compelled for to learn their own language, and for to construe their lessons and their things in French, and have since the Normans come first into England. Also gentlemen's children be taught for to speak French, from the time that they be rocked in their cradle, and can speak and play with a child's brooch. And uplandish men will liken themselves to gentlemen, and make a great business for to speak French for to be more accounted of."

From this it is plain that both the decay of the old Saxon grammar, and the importation into England of French words, were part of a natural movement of things, long anterior to the age of Chaucer, and quite independent of any innovation on his part. The total effect of the movement was to create a new composite language, which at present was without a literature, and which, if it was to become an instrument capable of expressing the thoughts and feelings of civil society, required to be subjected to the same refining influences as Dante's predecessors applied to the vulgar tongue of Italy. The question as to the poetry of the new language was, whether the main form or character impressed upon it should be Saxon or French. Langland decided for the Saxon; and you may judge of the metrical effects which he produced by the opening of *The Vision of Piers the Plowman:*

> In a somer seson · whan soft was the sonne,
> I shope me in shroudes · as I a shepe were,
> In habit as an heremite · unholy of workes,
> Went wyde in this worlde · wondres to here.
> Ac on a May morning · on Malvern hulles
> Me bifel a ferly · of fairy methoughte;
> I was wery forwandred · and wente me to reste
> And as I lay and lened · and looked on the wateres
> I slumbered in a slepynge · it sweyed so merie.

Here you will see that Langland has religiously preserved the traditional structure of the alliterative measure, two stressed syllables beginning with the same letter being placed in the first half of the verse, and one stressed syllable beginning with the same letter as the others in the second half. We also perceive in his verses the dactylic movement inherent in Anglo-Saxon. But I think we must, most of us, feel that, while this measure in the compact inflected form of the old Anglo-Saxon would have had a grand sound when chanted by the minstrel, the effect in Middle English, as a vehicle for allegorical narrative, is disagreeably monotonous. It is almost impossible to conceive that, by any variety of pause or period, a system of complex harmony could have been developed out of such an inflexible structure.

Let us now examine what Chaucer made of his effort to combine the uninflected remains of the Saxon vocabulary, and the analytic grammatical forms of the English which had grown out of the Saxon, with French rhythms and metres. The result of his experiment has been very variously judged. On the one side Dryden, writing when English had assumed a fixed form, and knowing nothing of the primitive stages of the language, says : " The verse of Chaucer, I confess, is not harmonious to us. They who lived with him, and some time after him, thought it musical ; and it continues so even in our judgment, if compared with the numbers of Lidgate and Gower, his contemporaries. 'Tis true I cannot go so far as he who published the last edition of him, for he would have us believe the fault is in our ears, and that there were really ten syllables in a verse where we find but nine. But this opinion is not worth confuting; 'tis so gross and obvious an error, that common sense (which is a rule in every thing but matters of Faith and Revelation) must convince the reader that equality of numbers in every verse, which we call 'heroic,' was either not known or not practised in Chaucer's age. It were an easy matter to produce some thousands of his verses which are lame for want of half a foot, and sometimes a whole one, and which no pronunciation can make otherwise."

I need hardly point out to-day that Speght, the editor referred to by Dryden, was perfectly right in his opinion; and that, with correct orthography, there are few verses in Chaucer which cannot be read harmoniously according to the pronunciation of the poet's day. So far indeed has opinion veered round on the subject, that the tendency now rather is to teach that any verse of Chaucer or his contemporaries, which sounds inharmonious in our ears, is to be defended on the assumption of some license recognised by the metrical composers of the time. I will not attempt to go into this question, but will confine myself to the point on which I wish to insist, namely, that Chaucer, by adapting French principles of versification to the peculiar conditions of Middle English, took the best means possible of harmonising the language, and that his practice, in its most essential features, was continued and developed by the poets who are recognised to be the chief masters in the use of the heroic couplet.

For it is this measure to which Dryden is alluding

in the criticism I have just read to you. Chaucer introduced it into England from France, modelling his usage on a popular French poet, rather older than himself, Guillaume de Machault. I can hardly doubt that the French decasyllabic or hendecasyllabic line, which is the basis of the metre, was remotely derived from the Latin trimeter iambic, shortened to meet the requirements of rhyme. At any rate the rhythmical accentual movement is equivalent to that of the iambus, the essence of the French metre being that the line should consist of five accents evenly distributed, and of ten or eleven syllables, the last sounded syllable in the second line of a couplet rhyming with the last sounded syllable of the first line. There must also be a cæsura or pause after the fourth syllable.

These characteristics are preserved in the English decasyllabic line of the normal type, whether used in the couplet or not, as, for example,

> They ál | so sérve | who ón | ly stánd | and wáit |

where the accent falls evenly on the second, fourth, sixth, eighth, and tenth syllables, and the cæsura after the fourth syllable. The English line, however, admits of much more variety than the French, partly because it combines the trochaic movement (that is to say, the accentuation of the first of two syllables rather than the second) with the iambic—as in Pope's line, "Die of a rose in aromatic pain"—and partly because in it the cæsura can fall after any syllable between the third and the seventh. Till the time of

Pope this latter peculiarity was not observed by the critics, though it was of course practised by the best poets; and George Gascoigne who wrote on English Prosody in the middle of Elizabeth's reign imagined that, as in French poetry, the cæsura must always fall after the fourth syllable. In the following couplet of Pope, for example, the cæsura in the first line is placed after the fifth, and in the second, after the sixth syllable:

> Where thou, great Anna, | whom three realms obey
> Dost sometimes counsel take, | and sometimes tea.

We see the cæsura falling after the seventh syllable in

> And universal Darkness | covers all;

and sometimes we find a line with a kind of double cæsura, one after the second syllable, one after the seventh, as

> Lawrence, of virtuous father, virtuous son.

Now while none of these shades and niceties of harmony are to be found in the early English poets who imitated the French rhyming system, and who for the most part did not venture beyond the facile octosyllabic measure, or the monotonous Alexandrine, they are all exhibited, in beautiful completeness, in the versification of Chaucer, as may be verified by any one who takes the trouble to analyse the opening lines of the Prologue to *The Canterbury Tales*. I will try to read them to you in such a manner that you may note at once the distribution of the accent and the place of the cæsura :

> Whan that Aprille | with his shoures sote
> The droghte of Marche | had perced to the rote
> And bathed every veyne | in swich licour
> Of which vertu | engendred is the flour ;
> Whan Zephirus | eek with his sote breeth
> Inspired hath | in every holt and heeth
> The tendre croppes | and the yonge sonne
> Hath in the Ram | his halfe cours y-ronne
> And smale fowles | maken melodye,
> That slepen al the night | with open yë,
> (So priketh hem nature | in hir corages) ;
> Than longen folk | to goon on pilgrimages,
> (And palmers | for to seken straunge strondes)
> To ferne halwes | couthe in sondry londes ;
> And specially | from every shires ende
> Of Engelond | to Caunterbury they wende,
> The holy blisful martir | for to seke,
> That hem hath holpen | whan that they were seke.

In this passage, then, you may observe the normal type of the iambic line, with the accent falling evenly on the second, fourth, sixth, eighth, and tenth syllables; the combination of the trochaic with the iambic movement, and the varied distribution of the cæsura. You find in the very opening of the first line an example of a trochee "Whan that"; while out of eighteen lines the cæsura falls in the French manner in eight after the fourth syllable; in five of them after the fifth; in two after the sixth; and twice only after the third and seventh respectively.

The lines further illustrate the perfectly regular process by which Chaucer naturalised French words in English, and which Skinner calls robbing "our language of its native grace and beauty." "Aprille," "March," "veyne," "licour," "vertu," "engendred," "flour," "Zephirus," "melodye," "nature," "corages," "pilgrimages," "palmers," "specially," are all words of Latin origin, yet they associate themselves in the most friendly manner with their neighbours of Saxon descent. The composition of the vocabulary throughout the entire passage is a marvellous monument of delicate perception, observation, and judgment. Chaucer saw that the two languages had been brought by different roads to almost exactly the same level, and that a bridge of communication existed between them in their common use of the final vowel *e*, which, as the uniform sign in each of ancient inflections, had assimilated the terminations of a very large number of French and English words.

Chaucer also availed himself of the perpetual migration into England of new words, to enrich and vary the resources of versification. He observed that, while the tendency of English was to throw back the accent as far as possible, the French accent fell on the final or penultimate syllables of words; and since the naturalised alien words, when they first settled in our language, retained their own native mode of accentuation, it was open to him to adapt his usage to the requirements of his metre. Thus we see in the Prologue that he uses "vertù" for "vírtue"; "Natùre" for "Náture," "licoùr" for "líquor"; but when it suits him he speaks of "vírtue" and "Náture"; hence it may be doubted whether the language was ever so richly equipped for rhyming purposes, as in the days when Chaucer was bringing about his much-abused fusion of the Latin and Teutonic stocks.

I pass on to consider poetry as a mirror of thought and culture; and I ask what would have been the intellectual character of English poetry, if the Saxons rather than the French, if Cædmon and not Chaucer, had determined the line of its development. The answer to this question plainly is, that the Character of its thought would have been, in the first place, so overwhelmingly religious as almost to exclude the principle of the secular imitation of life and action; in the second place, it would have been imitative rather than original; in the third place, it would have been insular, and little accessible to the great movement of art and learning proceeding from the Continent.

How entirely it would have been under the guidance and domination of the Church is shown by the consistently ecclesiastical character of the chief monuments of Anglo-Saxon or Middle English literature, the poems of Cædmon and Cynewulf, the homilies of Ælfric, the sermons of Wycliffe, the allegory of Langland. Imitative the English poets would no less certainly have been, yielding to the ideas presented to them with the readiness rather of docile scholars than of original inventors. The Saxon writers I have mentioned think mainly of instructing their hearers in the truth; they care little about pleasing their imagination with the beauties of form and expression. Hence they put a very small amount of their own thought into the ideas which they strive to popularise in the Saxon tongue. The writer who has the credit for the poems of Cædmon contents himself avowedly with a paraphrase of the Scripture narrative in Teutonic phrases and imagery. Alfred's attempts to found a school of Saxon prose-writing aimed only at translations of the works of well-known Latin theologians and historians. Cynewulf is even more completely submissive to ecclesiastical authority than Cædmon. The few Saxon poets who venture on a flight beyond the prescribed boundaries of religious instruction are generally tasteless imitators of Latin originals. Cynewulf's contemporaries, for example, greatly admired the riddles of a very poor Latin poet, Symphosius, and imitated them in their own phraseology; while in the reign of Edward III. several transcripts of tedious French romances were made into modern English alliterative verse. As to the insular tendencies of the native English genius we have only to listen to the sighs of the monastic author of *Cursor Mundi,* and the Puritanic reflections of Robert of Brunne on the sinfulness of dramatic entertainments not authorised by the Church, to see how strong was the antipathy of the Saxon portion of the nation to the movement of secular art and thought invading England from France and Italy.

All that is best and finest in the Saxon imagination is expressed in *The Vision of Piers the Plowman.* No one, I think, can study the great poem of Langland without feeling that he is in the company of a genius endowed with very admirable qualities of poetry. It is written with the faith of an apostle and the indignation of a satirist. Langland handles much of the subject-matter of Chaucer with an observation hardly less extensive, and with thought more profound. His imagination is at once sublime and humorous. At times it moves in regions of the most remote mystery; from these it passes abruptly to imitate the humours of real life, with all the relish and accuracy of a Dutch painter. Now we are with Antichrist and his forces, besieging the House of Unity; now keeping company with Tim the Tinker and Wat the Warrener in a tavern on Cornhill, or at the booths of Winchester Fair. But whether he be humorous or sublime, metaphysical or realistic, a prophet-like earnestness animates the archaism of his style, and sounds to us from a distant century the trumpet notes of truth and sincerity.

For all this there is something wanting to the poetry of Langland that prevents it from taking the same rank as that of Chaucer. It lacks the note of the Universal. Neither in the mode of conception nor in the form of expression can *The Vision of Piers the Plowman* be said to be an artistic imitation of Nature. The poet himself confesses that he is unable to interpret the confused view of life which presents itself to his imagination. He describes the vision that he saw of the Field full of Folk, of which, however, he could make nothing, till he was aided by Holy Church. Holy Church puts into his hands the key with which in the Middle Ages she provided all theologians and poets—the allegorical interpretation of Nature and Scripture. The adoption of this mode of imitation would not have been in itself a bar to the treatment of the subject on universal lines, for both *The Divine Comedy* and *The Pilgrim's Progress*, founded as they are on ideas common to the Christian world, are in their general scheme perfectly intelligible. But in order to understand even the framework of Langland's narrative, we must not only have a pretty extensive acquaintance with the history of his times, but also with the view of the triple division of Feudal society held by the scholastic theologians. And even when this has been mastered, the general idea of life presented in the poem is that of a mystic, the final impression left on the imagination a chaos of confused, though poetical, details.

No poem, in respect of its design, offers a stronger contrast to *The Vision of Piers the Plowman* than *The Canterbury Tales*. The Feudal system, with all the vast fabric of society built on its foundations, has, like the primæval vegetation converted into coal, been long ago metamorphosed by time into other forms; yet in the poetry of Chaucer, the image of the ancient structure abides for ever. The gathering of the pilgrims with a common purpose in the courtyard of the Tabard Inn; the wonderful composition of the wayfaring group, its religious equality, its social etiquette; the masterly figures of the Knight, the Monk, the Franklin, the Wife of Bath, vivid and clear-cut as the sculptures of the

Parthenon; the general air of freshness, simplicity, and nature, pervading the whole poem, and especially the Prologue; in all these features the great work of Chaucer furnishes perhaps the most instructive example in literature of the true methods of imitative art.

Push the comparison with Langland a little further, and you find that Chaucer's artistic superiority arises from his power of reconciling contrary principles of imagination. In the first place, we observe the complete fusion in *The Canterbury Tales* of the universal and the particular. The poet's first care is to form in his imagination a general plan and outline of ideal action. When this has been arranged, he is prepared to fill in the details with a minuteness of imitation which must satisfy the strictest Preraphaelite, and to justify himself, on dramatic principles, against some of the objections made to the realism of his painting.

> Who so shall telle a tale after a man,
> He moot reherce as ny as ever he can
> Everich a word, if it be in his charge,
> Al speke he never so rudeliche and large.
> Or elles he moot telle his tale untrewe
> Or feyne thing, or finde wordes newe.
> He may nat spare, althogh he were his brother;
> He moot as wel seye o word as another.
> Crist spak himself ful brode in holy writ,
> And wel ye woot no vileinye is it.
> Eek Plato seith, who so that can him rede,
> The wordes mote ben cosin to the dede.

Langland's imitation of details is equally minute;

but then Langland did not know how to frame the organic whole to which the real details should give life and colour.

Again Chaucer may be advantageously contrasted with Langland, and other of his immediate predecessors, in his treatment of the opposing principles of art and morality. Two extreme and rival opinions have always divided opinion on this subject. One side maintains that art must be the immediate servant of morality; that it is the business of the poet to decide how he will instruct and improve mankind, before he thinks of imitating Nature. Langland and all the Saxon poets before him took this didactic view. On the other side, it is contended that art is independent of morals; and is concerned only with imitation—an opinion which is brilliantly illustrated in the *Decameron*. For beauty and symmetry of structure Boccaccio's work is almost unrivalled; and yet the entire absence in its design of the ethical element deprives it of a claim to stand in the very highest rank among the monuments of human imagination. Chaucer, with rare insight, recognises that he must reconcile these two antagonistic views. His business as a poet was in the first place with story-telling, but he would have been untrue to all the traditions of English art and character if, in the composition of his stories, he had ignored the influence of the Catholic Church. It was from the Church that the *fabliau* had received its first refinement; collections of monastic tales like *Barlaam and Josafat* and the *Gesta Romanum* had pioneered the way for the *Decameron*. The Church too had preserved in her Ark, through the ages of barbarism, all the salvage of ancient art and science which enriched the active imagination of the early European poets. To eliminate the moral element in story-telling was therefore to be a traitor to the Church, of which Chaucer was a faithful son.

On the other hand, Chaucer knew that, as an artist, his first duty was imitation, instruction only his second. Moreover, he was the first English poet who was a layman; and he looked on Nature and society with the steady gaze of one who had been both a soldier and a diplomatist. In order to harmonise these conflicting claims, he bases his central scheme on a dramatic principle. In *The Canterbury Tales* most of the imitations of Nature are moral, but they are accommodated with perfect propriety to the character of the different story-tellers; and what is wanting to any speaker in the way of taste and refinement is corrected by the criticism of his companions. In this way Chaucer avoids, on the one hand, the tediousness of the sermon, which is a flagrant defect in the composition of Langland's *Vision;* and on the other, the shameless license which discredits the character of the gay company in the *Decameron*.

But the crowning triumph of Chaucer's art, as contrasted with Langland's, was his naturalisation in English poetry of the highest culture of continental Europe. The English people had been trained by degrees to accept a new standard of taste. Chastened and braced by centuries of stern discipline under Norman rule, they had become conscious of their revived power as a nation; at Crecy and Poitiers they had avenged the defeat inflicted on them by the French at Hastings. The new language, which had sprung out of the marriage between Saxon and French, had expelled the latter tongue, first from the law courts in the reign of Edward III., and afterwards from the grammar schools in the reign of Richard II. But as yet the dominant feeling in the English mind was a narrow insular patriotism, which expressed itself in the poetry of Laurence Minot, in a manner much resembling the spirit of those who are now called Jingoes, when they boast of the superiority of the English to all other nations. No English writer before Chaucer had shown himself alive to the nature of the spiritual forces which, in every country of Europe, were transforming the life of Catholic and Feudal society.

Chaucer introduced these new ideas to his countrymen. His position in the household of John of Gaunt obliged him to study the prevailing tastes of Norman chivalry, and these are reflected in his translation of *The Romance of the Rose*, *The Parliament of Foules*, *The Legend of Good Women*, and other poems. But of far more importance to the enlargement of English Culture was his intercourse with Italy, to which country he was twice sent on missions of diplomacy. He had a wide acquaintance with Italian literature. *The House of Fame* shows that he had studied Dante's *Divine*

Comedy; he translated, or rather re-wrote in English, the *Filostrato* of Boccaccio, embodying in his version a poem of Petrarch ; and though some would persuade us that he knew nothing of the *Decameron,* I cannot think that a man of such omnivorous reading was not well acquainted with that famous work.

From his studies of Italian life and literature he learned that humane and civic art which characterises the composition of *The Canterbury Tales.* Life, manners, and the general movement of things, disclosed themselves to his imagination in their true proportions, and the ideal reflection of his experience is seen in the admirable methods of good breeding, irony, and common sense, with which characters like the Knight and the Host regulate the behaviour of their fellow pilgrims. Equal consideration is shown to all the company, yet each member of it is kept in his proper place. We have none of the scolding dogmatism with which Langland's Abstract Personages tell the reader what he ought to think and do : the men and women of the pilgrimage, by their own behaviour, whether dignified, vulgar, absurd, or indecent, show us what is right and wrong in human conduct. The busy host interferes to put down the squabbles between the meaner persons ; when, on the other hand, the Monk wearies the audience with the insufferable length of his Tragedies, the Knight, as becomes his high station, is made to act as the saviour of society. Sometimes, again, the tale told is intended to cast ridicule on the taste for long-winded romances, and then the poet himself assumes the responsibility for boring his companions, and patiently puts up with their unceremonious criticism, which reflects the actual change of taste in society at large.

Hence, though Chaucer can in no sense be called the descendant of the Anglo-Saxon poets, and though he may be said to have imported into England not only waggon-loads of words from France, but streams of ideas from that country and Italy, yet is he justly accounted the father of *English* poetry. Since his time our poetry has continued from age to age to develop the mixed character which he was the first to impress upon it, reflecting the varying forces which played upon his own imagination. In *The Canterbury Tales* we see the first outlines of that mixed manner of conceiving the external contrasts of Life and Society which Shakespeare afterwards brought to maturity in his tragi-comedies; we see too the already mature development of a dramatic imagination which delights in representing the spiritual inconsistencies of human nature. Of this quality the main ingredient is *humour*, that peculiar creative power which can make an imaginary person expose his own weaknesses and absurdities without destroying all regard for him in the affections of the reader or spectator. Since the Wife of Bath related her experiences of marriage, this kind of oblique satire has made itself felt again and again in the mouths of ideal personages in English literature—Falstaff and Dogberry, Sir Roger de Coverley, Bailie Nicol Jarvie and the Laird of Dumbiedikes, Mr. Pickwick and Mr. Micawber, Mrs. Nickleby, and even Mrs. Gamp. No foreign nation having produced ideal work of a like character (with the single notable exception of *Don Quixote*), English poetry may fairly claim pre-eminence in creative humour, and as *The Canterbury Tales* are the first example of such imitation, the glory of having impressed this character on English poetry must be ascribed to Chaucer.

To Chaucer again, as I have already urged, is due the mixed character of our versification. He determined its course while the judgment of the poets was still wavering. Ennius first found out the way to naturalise Greek metres in the Latin language, thus converting it into a harmonious instrument for the expression of lofty thought and emotion; and in like manner did Chaucer refine the Saxon vocabulary with rhythms and metres, derived from France and Italy, which have served as the vehicles of ideas for many generations of English poets. The correctness of his intuition and the soundness of his procedure were at once acclaimed by the despairing emulation of his disciples and successors, Lydgate and Occleve; in the next age the new rhetoric he had established was carried north of the Tweed by James I. of Scotland: when Wyatt and Surrey introduced into our language the refinements of Italy, their experiments were still based on the vocabulary and syntax of Chaucer; and it was from that "well of English undefiled" that Spenser drew the enchanted words and images which enabled him to transport the fancy into Fairyland. It is no doubt true that Chaucer's poetry contains none of the dactylic and anapæstic movements, characteristic of Anglo-Saxon, which later ages have drawn out of our language: from the existing conditions of the tongue this would have been impossible; but of the large volume of our versification, up to the age of Tennyson, which is inspired by the iambic movement and derived from French sources, Chaucer is the fountain-head.

And as the mixed character of the English people has been the inspiring source of Chaucer's poetry, so is the poetry of *The Canterbury Tales* perhaps the most accurate of all mirrors for reflecting the English character. At first this may seem a paradoxical saying. Since the mirthful company of pilgrims rode out of the courtyard of The Tabard on a showery April morning, more than five hundred years ago, the feudal character of English society has vanished as completely as the material fabric of that famous inn. A new nation seems to have grown up vastly transcending the old in all the arts and amenities of life. The England of to-day possesses means of expression for its sentiments, ideas, and opinions, of which those simple pilgrims never dreamed. Every morning the journalist puts together for our instruction a coherent image of the world, in which the whole surface of life, with all its incidents and emotions, is photographed with marvellous accuracy, and in which the judgment of the spectator on the transient drama is expressed in a lucid form of words. So vivid to each mind is this reflection of its own experience, that, for the moment, what is really but the reflection of our environment seems to be the living portrait of ourselves. And yet the lapse of a month, a week, even a day, may so completely alter the external aspect of things, or our opinion of them may be so entirely revolutionised, that in the new kaleidoscopic figure presented to us by the journals we look in vain for a single feature of our former consciousness.

Compared with the confused and evanescent imagery of real life, how changeless and abiding is that ideal English landscape with its varied company of pilgrims, "ever on the march through the brilliant atmosphere of April," sparkling with many-coloured robes and exhilarated with cheerful sounds, as the cook rides out ahead playing on the bagpipes, and the abbot follows with his bridle jingling in the whistling wind! How English it all seems! The little society so lively and pugnacious, so petulant and free of speech, and yet so amenable to law and order! The pilgrims themselves, each alive with human follies and whims, —the demure gray-eyed Prioress, with her aristocratic daintiness, her pet dogs, and her motto derived from the Courts of Love—the physician, whose study was but little on the Bible—the bustling Serjeant at Law, who yet seemed busier than he was—the Friar, proud of his artificial lisp—the Wife of Bath, man-like in her scarlet hose and with her sharp spurs—the Host himself, large, and frank, and wise in his *savoir faire*, possessed of all the qualities required for a guide and leader of men! And as the imagination dwells with delight on the clear outlines of a scene vivid with all these jewels of description, it is marvellous to think that we are looking on the resemblances of men and women who have been in their graves for five centuries: setting aside their dress and a somewhat old-fashioned mode of expression, we might be in the company of our next-door neighbours of to-day. But Aristotle can furnish us with the key to the mystery: it is to be found, he would tell us, in the poet's knowledge of the law of Fine Art: " Poetry is a higher and more philosophical thing than history; for while history expresses only the particular, poetry tends to express the universal."

VII

MILTON

A PRELATE eminent in letters recently told me that he had tried without success to persuade the young men and women of his acquaintance to study *Paradise Lost*. On my asking him the reason, he said that his friends informed him that they could not put up with Milton's theology. The answer seemed to me a remarkable one for two reasons. In the first place, I was struck with the profound ignorance it disclosed of the first principles of criticism in those who thought it sufficient. To judge a poem by its theology, or even its morality, is very much like valuing a horse by its colour or the length of its tail; and I imagine that if there be any who attempt to make purchases in the horse-market on this principle they do not find themselves in possession of very excellent bargains. Some elementary knowledge of the "points" of a poem is required in the person who presumes to pass a judgment on it.

But again I was impressed with the extraordinary vanity and conceit implied in the judgment of the Bishop's young friends. Not to be able to "put up" with *Paradise Lost* involves a belief in the mind of the critic that the blame for this distaste is to be imputed to the defect of the poet rather than to his own insensibility. And perhaps at first sight it might seem as if there were something to be pleaded in defence of this conclusion, since Aristotle says justly that the end of Fine Art is to produce pleasure; and Addison says with equal justice that the art is to conform to the taste, and not the taste to the art. But then the pleasure and the taste which Aristotle and Addison are thinking of are not the pleasure and taste of the individual, but the permanent judgment of the world: "Quod semper, quod ubique, quod ab omnibus." An established classic, a work of fine art which has passed this ordeal, becomes an integral part of the law of taste; before any individual dissents from the general judgment he must understand thoroughly the grounds upon which it has been passed; and if he finally elects to abide by his own judgment in preference to that of the world, he must face the presumption that his taste is wrong.

Now *Paradise Lost* is one of the few supreme poems on which the opinion of competent judges has been practically unanimous. Critics have spoken of it in very different tones of sympathy and enthusiasm; but not one has ventured to question the presence in it of qualities denoting sublime genius. Algarotti, Addison, Voltaire, Johnson, Macaulay have in unqualified language paid a tribute to its colossal greatness. If, therefore, there be in the present day, with all its gushing appreciation, all its hurried exaggeration of the value of contemporary work, a tendency to under-estimate the rank of Milton in poetry, it is at least desirable that the question should be examined on clear technical principles, and I have therefore determined to ask you to-day to consider, as scientifically as possible, what those qualities are in *Paradise Lost* which ought to secure for it the reverence and admiration of all lovers of Fine Art.

The *locus classicus* for the appreciation of the poem is of course the series of papers written by Addison in the *Spectator*, and I should recommend every one who wishes to get a well-proportioned view of the whole composition to study carefully that excellent criticism. It contains, indeed, no profound thought; all the observations lie on the surface; but it gives the student a clear insight into the general structure of the work, and selects with admirable taste and judgment the specimens of its particular beauties. As a positive estimate of Milton's poetical performance, however, it is open to one objection, namely, that Addison, following the example of the French and Italian critics of his age, professedly applies in all its details the method of critical analysis adopted by Aristotle in his *Poetics*, thus leaving on the mind of the reader the impression that Milton's merit consists in satisfying Aristotle's rules. Now, as neither Milton nor any other great poet ever thought in his composition of Aristotle's rules, this line of analysis does not follow the order of nature; nor will it avail with any critic who, starting with a prejudice against Milton, is also indisposed to accept the authority of Aristotle. The real question is, to what extent is *Paradise Lost* an illustration of the laws of Fine Art, and these, as I have repeatedly said in the course of my lectures, ought to be declared, much more with reference to the fundamental philosophical principles discoverable in the *Poetics*, than with reference to Aristotle's technical analysis.

Taking then the fundamental reasoning on which Aristotle's philosophical ideas of poetry are based, every great poem ought to fulfil three conditions: (1) It must be an imitation of the Universal in Nature; (2) The conception of the Universal in it must possess an individual character; and (3) The opposite qualities which go to make up this individual character must be combined in complete harmony of expression. As to the first point, there are four great poems which may be said in a very special manner to illustrate the imitation of the Universal: *The Iliad, The Æneid, The Divine Comedy*, and *Paradise Lost*. Of these, the two latter exhibit a higher and wider conception of Nature than the two former. Homer, indeed, is unequalled in the various representation of human action and character; but the supernatural part of his conception—that which relates to the divine order and government of Nature,—being based on polytheistic fancy, is necessarily at variance with our ideas of "the probable." Virgil, inferior to Homer in the imitation of character, is unrivalled in the stateliness of his conception of human society; but as his reflection of the order of things is derived from the universal supremacy of the Roman Empire, which has long disappeared, it is local and partial; nor is his representation of the divine government of the world much more probable than Homer's.

Dante and Milton, on the other hand, present, each in their own way, an image of the whole constitution of Nature, physical, moral, and social. *The Divine Comedy* enables the imagination to pass from Hell, the earth's centre, right up, through the nine spheres recognised by the Ptolemaic astronomy, to the empyrean Heaven which is the seat of God Himself; and it treats on the way of every kind of human passion and character, and of their relations to the universal order of things. Of *Paradise Lost* Addison very well says in his remarks on the third book: "As Milton's genius was wonderfully turned to the sublime, his subject is the noblest that could have entered into the thoughts of man. Everything that is truly great and astonishing has a place in it. The whole system of the intellectual world; the chaos and the creation; heaven, earth, and hell, enter into the constitution of the poem."

The action of *Paradise Lost* relates in an ideal form the whole moral history of the human race between the Fall of Man and his redemption by the Son of God. Its universal character appears in the poet's invocation:

> Of man's first disobedience and the fruit
> Of that forbidden tree whose mortal taste
> Brought death into the world and all our woe
> With loss of Eden till one happier Man
> Restore us, and regain that blissful seat
> Sing Heavenly Muse.

He here announces a subject far more extensive than the consequences of the wrath of Achilles, or the foundation of the Roman Empire; and he elsewhere speaks with conscious pride of the greatness of the characters who support his action :

> Never since created man
> Met such embodied force, that, named with these
> Could merit more than that small infantry
> Warred on by cranes, though all the giant brood
> Of Phlegra with the heroic race were joined
> That fought at Thebes or Ilium, on each side
> Mixed with auxiliar gods.

It is plain, then, that as far as regards the first condition of a great poem, *Paradise Lost*, in its imitation of the Universal, stands above both *The Iliad* and *The Æneid*, and on a level with *The Divine Comedy*.

But to go on to the second point; while Poetry is an imitation of the Universal, the universal truths of Nature that it imitates are not of an abstract nature, like the universal truths of Mathematics. Poetry deals with truths of the imagination, and answers completely to the definition which Hamlet gives of the drama, when he speaks of "the purpose of playing, whose end both at the first and now was and is to hold as 'twere the mirror up to Nature"—that is, in the Aristotelian phrase, to imitate the Universal—and "to show virtue her own feature, scorn her own image, and the very age and body of the time his form and pressure." In other words, every great imitation of Nature in poetry will reflect in itself not only the abstract ideas of things in the mind of a chance individual, but the whole conception of order, of liberty, of religion, philosophy, and learning, which makes up the idea of Nature in the poet's generation. Poetry imitates universal Truth, but in such a way as to exhibit that characteristic idea of it stamped on the mind of society at large in a particular place and time.

There is no better way of realising the manner in which *Paradise Lost* shows "the age and body of the time his form and pressure," than by comparing Milton's conception with Dante's; for if there be one great poem that more than another furnishes an ideal image of contemporary society, it is *The Divine Comedy*. It is the most faithful and sublime mirror that exists of the idea of Nature in the Middle Ages. The main character of this idea may be summed up in a single word, Authority, both in Church and State. First of all, Dante's conception reposes on the Unity of Faith as defined by the Church in the scholastic philosophy, and more particularly in the *Summa Theologica* of S. Thomas Aquinas. According to that philosophy all truths, even the most mysterious, could be understood, or at least believed, if they were reasoned on syllogistically in the right way; and practically reasoning in the right way meant squaring the settled dogmas of the Church with the infallible philosophy of Aristotle, according to the method of Aquinas. How faithfully Dante adhered to this philosophical principle, in his poetical fashion, appears in a passage like the following, which is typical of the entire imaginative character of *The Divine Comedy:* "Let this be always a lead to thy feet, to make thee move as slow as a weary man towards the 'yes' and 'no' that thou seest not. Low down is he among the fools who affirms or denies without distinction; for in the one no less than in the other case the current opinion swerves in a false direction, and afterwards the desire binds the understanding." Here is the Scholastic Philosophy contained poetically in a nutshell. The universal idea of Nature having been formed by a process of syllogistic reasoning, starting from the First Cause of things, and being fortified by a series of almost mathematical proofs, all physical phenomena had to be explained on a hypothesis mainly theological. Hence the Ptolemaic theory of astronomy, which in the Middle Ages was regarded as unquestionably true, was incorporated by the Church as an article of faith, with the result, as we know, that Galileo's assertion of the rotation of the earth on its own axis was imputed to him for heresy.

Again, the theory of social order in the Middle Ages rested, like the unity of the Faith, on a hypothesis of universal political Authority. Europe was organised on the system of what was known as the Christian Republic; that is to say, as a single society under the joint rule of the Pope and the Emperor, the former being the earthly representative and Vicar of Christ, the latter the head of the Feudal Order, and heir, through the intervention of the Papacy, of the Roman Emperors of the West.

Unreal as was this theory, it was accepted, like

the Ptolemaic system, by the highest intellects of the Middle Ages, as part of the divine order of the Universe. In this respect *The Divine Comedy* gave back to "the age and body of the time" a perfect reflection of its "form and pressure." "Man," says Dante in his treatise *De Monarchia*, "has need of a double direction, that is to say, of the Supreme Pontiff, whose office is to bring the human race by the light of Revelation to Eternal Life, and of the Emperor, who must direct them to a temporal end by the teaching of philosophy." And the philosophical principle is illustrated with the most admirable poetical logic in the *Paradiso*. The uninstructed reader, for example, naturally asks why such a characterless person as the Emperor Justinian should have been exalted by Dante into Paradise; but the poet shows that the logic of his fiction is absolutely above criticism. Justinian appears in the Second Heaven as the representative both of theological orthodoxy and of the imperial law and justice typified by the Roman Empire. He undertakes to prove to Dante that the principle of the Holy Roman Empire is something superior to the party conception of it by Ghibelline and Guelph; and, in order to establish the point, he demonstrates how it enters into the scheme of God's Providence. Beginning with the far-off days when—in the words of the *Paradiso*—"Pallas died to give it a kingdom," he traces the secular growth and expansion of the Roman Empire, till it arrives at its destined climax, which he thus describes: "But that which the [holy] ensign, which causes me to speak, had done of old and was about to do through the mortal world which is subject to it, becomes in appearance little and obscure, if it be looked at in the third Cæsar's hand with clear eye and pure affection: for the living justice, which inspires me, granted to it by the hand of him of whom I speak the glory of working vengeance for his wrath." In less enigmatic language, the Roman Empire, in the time of Tiberius Cæsar, was a necessary instrument in the work of the Atonement. The argument leading up to this curious conclusion is given more fully in the treatise *De Monarchia;* it is as follows: "If the Roman Empire had not been of divine right, the sin of Adam could not have been [humanly] punished in Christ. . . . If Christ had not suffered under the ordinary judge, his penalty would not have been a lawful punishment; and the ordinary judge could only be one having jurisdiction over the whole human race. And Tiberius Cæsar, whose representative Pilate was, would not have had this jurisdiction, unless the Roman Empire had been of right divine."

When Dante with his clear vision looked abroad upon the world, he must have seen how ill the existing facts of society fitted in with this theory of universal Authority—how impossible, for example, it was to harmonise the Feudal System, its local fiefs and its rights of hereditary succession, its barbarous customs, its essential anarchy, with his civic idea of the Holy Roman Empire. But living as he did at a time when no one thought of questioning the soundness of the scholastic method of deductive reasoning, and when all the great nations of Europe were still in the chrysalis stage, he regarded the constitution of the Christian Republic as an emanation of the Love or Will of God, and held that its authority was not absolute only on account of the imperfection of human nature. In this respect he argued on the same principles as the physical philosophers of his age, who, when they observed that certain motions of the heavenly bodies were inconsistent with the perfectly circular movement of the spheres imagined by Ptolemy, immediately set to work to make the observed facts square with their system, by inventing what was called the theory of the Epicycle. Precisely in the same way Dante in Paradise asks King Charles Martel to resolve his doubt how it is that, if all authority proceeds from the will of God, good rulers can be succeeded by bad. The King explains to him that, for the regulation of civil society, there must be a diversity of functions; and that though ideas proceed pure from the mind of God, yet, entering into the habitation of different mortal bodies, they take various directions; and hence, by the influences of the planets, Fortune, under the control of the Divine Foresight, provides for the necessary fluctuations in human affairs.

Now in the three hundred and fifty years that intervened between the writing of *The Divine Comedy* and the publication of *Paradise Lost* the entire conception of Nature and Society had altered. It no longer rested on the basis of authority. The Spiritual Unity of Christendom, reposing on the authority of the

Scholastic Logic, had been shattered by the Reformation. In place of the political unity of Europe, involved in the theory of the Christian Republic, had arisen the European Equilibrium, constituted by the rivalry of various powerful nations, and shadowing forth the first faint outlines of diplomacy and the foundations of International Law. The Ptolemaic theory of the Universe had been, if not displaced, at least considerably discredited by the reasoning of Copernicus and Galileo. America had been discovered. Printed books diffused knowledge, only to be obtained in Dante's time from manuscripts or oral lectures. This knowledge, instead of being confined to the scholarly few who were able to acquire it in Latin, was propagated in the vulgar tongues of the different nations; on the other hand, the philosophy and literature of the ancients were no longer viewed through the scholastic medium, but were scientifically studied in the original languages.

Hence what chiefly characterises the seventeenth century is the altered attitude of the mind towards external authority. Milton's age is penetrated by *doubts* as to the truth about the movements of the heavenly bodies. The Ptolemaic theory is not absolutely rejected, but its authority is impugned. Bacon, for example, does not believe in the diurnal motion of the earth, but he says: "With no better reason is it affirmed that all the heavenly bodies move in perfect circles; that there are eccentrics and epicycles whereby the constancy of motions in perfect circles is preserved. . . . And it is the absurdity of these opinions that has driven men to the opinion of the diurnal motion of the earth; which I am convinced is most false." In the same spirit Milton makes the angel Raphael reply to the questions of Adam on the subject:

> To ask or search I blame thee not, for heaven
> Is as the book of God before thee set,
> Wherein to read his wondrous works, and learn
> His seasons, hours, or days, or months, or years.
> This to attain, whether heav'n move or earth,
> Imports not, if thou reckon right; the rest
> From man or angel the great architect
> Did wisely to conceal, and not divulge
> His secrets to be scanned by them who ought
> Rather admire; or if they list to try
> Conjecture, He his fabric of the heavens
> Hath left to their disputes, perhaps to move
> His laughter at their quaint opinions wide
> Hereafter, when they come to model heav'n
> And calculate the stars, how they will wield
> The mighty frame, how build, unbuild, contrive,
> To save appearances; how gird the sphere
> With centric and eccentric scribbled o'er
> Cycle and epicycle, orb in orb.

The conclusion of the whole matter is suspense of judgment:

> Heav'n is for thee too high
> To know what passes there; be lowly wise,
> Think only what concerns thee and thy being;
> Dream not of other worlds.

In these two passages we find an expression of the spirit of the Renaissance as regards Science, in opposition to the spirit of the Middle Ages—the inductive principle of reasoning, which, refusing to be bound by *a priori* authority, proceeds to its conclusions only by way of observation; and the humanist tendency, which inclines to concentrate observation on man and his immediate interests, rather than on those metaphysical questions which absorbed men's intellect in the Middle Ages. Nevertheless, the spirit of the Renaissance is not the predominant spirit in *Paradise Lost*. The purpose of the poet, as he tells us, is

> To assert eternal Providence,
> And justify the ways of God to men.

Hence, like Dante in *The Divine Comedy*, he still moves in a theological atmosphere; like Dante he feels the need of an infallible authority to set forth the true conception of Nature; but the authority on which he relies is not that of the Church, formulated and defined in the philosophy of Aquinas, but the inspiration of the Holy Scriptures interpreted by his own reason:

> And chiefly thou, O Spirit, that dost prefer
> Before all temples the upright heart and pure,
> Instruct me for thou knowest. . . .
>   What in me is dark
> Illumine, what is low raise and support.

To sum up, therefore, the fundamental difference between *The Divine Comedy* and *Paradise Lost* in a sentence: one conception of Nature is that evolved by the logic of the Catholic Schoolmen out of the opinions of the Christian Fathers, the other that of the reason of the English Independent, exercising itself on the text of the Bible; "the age and body of the time" reflected in one poem is the authority of the Latin

Church, in the other the liberty of the Teutonic Reformation.

I pass on to consider the third essential of a great poem, as it is illustrated in the form of *Paradise Lost*. Does the composition satisfy Sir Joshua Reynolds' definition of a work of Fine Art, namely, an ideal organism, made up of contrary parts harmonised into unity in such a manner that no one part is felt to predominate unduly over the others? Is the poet's conception of Nature communicated to the reader in a clear, characteristic, and appropriate form of expression? In deciding this point, I think that a very false impression of the merit of *Paradise Lost* has been created by Macaulay, who contrasts the style of Milton with that of Dante, without attempting to account for the difference. He says: "The poetry of Milton differs from that of Dante as the hieroglyphics of Egypt differed from the picture-writing of Mexico. The images which Dante employs speak for themselves; they stand simply for what they are. Those of Milton have a signification which is often discernible only to the initiated. Their value depends less on what they represent than on what they remotely suggest. However strange, however grotesque, may be the appearance which Dante undertakes to describe, he never shrinks from describing it. He gives us the shape, the colour, the sound, the smell, the taste; he counts the numbers, he measures the size. His similes are the illustrations of a traveller. Unlike those of other poets, and especially of Milton, they are introduced in a plain business-like manner;

not for the sake of any beauty in the objects from which they are drawn, not for the sake of any ornament which they may impart to the poem, but simply in order to make the meaning of the writer as clear to the reader as it is to himself."

Were it the case that Milton's form of expression did not make his conception as clear to the intelligent reader as it was to himself, this would be a fatal flaw in the art of his poem. But as a matter of fact, the ideal imagery of *Paradise Lost* is as clear and distinct as that of *The Divine Comedy;* only it is employed in a different way and for a different purpose. So far from its being true that in Dante—as Macaulay says—"the images speak for themselves and stand for what they are," the Italian poet tells us over and over again that he merely makes use of sensible images as a necessary mode of conveying spiritual truths to the weakness of human understanding. The great distinctness with which he describes external objects is due to his desire to give, by means of an allegorical symbol, a clear idea of the unseen world. Milton, on the other hand, employs images that do "speak for themselves and stand for what they are." His poem describes a real action, and though this action—the fall of the Rebel angels, the temptation of Man, and the loss of Eden—passes in a supernatural sphere, it is related in such a way as to give a probable account of events that actually happened in that sphere.

The form of *The Divine Comedy* is the most completely original that is found in the whole range of poetry. It is a narrative of the poet's own experience in the unseen world, an account of all that he saw and heard in his journey through Hell, Purgatory, and Paradise; and, as Macaulay justly says, he paints every object that he met with extraordinary distinctness; but this by the very conditions of his art he was bound to do, in order to make his fiction credible to his hearers. Moreover, it was easier for him than for Milton to make the composition of his whole poem pictorial, in proportion as the universal idea of Nature and Society in the Middle Ages—the Ptolemaic scheme of the celestial spheres, the syllogisms of the Scholastic Logic, the dual government of the Christian Republic—was more limited and symmetrical than the corresponding idea of the Universal in the seventeenth century. The framework of Dante's ideal conception was provided for him by universal authority and universal belief; all that he had to do was to communicate poetic life and colour from his own imagination to the ready-made organic form. This, it is needless to say, he did with unequalled genius.

Milton, on the contrary, chose to present his materials to the reader in the form of a regular epic. He had to relate in his poem not his own experience but that of others—of Man, of the Fallen Angels, of the Son of God. Instead of starting, like Dante, on his journey through the unseen world from Hell, the centre of the fixed and motionless Earth, and working up his way by symmetrical stages to the Empyrean Heaven, Milton calls on the Spirit of God to enable him to describe the external causes and events that led to the loss of Eden :

> Say, first,—for Heaven hides nothing from thy sight
> Nor the deep tract of Hell—say first what cause
> Moved our grand Parents in that happy state,
> Favoured of Heaven so highly, to fall off
> From their Creator, and transgress his will,
> For one restraint, lords of the world beside ?

In execution of this purpose, he begins his narrative, just as Homer does in the *Odyssey* and Virgil in the *Æneid*, at a point midway in the action described, and afterwards, in the body of the poem, employs—also in the Homeric and Virgilian manner—one of the leading characters to relate the preceding events necessary for the full comprehension of the action as a whole. The action of *Paradise Lost* practically opens with the departure of Satan from Hell to devise mischief against God's recently created universe, and whoever would form a clear conception of Milton's idea of Nature must take the trouble to follow, as on a map, the flight of the person whom Dryden rightly calls the hero of the poem, from his first encounter with Sin and Death, down to the moment when he makes his entrance into Eden. Macaulay, I should imagine, had never attempted to track the imagination of the poet with this minuteness, but if the reader studies *Paradise Lost* in the excellent edition of Professor Masson, he will find that Milton's ideal topography is quite as clear as Dante's. Like Dante, Milton assumes the Ptolemaic scheme of the heavens as the basis of his poetic description; but as, by the epic form of his poem, he is bound to view it from without, and to show the positions of Hell, of Chaos, and of the Empyrean, relatively to the universe, the imagery seems vaster and less symmetrical than that of *The Divine Comedy*. This is just as it should be. Compared with Dante's upward movement into Paradise, the wanderings of Milton's Satan outside the world of Creation, and his downward plunge to the earth through the spheres of the fixed stars and the planets, afford an exact reflection of the progress of astronomical knowledge between the age of the Schoolmen and the age of Bacon.

But though Milton triumphantly overcomes the first difficulty with which he was confronted, and presents to the reader a clear pictorial idea of Nature as a whole, he has still to solve the problem how to harmonise the action, which is his subject, with the epic form of poetical expression. This is an obstacle which no Christian poet, who attempts a regular epic, can avoid. Tasso, in his *Treatise on the Structure of Epic Poetry*, very frankly explains the nature of the task. The epic poet, he says, has to take into account two contrary conditions: first, that the reason of the reader postulates in the poetical narrative the appearance of probable truth; and secondly, that the imagination requires the presence of the marvellous, the supernatural, and all the embellishments and fictions with which this form of poetry is associated. By the epic poets of Greece and Rome the difficulty was not felt, both because they took for their subjects legendary events, which were supposed to have actually occurred, thus securing for their conceptions a basis of probability, and also because they could please the imagination with the appearance in their stories of the numerous gods and goddesses who were believed to intervene in the government of the world. When polytheism disappeared with the advent of Christianity, this supernatural machinery was no longer available for the purposes of the poet. Dante indeed, the first great Christian poet in the vulgar tongues of modern Europe, did not feel the want of it. The action which he described in *The Divine Comedy* was his own experience in Hell, Purgatory, and Paradise, and when, by the force of his genius, he had made his narrative seem probable to his hearers, his difficulties of invention were at an end, because his report of what he saw and heard was marvellous and supernatural in itself.

But Tasso, who, in his *Jerusalem Delivered*, attempted to preserve the traditional epic form of Homer and Virgil, was forced to deal with the standing difficulty, nor can it be said that he was quite successful in overcoming it. He sought to combine history with romance. He chose a historical subject, and thereby secured for his poem a basis of belief in the reader's mind; but when he came to elevate his historical truth by means of supernatural machinery, invention failed him. Allowing that it was not permissible for a Christian poet to introduce into his work Pagan deities, he contended that he might still enliven his narrative with the persons of diabolical agents, with magical enchantments, and with all the fictions of romance that Ariosto had introduced into the *Orlando Furioso*. But in this experiment Tasso, if I may say so, fell between two poetical stools. His historical and romantic elements are not harmonised. The real interest of the *Jerusalem* lies in the loves of Rinaldo and Armida, in the wanderings of Erminia among the shepherds, and in the beauty of the various descriptions. Admirable in themselves, these episodes, as the reader very clearly perceives, are not essentially connected with the main action of the deliverance of Jerusalem. The romantic parts have no real relation to the historical whole.

If a poet of Tasso's genius failed to conquer the difficulties inherent in the epic treatment of a secular historical subject, failure was ten times more inevitable in the case of the lesser artists who devoted their efforts to sacred themes. For here it was evident that no element of romance could be allowed to colour the severe outlines of historic Scriptural truth; and though several French poets in the seventeenth century ventured on the experiment, their attempts to raise their subject into the higher poetical atmosphere were both painful and grotesque. It is little wonder that Boileau, judging from these performances, and apparently without knowledge of Milton's great poem, should have pronounced the task of writing an epic on a sacred subject to be an artistic impossibility.

Such poetical failures and such a critical judgment give us an idea of the sublime art employed in the construction of *Paradise Lost*. From the invocation with which the poem opens, down to the noble melancholy of the last line—" Through Eden took their solitary way,"—the unity of the ideal organism is absolute and blameless. Yet in the entire narrative there is scarcely a detail that has not some warrant either in the text of Scripture or in sacred legend— the account of the Creation, for example, and of the Fall is merely an amplification of the Bible narrative, and the history of the fall of the Angels is founded on immemorial tradition—so that Aristotle's requirement of a basis of probability is fully satisfied. At the same time the scenes and incidents described are in themselves so vast and marvellous, that the imagination, transported beyond the range of experience, moves with delight amid the realities of a supernatural sphere. The same is true of the characters who conduct the action to its destined end. All but two are represented on a colossal scale, yet with attributes and qualities which Scripture authority and human experience render easy of conception. No divine, angelic, or diabolic personage is introduced whose name is not mentioned in the Bible or the Apocrypha. And Titanic as the imagination of character is, it is so dramatically conceived, so finely graduated, so exquisitely rendered, that we never feel ourselves chilled by an atmosphere of allegory and abstraction. Pity and Fear are always at work. Who can read without profound emotion the description of Satan about to address the host of fallen spirits whom he had led to their doom?

> Thrice he assayed, and thrice, in spite of scorn,
> Tears such as angels weep, burst forth; at last
> Words interwove with sighs found out their way.

Or what poetical rendering of despair ever equalled in tragic intensity the passion of the Devil as uttered in his speech to the Sun, or described in the feelings with which he gazes on the happiness of Adam and Eve?

Again, we have to admire in *Paradise Lost* the harmony that is effected between the spirit of the whole conception and the form in which it is expressed. The spirit of the poem is Christian, but the form is classical, and therefore Pagan, so that we at once find ourselves in the presence of that great opposition of thought which, from very early days, had divided the Christian Church. Tertullian ruthlessly condemned the study of all Pagan literature; Gregory the First used his authority to drive Virgil and Horace out of the schools; but human nature was too strong for them. A compromise was effected. The Pagan poets were in a way converted and Christianised—very much in the same manner as many of the Greek myths were transmuted into saintly legends,—and with so much success, that in the Middle Ages Virgil, Ovid, and Statius were accepted as established text-books in the course of Christian rhetoric. In consequence of this compromise the stories of Pagan mythology never gave Dante any trouble. His verse is studded with mythological allusions, rendered familiar to him by his scholastic education. He speaks of Icarus, and Glaucus, and Alcides, and the daughter of Latona, as if they were persons no less real than Belisarius, or Justinian, or the reigning Pope: all of them provide him with imagery which helps to illustrate some spiritual truth in the constitution of the unseen world.

But Milton, like Luther, and many of the leaders of the Reformation, judged of Pagan literature with something of the austere spirit of Tertullian. You will all remember the famous passage in *Paradise Regained* where Satan tempts the Saviour with the spectacle of the art, poetry, and philosophy of Athens. Not so familiar, but quite as characteristic, is the Saviour's reply :

> If I would delight my private hours
> With music or with poem, where so soon
> As in our native language can I find
> That solace ?   All our Law and Story strewed
> With hymns, our Psalms with artful terms inscribed,
> Our Hebrew songs and harps, in Babylon
> That pleased so well our victor's ear, declare
> That rather Greece from us these arts derived—
> Ill imitated while they loudest sing
> The vices of their deities, and their own,
> In fable, hymn, or song, so personating
> Their gods ridiculous, and themselves past shame.

Strange, indeed, it is to think that these lines should have been written by one who had deliberately adapted the matter of the Hebrew Scriptures to the requirements of Hellenic form, who, in the inmost nature of his genius, as illustrated by the regular structure of his poem, by the Homeric picturesqueness of his similes, by the Virgilian music in the roll of his proper names, and by the Latin turn of his diction, shows himself steeped in classic learning, penetrated with the spirit and character of classic poetry! Nevertheless, there is no contradiction in his style. *Paradise Lost* is free from every trace of cold formal imitation. The form of the poem is essentially original, and seems to spring spontaneously out of the central design; and the sublime art of Milton is nowhere more conspicuous than in the skill with which he turns the mythological imagery of a religion recognised as false to the illustration and embellishment of a Christian theme.

Let me remind you of a very few instances in which classical precedents have inspired him with the starting-point for his grandest imagery. The Catalogue of the Ships in the *Iliad* evidently suggested the magnificent enumeration of the false gods of the Gentiles in *Paradise Lost*. The tradition of the Church had long sanctioned the dim belief that the gods of the Greeks were devils, but I believe Milton was the first to appropriate the idea for poetical purposes, and to identify the Gentile deities with the fallen angels:

> Godlike Shapes, and Forms
> Excelling human; princely Dignities;
> And Powers that erst in Heaven sat on thrones,
> Though of their names in Heavenly records now
> Be no memorial, blotted out and rased
> By their rebellion from the Books of Life.

On this principle Mammon, the chief architect of Hell, is identified with Vulcan; but at the same time the errors of the Pagan mythology are most ingeniously and poetically corrected:

>   In Ausonian land
> Men called him Mulciber; and how he fell
> From Heaven they fabled, thrown by angry Jove
> Sheer o'er the crystal battlements: from morn
> To noon he fell, from noon to dewy eve,
> A summer's day, and with the setting sun
> Dropt from the zenith, like a falling star,
> On Lemnos, the Ægæan isle. Thus they relate,
> Erring; for he with this rebellious rout
> Fell long before; nor aught availed him now
> To have built in Heaven high towers; nor did he scape
> By all his engines, but was headlong sent,
> With his industrious crew, to work in Hell.

Ovid's ingenious but conceited description of Narcissus suggested to Milton Eve's most exquisite, most natural, relation of her feelings when she first saw her own reflection in the water. When Satan in the Garden of Eden stands confronted with the angel Gabriel, the situation reminds the poet of Jupiter in the *Æneid*, weighing in the scales the fates of Æneas and Turnus. This raises in his mind the sublime image of the Almighty hanging forth in heaven

>   The golden scales yet seen
> Betwixt Astræa and the Scorpion sign;

but since, as Bishop Newton justly points out, it would have been highly improper to represent Omniscience as ignorant of the event, the poet feigns that the action was intended to warn Satan of the fruitlessness of strife, by showing him the lightness of his own weight in the balance. And yet once more, the mixture of the Christian and classical imagery may be illustrated by the sublime invocation at the opening of Book VII.:

> Still govern thou my song,
> Urania, and fit audience find, though few.
> But drive far off the barbarous dissonance
> Of Bacchus and his revellers, the race
> Of that wild rout that tore the Thracian bard
> In Rhodope, where woods and rocks had ears
> To rapture, till the savage clamour drowned
> Both harp and voice; nor could the Muse defend
> Her son. So fail not thou who thee implores;
> For thou art heavenly, she an empty dream.

I am far from contending that Milton is invariably successful in blending the opposing elements of which his poem consists, that the form of *Paradise Lost* is always appropriate to the matter, the Christian spirit never out of harmony with the Pagan model. Parts of the narrative are undoubtedly dry and barren; the same may be said of every long poem, and notably of *The Divine Comedy*. Many of the details are out of place. In my opinion almost the whole of the Sixth Book, in which Milton, desiring to supply the obvious deficiency of incident in his subject, gives, through the mouth of Raphael, a very particular account of the War in Heaven, might have been omitted with advantage. Frequent conceits, puns, and satirical allusions, degrade the style in places below its usual lofty level; and on the other hand, the Latin idioms, by means of which the diction is exalted, are sometimes pushed beyond the point at which the sublime marches with a less admirable quality. But on the whole I should be prepared to maintain with confidence that, having regard to the unity and grandeur of the ideal scheme, the subordination of the parts to the whole, and the perfection of the workmanship, *Paradise Lost* satisfies more thoroughly than any epic poem of equal scope Sir Joshua Reynolds's definition of Fine Art.

Nor is the grandeur of Milton's art conspicuous only in its result; it is also to be measured by the greatness of the mental processes which produced it. *Paradise Lost*, *Paradise Regained*, and *Samson Agonistes* were Milton's latest works; like Chaucer's *Canterbury Tales*, like Shakespeare's *Hamlet* and *King Lear*, they were the offspring of a period when all his poetical faculties had been trained by long experience to work together. Brought into being in the midst of blindness, poverty, political and social disgrace, *Paradise Lost* gains in scope and grandeur by the adverse circumstances of its gestation. We see in its composition how the elements have been separated, sifted, recombined. As late as 1639 the evidence shows that Milton was meditating a quite different subject, a romantic one, the history of King Arthur, which, it is evident, could never have harmonised with the classic form he would certainly have attempted to give it. When, after the agony of the Civil War, his mind begins to weigh the possibilities of a Scriptural subject, his imagination stands doubtful in the choice of the necessary form. At first the drama suggests itself; and we know that Satan's address to the sun was composed for a work fashioned on the lines of the old Miracle Plays, an antiquated mould no longer suited to the character of the age. Finally, however, the poet reverts to the epic form, and the artistic judgment being now right, all the materials begin to settle themselves into their proper places; the recollections of the old romantic Arthurian theme are employed to embellish the narrative with simile and allusion; the stern heart of Puritanism circulates its life-blood through all the veins and arteries of the poetic organism.

From all this it follows that both in its conception and its expression *Paradise Lost* is a monument illustrating, in the highest form, not only the universal laws of poetry, but the operation of the English law of taste. In my last lecture I dwelt on the manner in which that law is illustrated in the poetry of Chaucer. I showed how the task of the great founder of our poetry lay in harmonising the genius of the Saxon and Norman-French languages, and how he expanded the insular religious spirit of Saxon poetry by uniting it with the more secular tendencies of art and science then manifesting themselves on the Continent of Europe, and particularly in Italy. Milton carried on the national tradition; but the problem he had to solve in poetry was of a different order. His destiny was to reconcile the genius of Humanism with the temper of the Reformation.

For nearly a century before the appearance of *Paradise Lost* two separate streams of thought had been running side by side in the English mind, as represented in the Universities, without any attempt being made to blend them into unity. One was the theology of the Reformation, whether represented by Luther, Calvin, or Arminius; the other was the imitation of classical forms, images, and idioms, encouraged by the Renaissance. The classical form had been made the vehicle for the Reformed theology, and the artistic result was grotesque enough. What could be more incongruous than to turn the serene beauty of the idylls of Theocritus into an allegorical weapon of Genevan divinity? Yet this was what had been done by Spenser in his *Shepherd's Calendar*. In Milton's youth the Humanist spirit had so much prevailed at Cambridge over the acrid temper of sectarianism, that his early poems, *L'Allegro, Il Penseroso*, and *Comus*, are inspired with an air of absolute classical repose, and even in *Lycidas* the note of theological controversy only faintly disturbs the pastoral calm of the elegiac style. Perhaps some epicures of art may even regret the exchange of outlines so sweet and chaste for the more complex harmonies of Milton's later compositions. But if, as at one time seemed probable, he had been sacrificed to the resentments of the Restoration, the world, while it would have had cause to deplore the loss of perhaps the most charming lyric poet in the English language, would have had no suspicion that there had perished in that imagination an epic poem of the same class as the *Iliad* and *The Divine Comedy*. The long fallow period, apparently so barren in poetical inspiration, devoted wholly to controversy, pamphleteering, and politics, was in reality needed to bring the fanciful and abstract imagination of the recluse poet into touch with the realities of the world about him. Plunging into the civil conflict equipped with his admirable artistic sense of order and proportion, a strong perception of actuality enabled him to give back an image of the war of life in an ideal form. The product of this strife of contraries was *Paradise Lost*.

In *Paradise Lost* are reflected all the contrary intellectual tendencies of the age—the energy of Hebraic faith, the aspirations of Hellenic art and philosophy, the romance of mediæval chivalry; but all these opposing elements are fused by a supreme judgment into a unity of conception which was beyond the reach of Spenser and Sidney. Verse, composed with the severe regularity of Sophocles, seems to swell into the sublime enthusiasm of the Psalms of David, or to breathe the stern ardours of the trumpets of Dunbar. In the commerce between the genius of the poet and his age there is something that resembles the joint action that produces the forms of the clouds, when the sun draws up the crude vapours from the bosom of the earth and fashions them into a thousand exquisite shapes of aerial architecture. The characteristics of the style of *Paradise Lost* can indeed be only fitly described by the word Miltonic, but through the inspiration of Milton we feel the presence of the life, the character, and the history, of the English People.

VIII

POPE

In my earlier lectures on Law in Taste I have endeavoured to arrive at my conclusions inductively and historically. Starting with the laws which govern the art of Poetry as a whole, and which are very clearly laid down in Aristotle's *Poetics*, we have seen that the first and greatest of these is that which defines Poetry to be the imitation of the Universal. I have shown that the second, and hardly less important, law of Poetry is the Law of National Character, whereby the Universal in nature is presented to the mind in such a particular form as the genius and circumstances of each nation require. In my two last lectures I attempted successively to draw out the law of character in English Poetry by reference to the practice of Chaucer, the father of our poetry, and to that of Milton, who, in one branch of the art, is acknowledged by all competent critics to stand in the same rank as Homer. In neither of these poets do we find any distinct declaration of the artistic principles on which they proceeded; the operation of the law of national character has to be inferred from their work.

I would now ask you to direct your attention to the genius of a poet who stands on a different footing from Chaucer and Milton, who consciously and deliberately schooled his imagination by a definite critical standard, and who has defined in the clearest possible manner what that standard was. I need hardly say that I refer to Alexander Pope, who, as you all know, proclaimed the end of his art to be correctness, and who embodied what he believed to be the law of poetical taste in his *Essay on Criticism.*

Nothing in criticism is more valuable than the attempts of eminent artists, who, if I may use a somewhat familiar metaphor, "know the ropes" of their art, to think out the first principles of procedure, and though it does not follow either that Pope's practice conformed to the highest law of English Poetry, or that his declaration of that law was entirely accurate, his opinions are at least deserving of the highest respect and consideration. This consideration, I am sorry to say, has not always been granted to it. Critics, who ought to have known better, have decried the *Essay on Criticism.* De Quincey, for example, who, himself only a prose writer, should have felt that he might appreciate imperfectly the motives of a writer in verse, arrogantly sneers at it as a collection of maxims, "the most mouldy with which criticism has baited its rat-traps." It has been also disparaged by poets like Bowles, because it gives prominence to a view of poetry with which they have little sympathy, and which they hold to be petty, restricted, and even, in a sense, "unpoetical." The position of these men is more intelligible than that of De Quincey; but their depreciation of Pope's poetry is discounted by their obvious incapacity to understand the peculiar conditions which gave rise to the declaration of law contained in the *Essay on Criticism*. I will, therefore, ask you first to consider what is the law of poetical conception declared by Pope; then, what is the nature of his law of poetical expression; and lastly, in what respects his principles and practice fall short of the highest law of English Poetry, as embodied in the work of poets like Chaucer and Milton.

Three main rules of guidance are laid down by Pope in his *Essay*. They are these: "Follow Nature;" "Avoid false wit;" "Imitate the Classics." The first of these principles is declared as follows:

> First follow Nature and your judgment frame
> By her just standard which is still the same.
> Unerring Nature, still divinely bright,
> One clear, unchanged, and universal light,
> Life, force, and beauty must to all impart
> At once the source, and end, and test of art.

So good a judge as Mr. Leslie Stephen regards this principle as one of what De Quincey calls "mouldy commonplaces," because he thinks that the maxim was common to critics in all ages. But that is just what it was not. Pope's advice as to following Nature was, in fact, a re-declaration of the law of Aristotle, as opposed to the practice of the poets of the Middle Ages. I do not mean to say that Dante did not imitate Nature; he would not have been the supreme poet that he was if he had failed to do so. I mean this, that though Nature has, as Pope says, "a just standard which is still the same," yet she reveals herself to men in different ages in different aspects, and therefore requires to be imitated in different forms. Let me illustrate this point by a concrete example, to which I have already referred for another purpose. Tasso, in his *Discourse on the Structure of Epic Poetry*, starts one of Aristotle's questions about a point on which his judgment is perplexed, namely, how far it is possible in a Christian epic to make use of supernatural machinery, as the Greeks and Romans did; since the gods and goddesses, on whose actions so much of the interest of the ancient epic depends, are in the Christian scheme of life condemned as false and delusive idols. In other words, the polytheistic conception of Nature, prevalent when Aristotle proclaimed that poetry was an imitation of the Universal, was abhorrent to the monotheistic belief of the Middle Ages. Tasso, therefore, could not imitate Nature quite in the same manner as Homer.

Nor would a poet of the Middle Ages have presented such an imitation of Man, and Society, and Human Life, as would have been characteristic of a Greek poet. The idea of man in Greek and Roman times was founded on a perfectly civic condition of things; the idea of man in the Middle Ages was founded on a system, partly ecclesiastical, and partly feudal, such as we see reflected in the philosophy of the Schoolmen: a view quite as universal as the civil view of the Romans—for it prevailed all over Mediæval Europe—and yet quite opposed to it. Dante, we know, conceived of the order of human society, as proceeding immediately from the mind of God, and he regarded the constitution of Europe in his day, whether this were called the Holy Roman Empire, or the Christian Republic, as part of the divine government of the Universe. Hence Dante's conception of Nature was primarily theological; and hence too the eminently suggestive remark of Boccaccio in his *Life of Dante:* "I say that Theology and Poetry may be said to be almost one where their subject is the same : nay, more, I say that Theology is nothing but God's poetry."

Again, as the Mediæval idea of the Universal differed fundamentally from the idea of the Universal in Greek and Roman times, so was the idea of Nature in the seventeenth century beginning to oppose itself to that of the Middle Ages. The Humanism of the Renaissance had something in common with the thought both of the Christian and pre-Christian eras. In its direct investigation of physical nature, and in its appreciation of the civic constitution of society, it had close affinities with the spirit of Greek and Roman philosophy ; on the other hand, the basis of its conception of things still rested on the traditional theology of the Church. But the framework of this theology was being immensely modified by circumstances, such as the speculation of Copernicus, the discoveries of Columbus, the invention of printing, and the new political system of Europe which arose out of the Reformation. Though, it was true, as Pope says, that Nature, both in itself and in the general constitution of the human mind, shone with " one clear, unchanged, and universal light," yet that light in the most representative conception of the seventeenth century was no longer mainly theological.

I turn to consider the second point, namely, the law of poetical expression, as it is declared in the *Essay on Criticism*:

> Expression is the dress of thought, and still
> Appears more decent as more suitable.
> A vile conceit in pompous words expressed
> Is like a clown in regal purple dressed.

These lines define very happily the law of expression, as embodied in the work of the best classical writers, who, imitating Nature on the polytheistic principle, conceived of her with admirable force and simplicity, as she lay before their eyes. But the passage also indicates very suggestively the nature of the revolution in thought, caused by the transition from mediæval to modern times. In the Middle Ages the centre of man's interest had been shifted from the visible world of sense to the world beyond the grave, and in order to express the theological conception of Nature, the poet had recourse to the forms of Allegory which were almost unused by his Pagan predecessors. Boccaccio, in the *Life of Dante*, to which I have already referred, says: " What is it, but a kind of poetic invention, when in the Scripture Christ is spoken of at one time as a lion, at another as a lamb, sometimes as a worm, at other times as a dragon, at others as a rock, and in many other ways to recite all which would be tedious. What else are the words of the Saviour in the Gospel, but a discourse of what is beyond the senses, which manner of speaking we in more ordinary language call *allegory*." It will be observed that Boccaccio here says almost exactly the same thing as Beatrice, when she explains to Dante the use of allegory: "Thus it is needful to speak to your wit, because from the object of sense alone it apprehends what it afterwards makes worthy of the understanding." In fact, the theological conception of Nature in the Middle Ages is the secret of the abundant use in those ages of the allegorical form of poetry.

The theological habit of thought continued to prevail in Europe long after Catholic unity was destroyed by the Reformation; and theological subjects were in special favour with the Humanist poets of the Reformed persuasion. But in none of these is Nature conceived in the same clear and universal light as she is presented to us in the *Divine Comedy*. Again, in consequence of their theological turn of thought, the allegorical form was extremely popular with the English poets of the first half of the seventeenth century; but no one can fail to observe that this form was employed by them, not as it was by Dante for the conveyance of spiritual truths, but for the purpose of pleasing the imagination with riddles, paradoxes, and far-fetched metaphors. The allegorical form at that period, in fact, became a poetical end in itself. Out of this decadent tendency of the imagination arose the practice of False Wit, so admirably defined by Johnson, who nevertheless failed to trace it to its native source. "Wit, abstracted from its effects upon the hearer, may," he says, "be more rigorously and philosophically considered as a kind of *discordia concors*, a combination of dissimilar images, or discovery of occult resemblances in things apparently unlike." And in this respect Locke contrasts the poetry still agreeable to the taste of his age with the operations of sense, judgment, and reason. "This," he says, "is a way of proceeding quite contrary to metaphor and allusion; wherein for the most part lies the entertainment and pleasantry of wit which strikes so lively on the fancy, and is therefore so acceptable to all people." Aiming persistently at the discovery of subtle resemblances, and the combination of contrary images, the poets of the seventeenth century altogether neglected the necessary basis of all true poetry, the Universal in Nature. Johnson describes with equal happiness and sagacity the unsoundness of their method: "Their attempts were always analytic; they broke every image into fragments, and could no more represent, by their slender conceits and laboured particularities, the prospects of nature, or the scenes of life, than he who dissects a sunbeam with a prism can exhibit the wide effulgence of a summer noon."

Let me illustrate these remarks by some concrete examples of what is called the "metaphysical" poetry of the seventeenth century. First, I will give you a specimen of the neglect of the Universal common in this kind of poetry, and nowhere more characteristically manifested than in Phineas Fletcher's *Purple Island*. The subject of the *Purple Island*, as the author declares, is theological. It professes to describe the State of Man's Nature after the Fall, and the conflict by which he is restored to a State of Grace, a theme, no doubt, of universal interest. The form in which the subject is embodied is allegory. Speaking in the character of a shepherd, the poet expounds to his companions the history and constitution of an island which typifies the body and soul of man; and so far the theological subject, and the allegorical form of the work, place it in the same category of composition as *The Divine Comedy*. But immediately the poet begins to execute his design, it is seen that his poem, unlike Dante's, is wanting altogether in unity of thought and action. What was really attractive to Fletcher in the poetical idea was the opportunity afforded of likening the different parts of the human body to the physical configuration of an island. Five or six cantos of his poem are devoted entirely to anatomy, and the ingenuity with which the particular resemblances are worked out is quite admirable. When, however, this essentially partial conception is expressed, the poetical impulse is exhausted. All that is moral in the subject, all that is organically required for the development of the action, is treated perfunctorily, and since the subject provides no natural exit, the author is obliged to conclude it with a fight between the Prince of the Island and a Dragon, in feeble imitation of Spenser in the first book of *The Faery Queen.*

From this neglect by the metaphysical poets of the Universal in their conceptions springs an essential impropriety in their forms of expression, which may be exemplified from a poem written by Giles Fletcher, brother of Phineas, *Christ's Death and Victory.* Here, too, we have a theological subject, almost identical with *Paradise Regained;* and here, again, there is a complete absence of unity of action. The four cantos of which the poem is composed deal separately with particular themes: The Contest between Divine Justice and Mercy; the Temptation; the Crucifixion and Descent into Hell; the Resurrection and Ascension into Heaven. The poet takes his start from the text of the Bible, but embroiders his narrative with a number of paradoxes, metaphors, classical similes, and strangely coined words, in such a manner as to produce an effect of brilliantly contrasted patchwork. His whole strength is thrown into his particular descriptions, the character of which may be inferred from a few examples; of which the following gives a portrait of the Redeemer evidently modelled on the description of Adonis by Marino:

> His cheeks as snowy apples, soft in wine,
> Had their red roses quencht with lilies white,
> And like to garden strawberries did shine,
> Washt in a bowl of milk, or rosebuds bright,
> Unbosoming their breasts against the light.
>   Here love-sick souls did eat, there drank and made
>   Sweet-smelling posies that could never fade.

The shocking effeminacy of this speaks for itself. Here, again, is a stanza followed by a simile which shows what havoc wit made of taste in the seventeenth century. The poet is describing the holy women returning from the Entombment:

> So home their bodies went to seek repose,
> But at the grave they left their souls behind:
> O who the force of love celestial knows
> That can the claims of nature's self unbind,
> Sending the body home without the mind!
>   Ah, blessed Virgin! what high angel's art
>   Can ever count thy tears or sing thy smart,
> When every nail that pierced his hand did pierce thy heart.

> So Philomel, perched on an aspen sprig,
> Weeps all the night her lost virginity,
> And sings her sad tale to the merry twig,
> That dances at such joyful misery,
> Ne ever lets sweet rest invade her eye,
>   But leaning on a thorn her dainty chest,
>   For fear soft sleep should steal into her breast,
> Expresses in her song grief not to be expressed.

But, after all, the most striking examples of the "false wit" of the seventeenth century are to be found in the lyric poets, of whom Crashaw may be taken as a notable example, since his work attracted the criticism of Pope himself, who calls him a "worse Cowley," and observes of him: "I take this poet to have writ like a gentleman, that is at leisure hours, and more to keep out of idleness than to establish a reputation, so that nothing regular or just can be expected of him. All that regards design, form, fable, which is the soul of poetry, all that concerns exactness or consent of parts, which is the body, will probably be wanting. Only pretty conceptions, fine metaphors, glittering expressions, and something of a neat cast of verse, which are properly the dress, gems, or loose ornaments of poetry, may be found in these verses. . . . His thoughts, one may observe in the main, are pretty; but sometimes far-fetched, and too often strained and stiffened to make them appear the greater. For men are never so apt to think a thing great as when it is odd or wonderful; and inconsiderate authors would rather be admired than understood."

Richard Crashaw was a convert to Roman Catholicism, with a soul possessed by the mystical piety characteristic of women like S. Teresa and Mme. Guyon. But he was also an excellent classical scholar, and he endeavoured to find a vehicle for his devotional feelings in the forms and images invented to express the wholly antagonistic sentiments of Anacreon and Catullus. His poetry is full of sighs, kisses, ardours, languors, and embraces, intended to express the amorous raptures of the soul in a state of religious ecstasy. To every one who can appreciate either the stern devotional style of Dante, or the exquisite taste of Virgil, the combination must appear deplorable. Here, for example, are some lines " On the Glorious Assumption of the Blessed Virgin":

> Hark, she is called! the parting hour is come!
> Take thy farewell, poor world, Heaven must go home.
> A piece of heavenly light, purer and brighter
> Than the chaste stars, whose choice lamps come to light her,

>   While through the crystal orbs, clearer than they,
>   She climbs, and makes a far more milky way.
>   She's called again! hark, how th' immortal Dove
>   Sighs to his silver mate: Rise up, my love,
>   Rise up, my fair, my spotless one,
>   The winter's past, the rain is gone :
>   The spring is come, the flowers appear
>   No sweets, since thou art wanting here.

He sends Mrs. M. R. the present of a Prayer-Book, and writes in it the following description of a soul transported by Divine Love:

>   O fair! O fortunate! O rich! O dear!
>   O happy and thrice happy she,
>   Dear silver-breasted dove,
>   Whoe'er she be,
>   Whose early love
>   With winged vows
>   Makes haste to meet her morning spouse,
>   And close with his immortal kisses ;
>   Happy soul, who never misses
>   To improve that precious hour :
>   And every day
>   Seize her sweet prey,
>   All fresh and fragrant as he rises,
>   Dropping with a balmy shower
>   A delicious dew of spices.

In a hymn to the name and honour of S. Teresa we find the following conception of the Saint's experiences in the moment of death :

>   How kindly will thy gentle heart
>   Kiss the sweetly killing dart :
>   And close in his embraces keep
>   Those delicious wounds that weep
>   Balsam, to heal themselves with thus ;

>   When these thy deaths so numerous
>   Shall all at once die into one,
>   And melt thy soul's sweet mansion:
>   Like a soft lump of incense, basted
>   By too hot a fire, and wasted
>   Into perfuming clouds, so fast
>   Shalt thou exhale to Heaven at last
>   In a dissolving sigh, and then
>   O what? ask not the tongues of men!

One of his favourite themes is the Weeping Magdalene, whose tears he likens to stars, cream on the Milky Way, gold, dew, pearls, and balsam, and nectar for souls on their arrival in Heaven:

>   When some new bright guest
>   Takes up among the stars a room,
>   And Heaven will make a feast,
>   Angels with their bottles come,
>   And draw from these full eyes of thine
>   Their master's water, their own wine.

Angelic tapsters! Poetry of this kind shows us very clearly what had happened to the religious imagination in the seventeenth century. We see the decay of the old austere theological method, applied to the interpretation of Nature by the Catholic Church. We see at the same time the perversion of the time-honoured forms of allegorical poetry, and their mixture with the pseudo-classical forms of the Renaissance, just as in the architecture of the period, and especially in the Churches of the Jesuits, we find fat and florid Cupids, as the only kind of image which can convey to men's minds the idea of angels.

This *discordia concors* of false wit was what Bacon

calls an idol of the Cave, because it had a superficial resemblance to fine art when truly defined, that is to say, "an assemblage of contrary qualities mixed in such proportion that no one part is felt to counteract another." But whereas fine art implies a union of contrary principles actually existing in Nature, false wit aims solely at the combination of dissimilar ideas of the mind without any reference to the actual truth of things. Pope fully understood that this practice was a violation of the law of Fine Art, and that it was the business of the poet to find a foundation for his conceptions in the Universal : hence his definition of True Wit :

> True wit is Nature to advantage dressed,
> What oft was thought but ne'er so well expressed.

The couplet sets forth the constant aim implied in his standard of correctness. His idea of correctness, therefore, may be defined as an imitation of Nature, in which an attempt is made to combine the Catholic spirit of the Middle Ages with the civic and philosophic ideas of the Renaissance, in the forms consecrated by the usage of classic poetry.

In many respects Pope was exceedingly well equipped both by nature and training for the accomplishment of this task. Born of Roman Catholic parents, he had also had a Roman Catholic education; but this strong initial tendency towards mediævalism was counteracted by his early introduction to the best society of London, which was of course emphatically Protestant. His temperament and perceptions naturally caused him to aim at a balance between the two religions, and he describes himself as

> Papist or Protestant, or both between,
> Like good Erasmus in an honest mean.

His age and the society about him impelled his genius in the same direction. The year of his birth, 1688, marked the opening in England of the new constitutional era. Proscribed from taking part in politics, in which, from his association with Swift and Bolingbroke, he was nevertheless deeply interested, he formed for himself a philosophic idea of the English constitution as a whole. While he was familiar with the nature of the controversy between the Roman and Anglican Churches, he had also read Bacon, and Locke, and Newton, to say nothing of the various Deistical writers who put forward their ideas so voluminously in the early part of the eighteenth century. Hence, in his conception of Nature, his imagination may be observed undergoing a development from Catholicism to what may be called a state of Catholic Deism. Listen, for example, to the impassioned lines in which he makes Heloïse address Abelard, and say if they do not breathe the very spirit of S. Benedict or S. Buonaventura:

> Of all affliction taught a lover yet
> 'Tis sure the hardest science to forget.
> How shall I love the sin yet keep the sense?
> How love the offender yet detest the offence?
> How the dear object from the crime remove?
> Or how distinguish penitence from love?
> Unequal task! a passion to resign

For hearts so touched, so pierced, so lost as mine.
Ere such a soul regain its peaceful state,
How often must it love, how often hate!
How often hope, despair, resent, regret,
Conceal, disdain—do all things but forget!
But let heaven seize it, all at once 'tis fired,
Not touched but rapt, not wakened but inspired!
Oh come, oh teach me nature to subdue,
Renounce my love, my life, myself—and you.
Fill my fond heart with God alone, for He
Alone can rival, can succeed to thee.

Or this, which has in it something of the spirit of Crashaw, though without his conceit:

> Vital spark of heavenly flame,
> Quit, O quit, this mortal frame,
> Trembling, hoping, lingering, flying,
> O the pain, the bliss of dying!
>   Cease, fond Nature, cease thy strife!
>   And let me languish into life.
>
> Hark they whisper: Angels say,
> Sister spirit, come away.
> What is this absorbs me quite,
> Heals my senses, steals my sight,
>   Drowns my spirit, draws my breath?
>   Tell me, my soul, can this be Death?
>
> The world recedes; it disappears!
> Heaven opens on my eyes! my ears
>   With sounds seraphic ring:
> Lend, lend your wings! I mount! I fly!
> O Grave, where is thy victory?
>   O Death! where is thy sting?

Compare this glowing enthusiasm with the Deistic rationalism of the address to the Creator in the Universal Prayer:

> Father of all! in every age,
> In every clime adored
> By saint, by savage, and by sage,
> Jehovah, Jove, or Lord.
>
> Thou first great Cause, least understood,
> Who all my sense confined,
> To know but this, that Thou art good
> And that myself am blind!

What a contrast! And yet both the youthful and the mature conceptions have one thing in common, the idea of Nature, of the Universal, apprehended by feeling and instinct in the one case, arrived at by an effort of Reason in the other. The latter perception expresses itself in the note of triumph animating the vigorous concluding lines of the *Essay on Man*, in which the poet defines his idea of Poetry, and, addressing Bolingbroke, declares:

> That urged by thee I turned the tuneful art
> From sounds to things, from fancy to the heart;
> For wit's false mirror held up nature's light;
> Showed erring pride whatever is is right;
> That reason, passion, answer one great aim;
> That true self-love and social are the same;
> That virtue only makes our lives below,
> And all our knowledge is ourselves to know.

You may say, How limited an idea of Nature, of the Universal, is this, compared with Dante's idea of the Universe as presented in *The Divine Comedy!* and you will say it justly. Still, it is fair to remember, in the first place, that this restriction of knowledge to self-knowledge is only the completion of a tendency of thought which reveals itself in *Paradise*

Lost, where, as I pointed out in my last lecture, the Archangel Raphael exhorts Adam:

> Be lowly wise,
> Think only what concerns thee and thy being,
> Dream not of other worlds.

And, in the second place, the just standard of comparison is not so much Pope's idea of Nature measured by Dante's, as Pope's contrasted with the False Wit of the poets of the seventeenth century, Phineas and Giles Fletcher, Donne, Crashaw, Quarles, and Cowley. Compared with any of these — for they had all of them given over the attempt to conceive Nature poetically as a whole — the view of Nature presented in the *Essay on Man* appears simple, harmonious, majestic. Moreover, it is the idea of Pope's age; it reflects the universal tendency of thought working in England and France during the seventeenth and eighteenth centuries, the movement, that is to say, of experimental and inductive philosophy, started by Bacon and carried on from him through Hobbes to Locke, and from Locke to Bolingbroke and Hume. That is the meaning of Pope's boast that he

> Turned the tuneful art
> From sounds to things, from fancy to the heart.

And that, too, explains why, by an inevitable inward movement, Pope's genius changed from romantic themes of pure fancy, like his *Pastorals*, to the moral, satiric, and didactic vein characteristic of his work in his later years.

Two main features distinguish Pope's conception of the Universal in Nature from that of poets like Milton and Chaucer. The first is the almost total elimination of the theological element, and the antagonism of the poet to the scholastic way of thinking—tendencies of reasoning which are reflected in passages like the following :

> For forms of faith let graceless zealots fight ;
> He can't be wrong whose life is in the right.
>
> Scotists and Thomists now in peace remain,
> Amidst their kindred cobwebs in Duck Lane.
>
> A second deluge learning thus o'errun,
> And the Monks finished what the Goths begun.
>
> Slave to no sect, who takes no private road,
> But looks through Nature up to Nature's God.

To sum up the character of Pope's idea of the Universal on the religious side : it is an attempt to reconcile the modern spirit with the spirit of antiquity, by eliminating the spirit of the Middle Ages.

The second feature is that, on the secular side, Pope's tendency is to harmonise the civic spirit of the Greeks and Romans with the national spirit of modern Europe by striking out the feudal element. The spirit of feudal chivalry, which, in the thirteenth century, found its abode in thousands of castles over the whole of Europe, and which in the sixteenth century concentrated itself in the Courts of powerful Monarchs, was, in the seventeenth century, languishing in the last stages of decay. The poetical forms, in which this spirit revealed itself to the imagination, had passed through corresponding stages of development, from the lyrics of the Troubadours and the romances of the Trouvères to the *Sonnets* of Petrarch, and thence to the *Arcadias* of Sannazaro and Sidney, until, in the seventeenth century, the approaching dissolution of chivalrous romance is shown in the *Grand Cyrus* of Mdlle. de Scudéry and in the *Mistress* of Cowley. Still, even in that late age, the old fire of poetry, animated by the principles of Love, Honour, and Loyalty, breaks through the smoke of conceit and paradox in some of the lyrics of the English cavaliers, the last representatives of the dying feudal order, as in Lovelace's lines :

> Yet this inconstancy is such
>   As you too shall adore :
> I could not love thee, dear, so much
>   Loved I not honour more.

Or in Montrose's charming verses :

> My dear, my only love, I pray
>   That little world of thee
> Be governed by no other sway
>   But purest Monarchy.
> For if confusion have a part,
>   Which virtuous souls abhor,
> And call a synod in thy heart,
>   I'll never love thee more.

Of this element of Romance there is no trace in the mature poetry of Pope; into his conception of society there enters neither the Petrarcan tradition of chivalrous love, continued through more than three centuries of sonnet-writers, nor the legendary spirit of the tales of Arthur and Charlemagne, which impressed itself so strongly on the imagination of Milton. In place of it reigns the genius of Satire, whether it be the satire of social manners, embodied in the exquisite mock-heroic style of the *Rape of the Lock*, or the satire of party politics and personal conflict, reflected in the didactic energy of the *Epistle to Arbuthnot*, the *Moral Essays*, and the *Imitations of Horace*. In this respect, too, Pope was the child of his age. The day of Sidney and Essex, even of Lovelace and Montrose, of the mediæval knight and courtier, with his refinements, his graces, and his caste sentiments, had passed; the day of Walpole and Pulteney and Bolingbroke and Carteret, of clubs and coffee-houses, had supervened; the aristocracy of England were no longer the followers of a semi-absolute Monarch; they were the leaders of a ruling Parliament.

As the elements of Theology and Chivalry vanished out of Pope's conception of Nature and Society, so did the form of Allegory disappear from his critical standard of expression. For allegory, in his judgment, had come to be identical with the form of False Wit, with that straining after remote and paradoxical ideas, and that hunt for unheard-of images and metaphors, which is the characteristic note of the typical poet of the seventeenth century. Correctness, on the other hand, which was Pope's constant aim, implies the rejection of all that is weak, superfluous, and irrelevant, in the conception of a subject viewed as an organic whole, together with the selection of the words best adapted for the clear conveyance of thought in a metrical form. As he himself put it in one of his *Imitations of Horace:*

> But how severely with themselves proceed
> The men who write such verse as we can read!
> Their own strict judges not a word they spare,
> That wants or force or light or weight or care.
> Howe'er unwillingly it quits its place,
> Nay, though at Court (perhaps) it may find grace;
> Such they'll degrade, and sometimes in its stead
> In downright charity revive the dead.
>
> . . . . . .
>
> Prune the luxuriant, the uncouth refine,
> But show no mercy to an empty line;
> Then polish all with so much life and ease,
> You think 'tis Nature and a knack to please.
> "But ease in writing comes from art not chance,
> As those move easiest who have learned to dance."

I think we are now in a position to determine both the extent of the service rendered by Pope to the art of English poetry and the limitations of his genius. His great, his pre-eminent merit is his clear declaration, his careful observance, of the paramount law of Poetry, the Imitation of the Universal. Assuming as a first principle of taste, that Fine Art lies in the harmonious reconciliation of contrary qualities, it must be acknowledged that Pope found out the way of harmonising the civic ideas of the Greeks and Romans, and the classical forms of expression, with the national English spirit of the eighteenth century, and with the genius of the then fully developed English language. This was a great achievement;

but we have to recognise at the same time that, in order to obtain his clear conception of the Universal, he was obliged to narrow and retrench his idea of the second great law of Fine Art, the Law of National Character.

As I said in my lecture on Chaucer, the English national character is made up of an extraordinary mixture of elements, and our highest poetry is a reflection of all these combined qualities. It reflects the Christian Religion, as it is formulated and defined in Mediæval Theology; it reflects the traditions of ancient art, in the full and perfect forms recovered for us by the Renaissance; and lastly, it reflects the movement of our national life and history made up by the fusion of different races and languages. Such is the mixed character of the poetry of Chaucer, of Shakespeare, of Milton, which may be described as theological, feudal, classical, and national; whereas, on the other hand, from the poetry of Pope the theological and feudal elements of our historic life are excluded. His poetry is therefore necessarily less elevated, and more restricted in its scope than that of his greatest predecessors; it may be added that it does not conform so completely as their's to Sir Joshua Reynolds's definition of Fine Art. Pope himself felt this and expressed the idea forcibly in a letter to Swift. He says: " My understanding indeed, such as it is, is extended rather than diminished; I see things more in the whole, more consistent, and more clearly deduced from, and related to, each other. But what I gain on the side of philosophy, I lose on the side of poetry; the flowers are gone when the fruits begin to ripen, and the fruit perhaps will never ripen perfectly." So, too, he puts it in the *Epistle to Arbuthnot*, when, speaking of the poetry of his youth, he says:

> Soft were my numbers; who could take offence,
> While pure Description held the place of sense?
> Like gentle Fanny's was my flowery theme,
> A painted mistress or a purling stream.

Following the inevitable bent of his genius and his time, he subordinated the play of imagination to the severity of reason and judgment, more than was consistent with the highest requirements of English Fine Art. A poem, in which the element of Fancy is so much subdued as it is in the *Essay on Man*, cannot be ranked, as an imitation of Nature, in the same class as *Paradise Lost;* nor can compositions, which exclude so completely the sentiments connected with romance and pastoralism as the *Moral Essays*, or which restrict the idea of society so rigidly to the representation of town life as the *Imitations of Horace*, be regarded as affording so complete a reflection of English feudal, rural, and domestic character as *The Canterbury Tales* or the *Allegro* and *Penseroso*.

The same kind of criticism must be passed on Pope's declaration of the law of poetical expression, as defined in his term Correctness. His idea of correctness, in so far as it consists in imitating the *spirit* of the great classical authors, is sound, and so is the principle which he lays down in the *Essay on Criticism*:

> Those Rules of old discovered, not devised,
> Are Nature still but Nature methodised;
> Nature, like Liberty, is but restrained
> By the same laws which first herself ordained.

And when he applies this principle of imitating the classics by the instinctive light of his genius, as he does in the *Epistle to Arbuthnot*, nothing can be more truly English, natural, and correct, than the style which results from it. But an excessive reverence for the classics often led him into formal imitation, which, judged by the Law of English Character in Poetry, was essentially incorrect. His attitude towards the Latin and Greek poets sometimes seems almost servile:

> Hail, Bards triumphant! born in happier days;
> Immortal heirs of universal praise.
> Whose honours with increase of ages grow,
> As streams roll down, enlarging as they flow;
> Nations unborn your mighty names shall sound,
> And worlds applaud that must not yet be found!
> O may some spark of your celestial fire
> The last, the meanest of your sons inspire
> (That on weak wings from far pursues your flights,
> Glows while he reads, but trembles as he writes),
> To teach vain wits a science little known,
> T' admire superior sense, and doubt their own!

Formal imitation of the classics, which produces the manner of writing found in Pope's *Pastorals* or his *Messiah*, cannot be said to be the following of Nature.

To sum up what has been said: Pope's conception of the law of taste determines his place in English poetry. There are certain modern critics who deny altogether his title to be ranked as a classic English poet. This is a judgment as bigoted as it is absurd. The pleasure with which his poetry is read by all who can appreciate art is a proof of the soundness of his own conception of the Universal in Nature. Pope is, and will remain, one of the great English classics. But not less unreasonable is it to proclaim him, as Matthew Arnold does, a classic not of our poetry but our prose; for this would imply that he and Dryden, whom Matthew Arnold couples with him, had made an artistic mistake in employing the metrical form of expression. Pope is one of the great English poets; howbeit, as the author of the Book of Samuel says of certain of David's mighty men, he attains not to the rank of the first three. He did not reflect to the same extent as Chaucer, Shakespeare, and Milton, *all* those complex principles which make up the Christian idea of the Universal in Nature, or *all* that fusion of tastes and tendencies which constitutes the English character. Hence he was not qualified to succeed in the highest walks of poetry, the epic and the dramatic: the inevitable development of his genius, directed by the character of his age, helped to suppress the lyrical and romantic vein in his imagination. On the other hand, in the ethical, the satiric, the didactic, in a word, the more familiar departments of poetry, he is supreme, and within this range his verse is deserving of the closest study, on account alike of the clear conception of Nature which it embodies, and of the severe self-judgment — so opposed to the indolence, the inaccuracy, and the obscurity of modern methods—with which he strives to give to every thought the highest polish of correct expression.

IX

BYRON AND TENNYSON

MACAULAY gives it as his opinion, in his *Essay on Milton*, that as civilisation advances poetry almost necessarily declines. This proposition seems to contain the misstatement of an important truth. As Macaulay states it, it is certainly not true, for the *Æneid*, *The Divine Comedy*, and *Paradise Lost*, were all produced at an advanced epoch of civilisation in their different communities. Nevertheless, it is a historical fact that, after a certain point of civilisation is reached, poems of this class cease to be produced; and further, we have complaints from late poets, such as Wordsworth, Byron, and Tennyson, that social circumstances are unfavourable to their art.

What, then, shall we say as to the truth of the matter? This, I think. The advance of civilisation necessarily involves a conflict between the principles of liberty and authority, because it necessitates, on the one hand, the strengthening of the central institutions on which the life of the community depends, and, on the other, the growth of a self-consciousness in each individual, which is to some extent adverse to the claims of society. A state is free and great in proportion as it succeeds in reconciling liberty with authority. This antagonism in the life of society is of course reflected in the life of Art, so that, whereas poetry is defined by Aristotle to be the imitation of the Universal in Nature, there is a strong tendency in late poetry to be transformed into the imitation of self-consciousness in the soul of the individual. When the authority of society is paramount, when, by virtue of a common belief, men think together about the principles of right and wrong, good and evil, then the poet can readily use the drama to imitate, before an audience, in the persons of actors, the universal idea of the conflict always proceeding in human nature. When, however, the right of the individual to dissent from the established creeds of society has been fully recognised, history seems to show that epic and dramatic poetry become inadequate forms of imitation. Thus we have no record of the production of any really great dramas on the Attic stage after the death of Socrates; nor has any great epic or dramatic poem been written in England since the establishment of the Parliamentary *régime* in 1688. Lyric poetry, on the contrary, may flourish, and has flourished, in the later stages of society, because this is a form of the art better adapted than the others for the expression of individual ideas. Hence Macaulay's proposition, if properly amended, may stand, that when society reaches the stage at which self-consciousness is widely diffused, the epic, dramatic, and it may be added the didactic, forms of poetry decline, and where poetry survives as an art, men mainly seek to express their ideas of Nature in the lyric form.

The series of lectures which I have had the honour of delivering to you have been an illustration of this general truth. I have shown that the course of modern European civilisation has been evolved out of the conflict between several distinct and contrary tendencies; the tradition of Art and letters derived from pre-Christian times, the formulated teaching of the Catholic Church, and the customs and institutions of the barbarous conquerors of the Roman Empire. From this struggle of forces have arisen those varying ideas of Nature which philosophers in successive ages have striven to define and poets to imitate, and according as one principle or another among them has gained the mastery, so has the balance varied in men's minds between social authority and individual liberty. But however the social equilibrium may have been determined, I have not hitherto passed in my lectures beyond the consideration of stages of Art, in which the universal idea of Nature is imitated in one of the more external forms—epic, dramatic, or didactic. We have seen the principles of liberty and authority harmonised by the poets in such ideal reflections of society as *The Divine Comedy*, *The Canterbury Tales*, the plays of Shakespeare, *Paradise Lost*, the *Moral Essays* of Pope; but in each and all of these, even in the last, the general and external imitation of men and things prevails over the self-conscious exhibition of the individual soul. We have now reached an epoch in which the centrifugal movement of the individual mind away from the authoritative beliefs of society makes itself apparent by a wide expression of self-consciousness in art. The poet begins to turn his gaze inward; he shifts the sphere of observation from the life and character of society to the seclusion of his own mind. As a natural consequence, during the period extending from the French Revolution to our own day, the lyrical form of poetry has prevailed; the last hundred years have been the age of the Odes on Immortality, the Skylark, and the Nightingale, the age of *In Memoriam*. And what is of main interest in relation to law in taste is to observe, first the indirect influence of society in imposing its own limitations and character on the ideas of the individual poet, and next the nature of the ideal form in which the poet attempts to give the appearance of universality to his own self-consciousness.

But let me, to begin with, illustrate what the self-conscious spirit in art is, by showing it, perhaps in its earliest, certainly in its most characteristic, shape, at the opening of Rousseau's *Confessions:* " I form," says Rousseau, " an enterprise which has had no precedent and will have no imitators. I wish to show my fellows a man in all the truth of Nature, and this man myself and nobody else. I feel my heart and I know men. I am not like any of those whom I have seen : I venture to believe that I have not been made like anybody else in existence. If I am not better than they are, at least I am something different. Whether Nature has done well or ill in breaking the mould in which she has cast me may be decided after reading me. Let the last trumpet sound when it will, I shall come with this book in my hand to present myself before the Sovereign Judge. I shall say boldly: Here is what I have done, and what I have thought, and what I was. I have told the good and the evil with the same frankness. I have kept back nothing bad: I have added nothing good; and if I have happened to employ some indifferent ornament, this has been only to fill up a void occasioned by want of memory. I may have supposed true what I knew might be so, never what I knew to be false. I have shown myself such as I was, good, generous, sublime, when I have been so; I have unveiled my inward nature as thou thyself, Eternal Being, hast seen it. Gather about me the innumerable crowd of my fellows; let them hear my confessions; let them blush for my unworthiness; let them bewail my sufferings. Let each of them in turn lay bare his heart at the foot of Thy throne with the same sincerity, and then let one of them say if he dare: 'I was better than this man.'"

This unqualified assertion of the rights of the individual conscience is indeed only the extension of a spiritual movement which may be traced back to the Renaissance. Shakespeare says in one of his *Sonnets:*

> For why should others' false adulterate eyes
> Give salutation to my sportive blood?
> Or on my frailties why are frailer spies,

> Which in their wills count bad what I think good?
> No, I am that I am, and they that level
> At my abuses reckon up their own:
> I may be straight, though they themselves be bevel;
> By their rank thoughts my deeds must not be shown;
> > Unless this general evil they maintain,
> > All men are bad, and in their badness reign.

But evidently self-consciousness must have become widely diffused in European society since Shakespeare's time, for you will observe that Rousseau goes very near relying on the principle against which Shakespeare protests: "All men are bad, and in their badness reign." He says frankly: "I am a poor, mean, pitiful, fellow, but I know that there is something interesting to the world in my poverty, meanness, and pitifulness; and I am sure that if I publish my weaknesses you, my neighbours, who are really no better than myself, will be fascinated with the picture I shall show you. This condition of mind is so universal that, although I am myself, and nobody is like me, still I may confess myself to mankind without any fear of forfeiting their sympathy and esteem."

As Rousseau's *Confessions* furnish the most striking, if not the earliest, evidence of the spread of self-consciousness in European society, so are his novels the first examples of the effects of that self-consciousness on imitative art. Like all men of ardent imagination, Rousseau was anxious to universalise his own ideas, but while the creative artists who preceded him sought to base their imitation of Nature on the actions and passions of men in civil society, Rousseau sought for his materials in his own breast. Over and over again he tells us in his *Confessions* that such and such incidents in *La Nouvelle Heloïse* and *Emile* are ideal reflections of his individual experience, but since he found the spectacle of his own passions and sentiments a drama too bare of incident for the demands of imagination, he endeavoured to extend it by his descriptions of external nature, for the sake not of imitating objects in themselves, but of showing them in their relation to the moods of the mind. As almost all imaginative writers since Rousseau have followed in his footsteps, he may fairly be regarded as the founder of the self-conscious, or romantic, mode of imitation.

The cause of this mood of mind, with the artistic practice which resulted from it, was the recoil from the system of Absolutism, which, during the eighteenth century, prevailed over the whole continent of Europe. The idea of Nature then almost universally established had been the work of a small circle of scholars and philosophers revolving about the different European courts, and since all the avenues to fortune were in the power of the governing few, organised society was well content with Leibnitz's creed of optimism, with Boileau's code of taste, and with the general conclusion of Pope's *Essay on Man*, "Whatever is is right." On the other hand, the governed many, excluded from all the privileges of political liberty, and oppressed with the spectacle of widespread misery among the masses of the people, were much more inclined to think,

"Whatever is is wrong." The men of letters, therefore, who represented this portion of the people, bending their imagination inward, naturally framed abstract ideas of society apart from the springs of political action. Certain it is that *Le Contrat Social* was the product of the most characteristic genius of the reign of Louis XV. in France, and that *La Nouvelle Heloïse*, followed in the next generation by *The Sorrows of Werther*, prepared the way for the final development of French and German Romanticism.

In England the case was different. There at least the *régime* of constitutional liberty was firmly established, and the spectacle of its exercise both in the sphere of politics and letters had influenced profoundly the Continental imagination. In England the spirit of compromise reigned supreme. The nation had grown up in the midst of Catholic and Feudal institutions, without suffering any check to its internal development. Humanism, established in the Universities by the efforts of the first scholars of the Renaissance, while it had enlarged and liberalised the old ways of scholastic thinking, had also helped to mitigate the moral rigidity of the Calvinistic Reformers. The Crown, without being deprived of its prerogative, was checked in the exercise of it by Parliament.

Nevertheless, this social and intellectual balance had not been attained without sacrifices, mainly at the expense of the mediæval order of things, and many individuals, who were in sympathy with that order, felt the restrictions in the idea of Nature and Society, imposed upon them alike by the political system of Walpole and by the poetical system of Pope. Their imaginations, dissatisfied with the ideals of national action, were forced into secret and subterranean channels. Many such underground streams of thought may be observed flowing in the English art and literature of the eighteenth century, quite apart from the visible river of national life, so deeply tinged with the colours of Deism, Materialism, Patriotism, and Classicalism. We see there the stream of Mysticism, represented equally in such a book as William Law's *Serious Call to a Devout Life*, and at a later date in the painting and poetry of Blake; the stream of Methodism manifesting itself in the preaching of the Wesleys and the poetry of Cowper; the stream of Romanticism obscurely passing from the French pastoral romance of the seventeenth century into the sentimental novels of Richardson, and thence again crossing to the Continent to inspire the imagination of Rousseau.

Swelled by all these different tributaries, there was in England, on the eve of the French Revolution, a great volume of romantic self-consciousness, running counter to the main stream of national taste, as we see it reflected in a periodical like the *Anti-Jacobin*, which, on one side, expresses the political conservatism of Pitt, and, on the other, the literary conservatism of Pope, Johnson, and Gifford. When the spiritual dykes burst, the waters of self-consciousness rushed forth in a torrent of lyric verse, of which the original impulse has continued to be felt for more than a hundred years.

They made for themselves two distinct channels—one, containing the active or, as it may be called, political spirit of self-consciousness, and seeking an outlet in a revolt against the creeds, customs, and institutions of society, the other, the reflective spirit which restricts itself to an analysis of the feelings and passions of the mind; both found an outward expression in ideal forms of art. The former movement, which includes the poetry of Shelley, may be studied in the work of Byron; the latter, embracing the genius both of Wordsworth and Coleridge, has its latest, and in many respects its most comprehensive, expression in the works of Tennyson.

Byron is the most self-conscious figure in the whole history of poetry; and as the operations of Rousseau's self-consciousness can best be observed in his *Confessions*, so is the key to Byron's self-consciousness furnished by his earliest volume, *Hours of Idleness*. Here he may be seen, contemplating his inward image and exhibiting himself to mankind, precisely as if he were some object in external nature. Though the book is announced as the work of " a minor," the writer moralises upon himself as an exhausted votary of pleasure. In an address to one of his acquaintance he speaks of himself as " a Timon of 19." He appears before the mirror of his imagination, sometimes as the impoverished lord of a half-ruined Abbey, sometimes as the last of a long line of wicked ancestry, or again, as the heart-broken lover of one whom marriage with a rival has separated from him for ever. Already his passion for solitary Nature and his antagonism to society, afterwards so powerfully expressed in the third canto of *Childe Harold*, is revealed in the germ, nor, in view of his history, is it possible to read without wonder the following lines, the work of a boy of nineteen:

> Few are my years, and yet I feel
>   The world was ne'er designed for me:
> Ah! why do darkening shades conceal
>   The hour when man must cease to be?
> Once I beheld a splendid dream,
>   A visionary scene of bliss.
> Truth! wherefore did thy hated beam
>   Awake me to a world like this?
>
> I loved—but those I loved are gone,
>   Had friends—my early friends are fled,
> How cheerless feels the heart alone,
>   When all its former hopes are dead!
> Though gay companions o'er the bowl
>   Dispel awhile the sense of ill;
> Though pleasure stirs the maddening soul,
>   The heart, the heart is lonely still.
>
> . . . . .
>
> Fain would I fly the haunts of men;
>   I seek to shun, not hate, mankind;
> My breast requires the sullen glen,
>   Whose gloom may suit a darkened mind.
> Oh, that to me the wings were given,
>   Which bear the turtle to her nest!
> Then would I cleave the vault of Heaven,
>   To flee away, and be at rest.

Truly, says the Scripture, "The heart is deceitful above all things, who can know it?" Little did Byron think, when he breathed, in all sincerity, his sentimental and monastic aspirations for the wings of a dove, that, within a year, he would be attacking in *English Bards and Scotch Reviewers*, the most famous and powerful names in the literature of the time; that his request for the sullen glen whose gloom might suit a darkened mind was to be followed by years of excitement, in which the creator of *Conrad* and *Cain* and *Sardanapalus* was to impersonate for the moment the spirit of all that was brilliant and revolutionary in the society about him. The truth is that Byron's nature was far too ardent and energetic to confine itself, like Rousseau, to the cloister of his own thought; he needed to project his imagination into action, whether as the leader of a national rising in Greece or as the satirist of society in England. He thirsted for distinction, and sought it sometimes in swimming, boxing, and even in cricket, sometimes in epic, dramatic, and satiric verse; nor can anything be more instructive to the critic than to observe the action and reaction between the self-consciousness of his powerful genius and the immutable necessities of these, the more external forms of the art of poetry.

Viewed strictly on their epic and dramatic side, the romantic tales and tragedies of Byron are wanting in most of the qualities which such compositions demand. This is a deficiency which, as I have said, is common to all late poets. The great minstrel, the born dramatist, must be above all things a creator. It is his business to produce what Aristotle calls τὸ πιθανόν, the effect of ideal probability, to invent a visionary world in which his own imagination and that of his audience can breathe freely outside themselves, to people it with beings unlike anything in actual experience, and yet capable of raising in the minds of his hearers images of men and women, expressing themselves in sentiments and diction recalling those of real life. Should any appearance of mechanism or artifice raise the suspicion that these actors are the lifeless puppets of the poet's brain, a sense of unreality intrudes on the sacred ground, and the illusion vanishes. For the creation of the illusion a groundwork of legend or history seems almost necessary, because, as Aristotle says, the mind most readily believes in things which are reported to have happened; certain it is that neither the Greek dramatists nor Shakespeare invented the matter of their dramas. But in the late days of poetry it is difficult to find legendary matter on which the imagination can work sympathetically; hence the creative instinct turns to the prose romance in preference to poetry, and probably the only example of an ancient legend being conceived by a self-conscious poet with unerring instinct, and expressed with perfect propriety, is Goethe's *Faust*.

But while all self-conscious art is liable to these drawbacks, Byron's poetry suffers from them in a more than ordinary degree. His method of composing a drama, for example, is entirely undramatic. He never selects his action for its interest as a whole, but because it gives him an opportunity for the exhibition of certain special characters, sentiments, and descriptions, a method which is of course an inversion of the method of Sophocles or Shakespeare. Nothing can be more absurd than the plot of *Manfred* or *The Deformed Transformed*; nothing more bare of dramatic situation than *The Two Foscari* or *Sardanapalus*. Of the arts of complication, change of fortune, and *dénouement*, necessary to the construction of a good play or a good story, Byron was either ignorant or careless, as must be evident to every reader of *Lara* or *The Corsair*. Nor are these defects of ideal structure atoned for by the interest and sympathy excited by the characters represented. We do not think of Byron's *dramatis personae* as we do of Ulysses, or Thersites, or Shylock, or Meg Merrilies, that is to say, as beings who have an ideal existence of their own; Cain, and Manfred, and Lara, and Conrad, are felt to be nothing but externalised reflections of the poet himself.

But when we turn from the epic and dramatic forms of Byron to the lyrical impulse out of which they spring, the whole aspect of the question changes. We see then that the characteristics of his poetry are the result of an effort to find what is universal in nature in his own self-consciousness, and to bring himself into touch with society by clothing his self-consciousness in an external shape. The epic form of verse is employed by him, because it gives him an opportunity of describing his own moods and those appearances of inanimate Nature which are akin to them; the drama enables him to multiply himself in a variety of *dramatis personae*, and by means of frequent soliloquy; in the satire, especially the personal form of satire, developed by Pope, he can

2 D

indulge fully his spleen against the established order of society. Hence we are necessarily brought to judge of his work from the starting-point fixed by Rousseau, and setting aside the question whether any man has a right to confess himself to the reader without reference to the supreme authority of moral law, the points for the critic to decide are, first, whether the poetry of Byron raises in the mind the idea of the Universal, and secondly, whether the form of his expression is an adequate vehicle for communicating this idea to the world.

As to the first question there can be but one answer. Byron, the most self-conscious, the most individual, of English poets, is also, in a sense, the most representative of all English poets since Shakespeare. Whatever there is in human nature of consciousness of good and evil, of rebellion against the law and order of the universe, of discontent with the standards of society, seems to have concentrated itself in the mind of this child of genius, convulsed by the violence of his own passions, morbidly sensitive to a single physical defect, haunted by the fear of madness and the sense of inherited crime, always revolving in his heart the real or imaginary injuries he had suffered from mankind. The meeting of so many outward and inward forces in Byron's imagination produced in him two typical moods, both of which had been expressed long before in dramatic and epic poetry. One was the intellectual ennui of Hamlet: " What a piece of work is a man ! How noble in reason ! how infinite in faculties ! in form and moving how express and admirable! in action how like an angel! in apprehension how like a god! the beauty of the world! the paragon of animals! And yet to me, what is this quintessence of dust? Man delights not me; no, nor woman neither, though by your smiling you seem to say so."

Under the influence of Rousseau, the discontent with self and society, thus expressed in the character of Hamlet, grew into the feeling for external Nature, so widely experienced in the modern mind, which Byron expresses in *Childe Harold:*

> I live not in myself, but I become
> Portion of that around me; and to me
> High mountains are a feeling, but the hum
> Of human cities torture : I can see
> Nothing to loathe in nature, save to be
> A link reluctant in a fleshly chain,
> Class'd among creatures, when the soul can flee,
> And with the sky, the peak, the heaving plain
> Of ocean, or the stars, mingle, and not in vain.
>
> . . . . .
>
> Are not the mountains, waves, and skies a part
> Of me and of my soul, as I of them?
> Is not the love of these deep in my heart
> With a pure passion? should I not contemn
> All objects, if compared with these? and stem
> A tide of suffering, rather than forgo
> Such feelings for the hard and worldly phlegm
> Of those whose eyes are only turn'd below,
> Gazing upon the ground, with thoughts which dare not
> glow?

Here is the sentimental mood sketched in *Hours of Idleness*, developed to sublime intensity. But just as *Hours of Idleness* was followed by *English Bards and Scotch Reviewers*, so, in *Don Juan*, Byron almost immediately abandons the monastic impulse, embodied in *Childe Harold*, for his still more characteristic *rôle* of reckless defiance, and, in his inflexible opposition to all forms of established authority, seems to appropriate the attitude of him whom Dryden called the hero of *Paradise Lost* and Johnson the first of the Whigs:

> All is not lost; the unconquerable will,
> And study of revenge, immortal hate,
> And courage never to submit or yield,
> And what is else not to be overcome.

Who does not hear the accents of the lost Archangel in this stanza of *Don Juan?*

> And I will war, at least in words, and—should
>   My chance so happen—deeds, with all who war
> With Thought; and of Thought's foes by far most rude,
>   Tyrants and sycophants have been and are.
> I know not who may conquer: if I could
>   Have such a prescience, it should be no bar
> To this my plain, sworn, downright, detestation
> Of every despotism in every nation.

If any proof were needed of the universal character of Byron's conception, it would be found in the splendid natural force of his expression. His verse may be of course blamed, and justly, for defects of execution, for tawdriness, slovenliness, negligence, and obscurity; but, when all is said, no poet equals him in the irresistible power with which he moulds ideal forms to embody inward emotions. His genius is above all things lyrical; as I have said, he uses epic, dramatic, and satiric forms only for the sake of self-expression; but the ease and vigour with which he adapts each in turn to his purpose are wonderful. He is at home in every kind of metre. He employs the Spenser stanza for analysis of feeling and descriptions of scenery, turns the classic heroic couplet into a vehicle for the swift rush of romantic passion, seizes on the soliloquy and blank verse of the drama, as the mirror to reflect his feeling for nature and his loathing for the world, and transforms the light mock-heroic of the Italian *ottava rima* into savage satire on English society. His best work is done when he can assume a point of vantage or a character which allows him to comment on himself and mankind, whether this be contemplative, as in *Childe Harold*, or cynical, as in *Don Juan*, and he himself is quite aware of the characteristic tendency of his genius.

> If I have any fault it is digression,
> Leaving my people to proceed alone,
> While I soliloquise beyond expression.

As a rule self-consciousness and soliloquy lead to affectation; but it was not so with Byron, whose modes of expression are absolutely natural. Theatrical as his thought often is, he was saved from the worst of all literary vices, partly by the immense force of his genius, partly by the excellence of his literary judgment, and partly also by his knowledge of social conventions and language. Whether his judgments of the world and himself are sound or not, they are at least sincere, and they are delivered with the frank defiance of one who is confident of having taken the measure of his audience. In this respect his style differs from that of most of his contemporaries, particularly the Lake School, who contended against the world without having mixed in it, thus drawing from Byron a criticism which was not altogether unjust:

> You—gentlemen! by dint of long seclusion
> From better company, have kept your own
> At Keswick, and through still continued fusion
> Of one another's minds, at last are grown
> To deem, as a most logical conclusion,
> That Poesy has wreaths for you alone.

Completely versed in the conditions of the eighteenth century style, Byron was able to harmonise it with the opposite tendencies and characteristics of his own age, and his verse admirably illustrates our postulate of English Fine Art, namely, the fusion of contrary qualities. Macaulay says of him with truth: " He was the man of the last thirteen years of the eighteenth century, and of the first twenty-three years of the nineteenth century. He belonged half to the old and half to the new school of poetry. His personal taste led him to the former; his thirst for praise to the latter; his talents were equally suited to both. His fame was a common ground on which the zealots of both sides, Gifford, for example, and Shelley, might meet. He was the representative not of either literary party, but of both at once, and of their conflict, and of the victory by which that conflict was terminated. His poetry fills and measures the whole of the vast interval through which our literature has passed since the time of Johnson. It touches the *Essay on Man* at the one extremity and *The Excursion* at the other."

Tennyson, not much more than twenty years younger than Byron, naturally fell to some extent under the same poetic influences, and his earliest published work which appeared in the little volume called *Poems by Two Brothers* (1827) is suffused with the colours of the Byronic after-glow. In the volume of his poems printed in 1830 appeared a composition of some length (since suppressed) entitled "Supposed Confessions of a Second-rate Sensitive Mind not at unity itself," full of that morbid introspective spirit, generated by "the self-torturing sophist wild Rousseau," which breathes through *Hours of Idleness*. This vein of self-analysis is, at a somewhat later date, worked out with more art in *The Two Voices*, and, not unnaturally, it is accompanied in *Locksley Hall* by an anti-social and misanthropic mood, almost as gloomy as Byron's own :

> Cursed be the social wants that sin against the strength of youth !
> Cursed be the social lies that warp us from the living truth !
>
> Cursed be the sickly forms that err from honest Nature's rule !
> Cursed be the gold that gilds the straiten'd forehead of the fool !

The misanthropic view of Nature and Society is carried still further in *Maud :*

> I keep but a man and a maid, ever ready to slander and steal ;
> I know it, and smile a hard-set smile, like a stoic, or like
> A wiser epicurean, and let the world have its way :
> For nature is one with rapine, a harm no preacher can heal ;

> The Mayfly is torn by the swallow, the sparrow spear'd by the shrike,
> And the whole little wood where I sit is a world of plunder and prey.

From the soliloquising habit of Byron, too, Tennyson took the form of lyrical monologue in character, in which he is fond of embodying his self-conscious moods. But when his modes of conception and expression are more closely compared with Byron's, the self-consciousness of each is seen to spring from a totally different source. Byron's is personal, the product of character, temper, inheritance; Tennyson's is reflective, the result of the pressure of society on the individual mind, of the decay of inward faith in the midst of the weakening of external creeds and institutions. As he says in the "Supposed Confessions of a Second-rate Sensitive Mind":

> How sweet to have a common faith!
> To hold a common scorn of death,
> And at a burial to hear
> The creaking cords which wound and eat
> Into my human heart, whene'er
> Earth goes to earth, with grief, not fear,
> With hopeful grief, were passing sweet!

Byron's self-consciousness always expressed itself in some form of action; Tennyson's ends in reflection. He says in the spirit of Hamlet:

> O weary life! O weary death!
> O spirit and heart made desolate!
> O damned vacillating state!

Moreover, the poetical forms which each poet

chooses for the vehicles of his emotion are radically opposed. Byron describes himself in the epic, and makes his characters soliloquise of himself in the drama; he would never have dramatised his self-consciousness in a lyric form as Tennyson does in *Locksley Hall* and *Maud*. What Byron was in his attitude towards society at the beginning, that he remained to the end, rebellious, irreconcilable, scornful, satiric; the lyric and satiric impulse, disclosed in *Hours of Idleness*, exhibits itself, only with matured power, in *Don Juan*. Tennyson, on the contrary, seems to be always advancing in endeavour towards some point of art in which his mind may attain repose and unity; he seeks to merge his own self-consciousness in the larger consciousness of society, and in proportion as he approaches to this external point of contemplation, he leaves behind him the fluid lyric impulse of his youth, seeking to imprison his ideas in the visible and abiding forms peculiar to the arts of painting and sculpture. Of these self-conscious movements of his imagination he gives us in his poems many interesting autobiographical glimpses. How suggestive, for example, are the following lines from *In Memoriam*—written with reference to the remark of a woman that "doubt is devil-born"—when read in connection with the interjections of "the second-rate mind not at unity with itself"—"O damned vacillating state!"

> I know not: one indeed I knew
> In many a subtle question versed,
> Who touch'd a jarring lyre at first,
> But ever strove to make it true:

> Perplext in faith, but pure in deeds,
> At last he beat his music out.
> There lives more faith in honest doubt,
> Believe me, than in half the creeds.

And so again, in illustration of the sensitiveness with which the poet's self-consciousness shrinks or expands with the self-consciousness of society, it is interesting to contrast the conclusion of *Locksley Hall* with the conclusion of *Maud*. The jilted lover in the former cries:

> Comes a vapour from the margin, blackening over heath and holt,
> Cramming all the blast before it, in its breast a thunderbolt.
>
> Let it fall on Locksley Hall, with rain or hail, or fire or snow;
> For the mighty wind arises, roaring seaward, and I go.

But the semi-madman of *Maud* gets rid of his "old hysterical mock-disease" thus:

> And I stood on a giant deck and mix'd my breath
> With a loyal people shouting a battle cry,
> Till I saw the dreary phantom arise and fly
> Far into the North, and battle, and seas of death.
> . . . . . .
> Let it flame or fade, and the war roll down like a wind,
> We have proved we have hearts in a cause, we are noble still,
> And myself have awaked, as it seems, to the better mind;
> It is better to fight for the good than to rail at the ill;
> I have felt with my native land, I am one with my kind,
> I embrace the purpose of God, and the doom assign'd.

But whether the poet's haunting self-consciousness finds relief in this manner, or whether, as in *Locksley Hall Sixty Years After*, it relapses into something of the "old hysterical mock-disease," the artistic resolve to arrest the transitory feeling in a perfect and abiding ideal form remains. How intimately this poetic impulse is associated with the centrifugal movement of the individual apart from society is shown by a very fine passage in *The Palace of Art:*

> No nightingale delighteth to prolong
>   Her low preamble all alone,
> More than my soul to hear her echo'd song
>   Throb thro' the ribbed stone;
>
> Singing and murmuring in her feastful mirth,
>   Joying to feel herself alive,
> Lord over Nature, Lord of the visible earth,
>   Lord of the senses five;
>
> Communing with herself: "All these are mine,
>   And let the world have peace or wars,
> 'Tis one to me."
>
>   .   .   .   .   .
>
> "I take possession of man's mind and deed.
>   I care not what the sects may brawl.
> I sit as God holding no form of creed,
>   But contemplating all."

Almost inevitably an imagination thus affected seeks to develop in the art of poetry those elements which are most akin to the plastic arts and to music. Among the English poets Tennyson is the greatest word-painter. Whatever form of poetry he attempts —and he has attempted all—this tendency is stamped upon it, and success attends him in proportion as the form is capable of being used for sculpturesque, or pictorial, or musical, purposes. The genius of painting inspires to perfection the monologues and lyrical idylls—*Tithonus, Ulysses, Mariana in the Moated*

Grange, and the like—which form the bulk of Tennyson's earlier work. It attains its meridian in *In Memoriam,* where, joined with the penetrating force of intense self-analysis, it succeeds in giving dignity of form to the most familiar objects and associations. What other poet has ever written thus of a picnic?

> Nor less it pleased in livelier moods,
>   Beyond the bounding hill to stray,
>   And break the livelong summer day
> With banquet in the distant woods;
>
> Whereat we glanced from theme to theme,
>   Discuss'd the books to love or hate,
>   Or touch'd the changes of the state,
> Or threaded some Socratic dream;
>
> But if I praised the busy town,
>   He loved to rail against it still,
>   For "ground in yonder social mill
> We rub each other's angles down,
>
> "And merge," he said, "in form and gloss
>   The picturesque of man and man."
>   We talk'd: the stream beneath us ran,
> The wine-flask lying couch'd in moss,
>
> Or cool'd within the glooming wave;
>   And last, returning from afar,
>   Before the crimson-circled star
> Had fall'n into her father's grave,
>
> And brushing ankle-deep in flowers,
>   We heard behind the woodbine veil
>   The milk that bubbled in the pail,
> And buzzings of the honied hours.

Analogous to this power of word-painting in Tennyson is the delight in novel metrical experiments for the purpose of embodying moods of self-consciousness, as in

Maud; memories of travel, as in *The Daisy;* impressions of character, as in *The Northern Farmer;* or the movement of ancient rhythms, as in his imitation of Latin Alcaics and his translation of the *The Battle of Brunanburh.* Rare, indeed, is the skill with which he arrests the fugitive impression ; but it is to be observed that his musical and pictorial methods only avail him so long as he confines himself to the lyrical sphere. When his ambition carries him to the composition of dramatic or epic verse, self-consciousness destroys the ideal illusion, and fails to conceal the labours of his art. Tennyson is even less dramatic than Byron. *Marino Faliero* and *Cain* at least raise the idea of the poet's energetic and typical personality, but *Queen Mary,* and *Harold,* and *Becket* imitate no universal idea. The same is true of Tennyson's epical efforts, *The Idylls of the King,* for example. In my opinion the poet was ill-inspired in his attempt to make that beautiful and suggestive *tour de force,* the *Morte d'Arthur* of the early poems, the foundation of an epic without unity, in which the actions and characters of knights are employed merely to decorate the transient phases of modern self-consciousness. Still more inappropriate are these pictorial and metrical effects, when applied to heighten and dignify the familiar incidents of life. Take, for example, the manner in which the poet, in *Aylmer's Field,* narrates the discovery by Sir Aylmer, in a tree, of the clandestine correspondence between Leolin Averill and Edith Aylmer:

> There the manorial lord too curiously
> Raking in that millennial touchwood-dust
> Found for himself a bitter treasure-trove;
> Burst his own wyvern on the seal, and read,
> Writhing, a letter from his child, for which
> Came at the moment Leolin's emissary,
> A crippled lad, and coming turn'd to fly,
> But scared with threats of jail and halter gave
> To him that fluster'd his poor parish wits
> The letter which he brought, and swore besides
> To play their go-between as heretofore,
> Nor let them know themselves betray'd; and then,
> Soul-stricken at their kindness to him, went
> Hating his own lean heart and miserable.

I venture to say that a more un-English mannerism, in the form of narrative poetry, was never invented.

The poetry of Byron and Tennyson furnishes a striking illustration of that law which I endeavoured to define at the opening of my lecture. Great as the position of each is in the history of our poetry, their success has not been achieved in the epic and dramatic departments of the art. They have not enriched our imagination with those ideal scenes of action and passion, which in the earlier stages of society the poet, breathing the atmosphere of common beliefs and customs, is able to call up before the mind of a public audience. Their task has been accomplished in the lyrical sphere; it has been theirs to find the metrical form fitted to express emotions which, though universal, find as a rule no outlet in the life of society, and remain buried in the secret consciousness of the individual soul. Byron's power lies in the intense force and naturalness of the language in which he communicates his own consciousness to the reader; Tennyson's in the art with which he uses words so as to place the most subtle movements of the reader's consciousness before the imagination in an almost visible form.

It is by virtue of this representative form that both poets satisfy the law of the art as defined by Aristotle. Though it is, of course, impossible to test the presence of the Universal in lyric poetry in the same way as in epic and dramatic poetry, by comparing the imagery of the poet with the life of Nature itself, yet, viewed in a certain aspect, the imitation of self-consciousness may assume an external shape. If the lyric poet does not, like the dramatist, "hold the mirror up to nature," he can, nevertheless, "show the very age and body of the time his form and pressure." And as, by the Aristotelian canon, the art of the dramatist is seen in the representation of ideas of action and passion which seem always natural, always probable, so the art of the lyric poet is felt by his touching those sentiments and emotions which are common to society, or have been common to it in some stage of its historic life. Judged by this standard both Byron and Tennyson will be found to satisfy the law of their art. Each in his own way is a thoroughly representative poet. Byron expresses the passions of a ruling caste, the impulse of revolt widely felt in the last days of the ascendency of that great and powerful class, which directed the government of England after the Revolution of

1688. Blended in his verse there is perceived a conflict of opposing tendencies, the desperation of a Catiline and the patriotism of a Cicero, the selfishness of the debauched and gambling companions of the Prince Regent, and the public spirit of the men who defended the liberties of Europe against the armies of Napoleon. Who does not feel the self-conscious emotion of aristocratic English society in the speech which Byron puts into the mouth of Marino Faliero, when urged to destroy the Venetian Senate? Isaac Bertuccio says to him:

> You passed their sentence, and it is a just one.

Faliero replies:

> Aye, so it seems and so it is to *you*:
> You are a patriot, plebeian Gracchus—
> The rebel's oracle, the people's tribune—
> I blame you not—you act in your vocation;
> They smote you, and oppressed you, and despised you;
> So they have *me*: but *you* ne'er spoke with them;
> You never broke their bread, nor shared their salt;
> You never had their wine-cup at your lips;
> You grew not up with them, nor laughed, nor wept,
> Nor held a revel in their company;
> Ne'er smiled to see them smile, nor claimed their smile
> In social interchange for yours, nor trusted,
> Nor wore them in your heart of hearts, as I have.

This is not good dramatic poetry, for nothing can be more improbable than that one conspirator should so address another, but, regarded as an ideal lyrical reflection of the sentiments towards society of Byron and a large number of his contemporaries in the period just antecedent to the first Reform

Bill, it would be difficult to find finer verse. And the imitation of these emotions will always be interesting to those who care for the history of their country.

Tennyson's lyrical mode of expressing social self-consciousness is equally characteristic. His verse does not reflect, like Byron's, the personal discontent of a class, but rather the inward suffering of the individual who cannot bring his mind into harmony with the ideals of a free and expanding community. The self-consciousness he represents is that of a large portion of educated society, caused by the change from oligarchical to democratic self-government effected by the Reform Bill of 1832. As a poet, sensitively alive to all outward change, he is aware of the material growth of the nation in numbers, in wealth, and in all the external arts and refinements of life. At the same time, as an individual, his imagination fails to find satisfaction in the public life of the nation, expressed in the acts of its government, while his own consciousness is distracted by a perpetual analysis of the beliefs and customs on which the historic character of society is founded. This conflict between the spirit of action and the spirit of reflection has stimulated the genius of every prominent English writer in the last two generations: outlets of expression have been sought for it in the self-torturing prose of *Sartor Resartus;* in the analytical psychology of *Middlemarch;* in the quasi-dramatic monologues of *Men and Women.* But as it is in its essence self-conscious, the true form for its utterance would seem to be lyrical; and nowhere, I think, has a lyrical vehicle been found for it equal in harmony, in lucidity, in repose, in dignity, in all those conditions which Fine Art demands, to the verse of *In Memoriam*.

X

CONCLUSION

Now that I have come to the close of this series of lectures, it only remains for me to look back over the ground that has been covered, and to sum up the results of the argument that I have endeavoured to develop. But before doing so it is perhaps not unnatural for me on this, the last occasion on which I shall have the honour of addressing you, to review for a moment the general circumstances of the period, during which I have held the Chair of Poetry—circumstances which have doubtless exercised an unconscious influence in directing me to the choice of my subject, and I suppose also in shaping to some extent the tendency of my thought. By a curious coincidence I was chosen Professor of Poetry just after a general election had decided an issue of the gravest importance to the fortunes of the United Kingdom; I lay down my office after another general election has given the verdict of the people on a policy which, for good or ill, must be regarded as a turning-point in the destinies of the British Empire. Unless we are to look on art as an abstract almost inhuman region, remote from the actions and emotions of the living world, it is impossible not to feel that great events like these must reverberate in the spiritual sphere, and perhaps awake fresh movements of taste and imagination.

By another coincidence, not less noteworthy, I bring my term of office to an end with the close of a century. It may be the effect of fancy or superstition, but we are certainly moved by a common instinct to look on each cycle of a hundred years as marking by itself a definite stage in the course of human affairs. Successive centuries present themselves under separate and distinctive aspects, and seem to carry forward the stages of the world's history like the connected acts of a drama. If we turn our imagination back to the time when the distinctively modern era begins, we see in the sixteenth century the great movements of the Renaissance, and the Reformation at work to undermine the Catholic fabric of the Papacy and the Empire, which constituted the order of mediæval Europe, and to lay the foundations of the Balance of Power, which holds together the society of our own times. Here we have the opening of the drama—the δέσις as Aristotle would have called it, or the evolution of the situation. A second act seems to begin with the seventeenth century, as we watch the progress of the disintegrating movement in the heart of each nation, and the struggle of rival monarchies, representing separate national interests, to obtain the preponderance of power within the newly balanced European system. The eighteenth century is the third act, in which the structural interest of the drama reaches its climax: from the dawn of the century to its last decade the solvent of Philosophy continues to loosen the exterior framework of Feudal Absolutism, raised up by the joint labours of the Renaissance and the Reformation, till it is on the point of toppling to its fall in the French Revolution.

The fourth act brings us to the close of our own century. And as we look back on its long scene of change and transformation, we recognise that the master passion of the dying era has been Liberty. Liberty, in the first place, for peoples. From the carnivals of the first Revolution, in the streets of Paris, down to the last earthquake shocks of 1848, races and nationalities start into infant life, and strive after ideals as yet but dimly understood amid the chaotic struggle for existence. Liberty is aimed at, in the second place, for the individual. In one way or another the tendency of the century, at any rate the first half of it, has been to seek to confine the functions of the State within the narrowest possible limits, so as to allow the individual the fullest play in developing his capacities as he chooses. Each individual must have complete freedom of action. Every householder must have his individual share in the government of the country. The workman must be freed from all restraints upon his right to sell his labour to whom, at the place where, and at the time when, he chooses. The merchant, freed from the trammels of Navigation Laws and protective duties, has to think simply and solely of buying in the cheapest market, and selling in the dearest.

Again, the individual must enjoy the largest liberty of thought; the religious sectarian is not only to be permitted the freedom of worshipping undisturbed in his own way, but of attacking, if he wishes, the foundation of the corporate Religion of the State; the advanced thinker must be free to push his intellectual theories in public up to that dim and doubtful point, at which the expression of obscenity or blasphemy may seem to imperil the well-being of society. And this because Liberty is regarded—and in a sense rightly regarded—as being an end in itself; so that the aim of philosophy in England, at least up to the middle of the nineteenth century, might be summed up in the phrase *laisser faire*, "let be," and has consisted rather in preventing the State from interfering with the liberty of the individual than in directing its energies to a constructive social end.

Those who can carry back their thoughts as far as I can will remember the enthusiasm with which young University men, in the sixth and seventh decades of the century, embraced the doctrines of the most influential teacher of this school, John Stuart Mill, especially as expounded in his book on *Liberty*. Their thoughts and feelings were those described by Wordsworth—pre-eminently the poet of Individualism—as prevailing at the opening of the Revolutionary era:

O pleasant exercise of hope and joy,
For mighty were the auxiliars which then stood
Upon our side, us who were strong in love.

> Bliss was in it in that dawn to be alive;
> But to be young was very heaven.

And the ideals of young Oxford were those of which the same poet speaks afterwards in a passage less well known:

> What delight,
> How glorious, in self-knowledge and self-rule,
> To look through all the frailties of the world,
> And with a resolute mastery, shaking off
> Infirmities of nature, time, and place,
> Build social upon personal Liberty,
> Which to the blind restraints of general laws
> Superior, magisterially adopts
> One guide, the light of circumstances, flashed
> Upon an independent intellect!
> Thus expectation rose again: thus hope,
> From her first ground expelled, grew proud once more.
> Oft as my thoughts were turned to human kind,
> I scorned indifference, but inflamed with thirst
> Of a secure intelligence, and, sick
> Of other longing, I pursued what seemed
> A more exalted Nature; wished that Man
> Should start out of his earthy worm-like state,
> And spread abroad the wings of Liberty,
> Lord of himself and undisturbed delights.

Such were the aspirations of that individual self-consciousness, generated by the atmosphere of Revolutionary liberty, which prevailed till about the year 1870. Then came the necessary reaction. From the exaggerated hopes of human progress men passed into a fit of revolutionary pessimism, and the world of Culture began to exchange the somewhat bourgeois Liberalism of Mill for the gloomy disdain of Schopenhauer. Nevertheless, throughout the remainder of the century individual liberty has still asserted itself as the end and goal of existence, individual consciousness as the standard of all intellectual measurement; only instead of looking forward with Wordsworth to political Liberty as the aim of human society, the Decadents, the Symbolists, the votaries of the *Fin du Siècle*, and other philosophical sects which have sprung out of the study of Schopenhauer, now aspire to the freedom of Art and Imagination, as a kind of heaven of self-culture, in which each man can, if he thinks fit, find a refuge and solace from the evils of existence. From the enthusiastic dreams of Revolutionary progress we have turned to the opiates of intellectual Buddhism.

Men of sense and manliness will not allow themselves to be infected with the despair of fantastic sects; pessimism is merely the unbalanced recoil from an exaggerated optimism, not warranted by facts and experience. One of the greatest benefits of increased individual liberty has been that it has stimulated the conscience of society; and the vast development of a free press, while it perplexes us with the multiformity of facts and opinions converging on all sides upon our consciousness, enables us to face these in a spirit free from prejudice. No right-thinking man has given up his belief in the advantages of rational and constitutional liberty; but, on the other hand, every sound reasoner is much more ready than he was to acknowledge that Liberty itself is not the solution of human ills; that much more is to be said than was supposed for such old authoritative methods of dealing with men and things as were not long ago accounted relics of benighted barbarism; that, in fact, the remedy of *laisser faire*, of letting things go, of leaving each man as a separate unit to think, speak, and do as he likes, however simple and attractive it seemed in the outset, has itself been the cause of a thousand difficulties, which require to be dealt with on quite another principle.

It is well to look at concrete examples of these truths, in order to realise exactly wherein lies the fallacy of the doctrine of *laisser faire*. Take the philosophy of the Manchester School—why has not Cobden's prophecy been fulfilled, that, if the principle of Free Trade were once proclaimed, it would be universally adopted? Is it not plain that Cobden, regarding the world as if it consisted only of a number of money-making units, left out of his calculation most important factors? On the external side he omitted national organisation and the European Balance of Power, and, on the spiritual side, the passion of envy and the mutual antagonism of class interests; he formed therefore quite a wrong estimate of the strength of the forces which have resulted in the ideals of Protection and Socialism.

Look again at the principle of *laisser faire* in its operation within the sphere of Religion. How has it worked in France, the classic land of Revolution, where the doctrine of Liberty, Equality, Fraternity, when first proclaimed, was understood to mean, in spiritual matters, that each individual was free to think as he chose? At the present moment the

Waldeck-Rousseau Ministry, which is supposed to reflect in its composition all shades of Republicanism, has proclaimed that, though the doctrine still applies to everybody who chooses to restrict his active energies within the sphere of private life, it must be so interpreted as to exclude from the service of the State every man whose character and opinions have been formed in a place of religious education. I am not so presumptuous as to cast obloquy on the legislation of a foreign state, with the inner concerns of which no Englishman has a right to interfere; I merely wish to show how the doctrine of *laisser faire* has been qualified in practice, and to call your attention to the practical rejection by French Liberals of their old ideal : " A public career open to all the talents."

In the sphere of imagination we find a phrase exactly analogous to the phrase of *laisser faire* in commerce and politics : *De gustibus non est disputandum.* The soundness of this maxim was some months ago asserted by a leader of English thought and action, justly exercising great influence over the opinions of his countrymen, and I doubt not that he arrived at his conclusion from his observation of the multiplicity and self-contradiction of modern tastes, and the complete absence of any recognised standard of judgment in contemporary literature. But in the first place, it is to be remembered that this state of anarchy did not always exist; it is, in fact, itself the result of a reaction against the absolute and authoritative method of criticism, which used to be applied to works of art by men of taste in almost all European countries in the eighteenth century. The revolt, in the name of Liberty, against the classical conventions accepted as a starting-point by the critics of that age, has ended in a demand for the emancipation of the artist from all rules whatever. But as to this we have to observe that the violent assertion of individual liberty is one of the inconsistencies of human nature: men are not content to differ. Look at the antagonism between the Classicists and the Romanticists in the early part of the century, between the Naturalists and the Impressionists in the latter half; how idle is it to say that there should be no disputing about taste, when men dispute, and will continue to dispute, about it every hour of their lives! If they reject the technical standard imposed on them by authority, they erect a metaphysical authority for themselves, and seek to impose this on as large a circle of true believers as they can rally to the worship of their particular Cult.

We have then to recognise the existing condition of things: there is now a general consciousness—we may almost call it a consciousness of the State—that the problems with which we are obliged to deal must be considered, with a view, not so much to enlarging the liberty of the individual, as to promoting the welfare of society. Granted that the development of all the faculties of the human intellect is good in itself, the result will not be good, unless these energies are directed to the promotion of some social end. It is perceived that the task of the new century will be to discover what St. James in his Epistle calls "the perfect law of liberty," the discernment of design in the constitution and tendency of things, which is always being more or less defeated by the corruption of human nature. And hence, just as in religion and politics so in the sphere of taste, we are bound to examine whether there be not an eternal law, above and beyond the æsthetic perceptions of the individual, binding the poet and painter to direct their conceptions towards some social end, which must be understood alike by artist and critic before either can produce or judge a work of Fine Art. To search for and define this law has been my object in the series of lectures I am bringing to a close, and my last words shall be devoted to reminding you of the course we have taken.

I pointed out, in the first place, the existence of that general law, or prevailing instinct, in human nature, on which Aristotle bases his reasoning about Fine Art, the motion of the spirit, that is to say, which, on the one hand, impels the artist to put the idea of his own mind into his imitation of Nature, and, on the other, justifies the critic in requiring that the artistic imitation shall express the general sense of what ought to be. This is Aristotle's Law of the Universal; it is founded on the consideration that all human beings, however great their individual varieties, are constituted fundamentally in the same way, and therefore that it is the duty of the artist to be acquainted, not only with the workings of his own imagination, but with the imaginative expectations of men as such. The validity of this law is proved equally by its theoretical certainty, and by the fact that it has been obeyed by all the greatest artists of the world; so that the kind of pleasure which is felt *semper, ubique, ab omnibus*, becomes necessarily the standard to which every work, claiming to be one of Fine Art, is brought for the determination of its value.

The definition of the Law of the Universal, however, only carries us to a point at which our minds are steadied with a belief that, amid the infinity of tastes and opinions, there is a stable foundation of judgment. We are immediately confronted with the further fact that each great master-work of genius has a life of its own, distinguishing it from every other work of genius that the world possesses. Are we to conclude from this that genius is a law unto itself, and not to be made subject to any discoverable law of art? By no means: for that would destroy the validity of the Law of the Universal. The fact is explained when we consider that, though the Universal is something absolutely existing in itself, it can only be reflected through the medium of minds differing in constitution and character. Besides the Law of the Universal noted by Aristotle, we have to recognise the existence of another law, the operation of which Aristotle himself did not observe, and indeed had no opportunity of observing, the Law of National Character. By this I mean the social instinct which compels the artist unconsciously to individualise his idea of the Universal in the light of the race tendencies, the methods of education, and the political history and character of the nation to which he belongs. In so far as his view of the Universal represents faithfully the sum of the national life, the man is a great painter or poet, and his work becomes a monumental standard by reference to which the quality of other artistic work produced in his nation can be judged. But in order that the critic may be able to declare and apply this Law of National Character, he must, by means of conscious analysis, investigate the nature of the spiritual forces by which the artist has been unconsciously inspired, observe the modes in which these operate at different periods and in different nations, and finally judge in what respect each work of Fine Art is a faithful reflection of the life of the society out of which it springs.

I have endeavoured in several successive lectures to illustrate the actual existence and operation of the Law of National Character. I have shown the permanence of the four great forces—Catholicism, Feudalism, Humanism, and Protestantism—by which the course of life in European nations has been determined, and the different way in which they have operated in each nation according to the character of the people ; and further, how the bent of the national character and history has been in each country reflected in the course of the national poetry. We have seen, for example, how the French character seems to have given a definite direction to French history in striking contrast with that of Germany, and how the English character, as manifested in history, differs from them both : we have noted with what rare representative fidelity poets like Dante, Chaucer, Milton, Molière, La Fontaine, Goethe, and Heine, reflect the character of their countrymen, and how their works may be taken as the abstract and brief chronicles of their time.

Phenomena so regular, so invariable, as those which I have illustrated in my lectures ought, I think, to furnish sufficient proof of, at least; the unconscious operation of the two great Laws of Taste. But it may be asked : Granting their existence, can these laws be consciously applied ? Can we, when we are judging of a newly-created picture or poem, submit it to the practical test of law so as to decide with any confidence as to its possession of permanent qualities ? I think we can, on certain conditions. The first, and the most indispensable, is the acknowledgment of the principle of Authority. We must allow the existence of law in an external form—that is to say, in the work of the greatest artists, not because these have in an arbitrary manner created the law, but because the universal and enduring pleasure which their work affords is a sufficient proof that they have obeyed it. Their work is therefore to be studied in a liberal and intelligent spirit, in order that we may discover the reason of their method and procedure, which the method of all genuine artists is bound to resemble, though not slavishly to reproduce.

When the source of authority has been recognised in principle, it should be practically used in education. Besides collecting the law of art from the practice of the greatest artists, we must also study it in the treatises of those who have most scientifically declared it—that is to say, of the most philosophical critics. The head and source of this study is to be sought in the *Poetics* of Aristotle, not for the reason that made the scholars of the Italian Renaissance turn to the authority of Aristotle, as being an absolute Dictator in the sphere of taste, but because he was the first to investigate by analysis the imaginative principles underlying the creations of the most artistically constituted of all races, so that the elementary conditions of fine art are more clearly defined in his treatise than anywhere else. The long and persistent misinterpretation of Aristotle's meaning was, it is true, the cause of much artistic aberration in the sixteenth, seventeenth, and eighteenth centuries; but the patient labours of modern scholars have removed the old stumbling-blocks, and any English reader, who studies the *Poetics* with the aid afforded him by the admirable essays of Professor Butcher, may now make himself acquainted with all that is essential in the Theory of Fine Art.

Though the Law of the Universal can be most thoroughly studied in the *Poetics* of Aristotle, the student of taste ought not to let this treatise monopolise his attention. The Law of National Character has to be collected from other critical sources. No doubt almost all Aristotle's critical successors into quite modern times have looked at the Universal more or less through his reasoning; but most of them, in so far as they have been men of original thought, have made some contribution of value to Criticism, derived from the peculiar character and complexion of the society to which they have belonged. Roman, Florentine, French, German, and English—Quintilian, Dante, Boileau, Lessing, Johnson, and many others—have formed their own characteristic idea of the Law of the Universal; and if any one desires to satisfy himself of the identity and permanence of the problems of taste from the dawn of Greek civilisation downwards, he will find the subject exhaustively treated in the excellent *History of Criticism*, of which the first volume has recently been published by Professor Saintsbury. It is certain that a critic who comes to the judgment of a modern work of imagination equipped with the knowledge of the varied operations of the universal Law of Rhetoric need not be doubtful of his right to decide with authority.

You will see that the authority in taste for which I am pleading is something quite different from the authority of an Academy. The Italian Academies of the sixteenth century and the French Academy were simply assemblies of representative men who discussed points of taste among themselves, and laid down rules in an arbitrary manner which carried with them just so much conventional authority as was due to the collective agreement of able and learned scholars. But almost all of them regarding the reasoning of Aristotle as axiomatic, and their misinterpretation of the text of the *Poetics* being frequent, the rules and regulations which they endeavoured to impose upon the taste of the world were devoid

2 F

of a really rational basis. There is nothing *a priori* or abstract in the critical method I have suggested. The two Laws we have been considering are founded in the constitution of the human mind; their operation is discovered by inductions from observation and experience. The only surrender of liberty demanded from the individual taste is, in the first place, the suspension of judgment till the æsthetic perception has been justly trained, and, in the second place, a submission of the intellect, in the early stages of its schooling, to the judgment of the world on the works of art deemed most worthy of admiration. When the judging faculty has been disciplined to view things in all their bearings, and has become robust and mature, the mind resumes its native liberty, and is free to revise its early decisions. Such is the course of what has been well called Humanism in Education.

I am well aware that the recognition of lawful authority in the sphere of imagination is not likely to be attained without a painful effort. The passion for novelty in the human breast; the instinct of democracy which makes the majority of the moment the supreme Court of appeal; commercial interest which finds its account in following the law of demand and supply; all these influences favour the assertion of unrestricted liberty of taste. But the dangers to civilisation and refinement, arising out of the present anarchical condition of things, ought to show the lovers of true liberty the necessity of rallying round an authoritative standard of taste. " I do not think," says Sir Richard Jebb, in his lecture on Humanism in Education, "there is any exaggeration in what Mr. Froude said thirteen years ago, that if we ever lose those studies our national taste and the tone of our national intellect will suffer a serious decline. Classical studies help to preserve sound standards of literature. It is not difficult to lose such standards, even for a nation with the highest material civilisation, with abounding mental activity, and with a great literature of its own. It is peculiarly easy to do so in days when the lighter and more ephemeral kinds of writing form for many people the staple of daily reading. The fashions of the hour may start a movement not in the best direction, which may go on until the path is difficult to retrace. The humanities, if they cannot prevent such a movement, can do something to temper and counteract it; because they appeal to permanent things, to the instinct for beauty in human nature, and to the emotions, and in any one who is at all susceptible to their influence, they develop a literary conscience."

Nothing can be added to the force of these admirable words. My only regret is that, in placing before us the advantage, nay the necessity, of recognising a definite standard of taste for the purposes of education, Sir Richard Jebb did not at the same time insist on the duty of promoting this aim by organised endeavour. He seems to rely on the permeating influence of our old established system of Humanism in Education, and on the inspiring example of individual scholars—that is to say, he is content to trust to the principle of *laisser faire*. Great and beneficial as the indirect effect of the labours of eminent scholars may be on the thought of society, it is impossible that the ideal they represent should stand against the overwhelming pressure of the forces of materialism around us, unless it is proclaimed, defined, and systematically defended. For this end we need the concerted efforts of all who desire to maintain the Humanist tradition; above all, we need a deliberate and sustained assertion of the principle on the part of the Universities.

I venture to think that, at the present moment, the English Universities are hardly acting up to their traditions in the amount of attention that they bestow on the training of taste. From very early days, Oxford and Cambridge assimilated with their system of mediæval education all the ideas that flowed in upon them with the rise of the New Learning. But they did not, like the later Italian Humanists, regard art and learning as something to be pursued for its own sake, and without reference to the active life of the State. On the contrary, as the College system expanded, the ideal of civic education grew always stronger; the Universities shared to the full in the sympathies and interests which were moving the mind of the nation at large, and instead of developing into monasteries devoted to the purposes of knowledge and research, they became rather schools for preparing the minds of youth for the discharge of public affairs. Oxford and Cambridge, having participated to the full in the internal struggle caused by the Reformation and the Civil Wars, continued to send from their seminaries the men who presided over the business of the country as judges and statesmen; poets and essayists went forth from the seclusion of their colleges to apply the stores of knowledge, there derived from the study of antiquity, to the problems of living thought. This bracing political atmosphere helped to invigorate the studies of the Universities themselves, making the scholar sympathise with the civic spirit of the great classical authors, and vivify the literatures of Greece and Rome with analogies drawn from the society about him.

While my own official duties permit me to observe with satisfaction how largely the public service is still recruited from the Universities, I am doubtful whether Oxford, at all events, derives as much nourishment as was formerly the case from the outer world. There seems within the last fifty years to have been some diminution in the intercourse between the life of this University and that of the State. Perhaps the tendency arises from a natural antipathy to the utilitarian forces in society, generated in the atmosphere of democratic politics, a reaction which has driven the scholar to seek his own ideal of liberty in Self-Culture. At any rate no one, I think, can read the books of my eminent predecessor, Matthew Arnold, without perceiving that a certain exclusive instinct of self-esteem has been for a long time impelling Academic society to exalt itself at the expense of the Gentile world, classified as Barbarians,

Philistines, and Populace. The University man has his own æsthetic aim, his own ideal of Self-Culture, to pursue, apart from the main impulse of social action in the State. And the result of this Academic monasticism has been, if I may dare to say so before such an audience as this, a decline in the robustness of Oxford taste. I seem to find evidence of a falling off in the prize exercises I have been called on to judge as Professor of Poetry. I note in the Essays, for example, a failure of power to treat a subject as a whole, a tendency to cultivate style as a thing desirable in itself apart from the subject-matter, and, on the other hand, a passion for making points and epigrams without any regard to perspective and proportion.

This is one of the mischiefs that arise out of separating the interests of Art or Taste from the movement of life and action; Taste tends to become effeminate. There is a danger of an opposite kind, also encouraged by the prevalent tendency of *laisser faire* and the principle *De gustibus non est disputandum*. I mean the excess of scientific curiosity which prompts the inquirer to study all tastes alike in a spirit of Epicurean indifference. In the enjoyment we derive from watching the operations of the human mind, we are inclined to leave out of account the moral bearing of taste, and to content ourselves with a mere analysis of artistic motives, without determining whether these are good or bad, right or wrong. Such a habit of thought is readily engendered by the study of history; and I venture to think that Professor Saintsbury, the value of whose *History of Criticism* can hardly be overestimated, comes perilously near the encouragement of dilettante trifling when he says: "The point on which I am content to be called a critical Pangloss is this: that I have hardly the slightest desire to alter—if I could do so by the greatest of all miracles, that of retroactive change — the literary course of the world. No doubt things might have been better still: but one may also be perfectly contented with the actual result."

If it be the case that Aristotle—as Professor Saintsbury says, and Mr. Bosanquet, in his *History of Æsthetic*, seems to be of the same opinion—"oversteps the genus a little in his generalisation, and merges Poetics in Ethics," then I am well content to err with Aristotle. But, in truth, I do not think that he does err. I have said, in my lecture on Aristotle, that all his philosophy about human affairs regards man, not from the mere metaphysical standpoint of Kant and modern philosophers, as an isolated individual, but as πολιτικὸν ζῷον, a social being. It would therefore have been impossible for him to eliminate moral considerations from the theory of Fine Art, and in all his reasoning about Pleasure as the end of Art, there is the underlying assumption that the pleasure produced by Art must be such as is to promote the health and well-being of the State. Those who think that his reasoning in this respect is sound will conclude that, beyond the Law of the Universal, there is no absolute law in Æsthetics, and that the only law binding on the artist is the Law of National Character, as interpreted by the educated conscience of society, which necessarily includes those religious and moral considerations that determine our conduct as individuals.

By pursuing, or seeming to pursue, too exclusively the aim of Self-culture, by failing to direct liberal or Humanist Education to a moral, a practical, a social end, I think we have brought ourselves within measureable distance of a great danger. This may be seen dimly approaching in the light of the address recently delivered by Lord Rosebery as Rector of Glasgow University. I read with sympathy Lord Rosebery's saying that the affairs of the British Empire ought to be conducted on business principles; but when I ask how this ideal is to be translated into action, I find that, in his view, the tradition of education in the Universities should be altered so as to make them into schools of technical training in the business of commercial and professional life. Hence the old foundation of the Humanities is to be abandoned. "The protest," says Lord Rosebery, "against the educational bondage of the dead languages is being raised in Edinburgh again to-day, but this time by the voice of the mercantile community. The leading bodies of that calling lately appointed a Committee to consider the subject of Commercial Education. Their Report is well worth reading. They speak of the ancient tongues with courtesy and respect, but they demand something more practical, useful, less divorced from everyday life. . . . There is required, they say, on the part of the educational authorities an admission that a man may be an educated, and even a cultured gentleman, although he has not studied Latin or Greek; and they further point out that both France and Germany possess invaluable literatures, with the advantage that they are in languages which are living and are not dead."

The fallacy underlying this reasoning is as transparent as it is time-honoured. The *raison d'être* of our Universities is to promote liberal education, and the aim of liberal education is not to impart knowledge for utilitarian purposes, but so to cultivate the moral and intellectual faculties of the scholar as to fit him, on his entrance into life, for the duties of a citizen. Such has been the fundamental idea of the English University course from the days of the Renaissance; such is still the effect on the mind of our great Oxford school of *Literæ Humaniores*. To depart from this ideal, to do away with this foundation, to attempt to build up a fabric of culture on the study of modern languages and literatures, without reference to the art and literature of antiquity, would be to reduce the system of liberal education to anarchy. Men of independent minds no doubt make their way by native force of character; but education in itself must be organised, and how is it possible for a man to be comprehensively instructed in the history of human society, in the meaning of law and government, in the various relations of thought, and in the useful and beautiful arts of expression, unless he begins at the beginning?

At the same time, the demand that liberal education shall be practical in the high and imperial sense of the term is a just one. The Universities should be prepared to show that their schools are animated with the public spirit of the πολιτικὴ παιδεία, the civic training, that was given in the city states of Greece in the days of their greatness and liberty. Our educational aims ought to be brought into conformity with the law of our social being as disclosed in the course of our national history, and they will then be seen to be equally remote from a narrow utilitarianism and from the pursuit of art and science as ends in themselves.

Let us recognise the principle that the tendency of our time towards the consolidation of the Empire carries with it a corresponding ideal of imperial Culture. The Universities are the natural guardians of the traditions of Humanism. It is for us to show our scholars that, in submitting themselves to a course of education founded on the study of the "ancient tongues," they are not "divorcing themselves from everyday life," not dissecting a dead body, not learning Greek and Latin in a mere spirit of archæology, but are familiarising themselves with a science that can reveal to them the genius of their own ancient customs and Christian institutions, inseparably associated as these are with the civic spirit of free Pagan antiquity. From the vantage ground of historic science it is the privilege, and should be the aim, of the Universities to maintain the standard of purity in the English language. In our school of English Language and Literature—at least as it might be—the student may learn to trace from age to age the development of our tongue, and to observe the flexibility with which its character has adapted itself to the gradual changes in our national life and society. Nor ought we to study our own language and literature in a mere insular temper, but, by comparing it with the genius of the languages and literatures of the Continent, to teach the scholar how to appreciate justly the relative character of English Art and Poetry, as the vehicle of ideas common to all the Christian nations of Europe.

Such was, in principle, the method of English University education that called forth the ever-memorable tribute from the illustrious Döllinger, cited in my Inaugural Lecture: "The colleges of Oxford and Cambridge have many a time, as I observed their working on the spot, awakened in me feelings of envy, and led me to long for the time when we might again have something of the kind; for I could plainly perceive that their effect was to make instruction take root in the mind, and become a part of it, and that their influence extended beyond the mere communication of knowledge, to the ennobling elevation of the life and character." *Nolumus leges Angliæ mutari:* we will do nothing to weaken the groundwork of the national character; for, as was asked of old, "if the foundations be destroyed, what can the righteous do?" If, on the other hand, these ethical foundations are kept sacred and untouched, the most ample opportunity is given for expanding the principle of individual liberty, according to the ever-changing needs of our imperial society:

Nought shall make us rue,
If England to itself do rest but true.

Do we ask for some practical guide in the exercise of rational freedom in taste and politics, I know not what more majestic monument of Law we can find than the continuous growth of our institutions as reflected in our language and literature. In that ideal mirror, illuminated by history, may be seen an image of the life of the people which will enable the statesman to proceed safely on his path of necessary reconstruction, stimulate the invention of the painter and the poet, and prove to the philosopher that the perfecting of the law of liberty consists in maintaining the standard of duty imposed on us alike by the actions and by the art of our fathers.

CORRIGENDA

P. 250, last line, *for* " through walled towns," *read* " through once-walled towns."

P. 294, line 3, *for* " general and moderating guidance," *read* " genial and moderating guidance."

P. 431, line 9, *for* "to furnish sufficient proof of, at least; the unconscious operation of the two great Laws of Taste," *read* "to furnish sufficient proof of, at least, the unconscious operation of the two great Laws of Taste."

INDEX

Absalom and Achitophel, 41
Absolutism, 394
Academies, 15, 16, 37, 279
Academy, the French, 13-14, 15-16, 19, 228
Addison, 23, 150, 330, 331, 333
Æneid, 50-2
Æschylus, 101, 103, 104, 119, 126, 217
Æsthetic philosophy, 161, 168-9
Affectation, 32, 297, 405
Agathon, 93, 122
Allegory, 344, 365-6
Analysis in Art, 148, 249
Analysis of Beauty, 172
Anglo-Saxon Culture, 315-23
—— Language, 307
—— Race, 300-4
—— Versification, 304-15
Anthology, the Greek, 98-9
Antigone, 26, 216
Anti-Jacobin, The, 396
Apollo Belvedere, 293
Apollonius Rhodius, 94-7, 109
Apology for Poetry, 69
Argonautica, 94
Aristocracy, English, 130-1
Aristophanes, 27, 103, 216, 217
ARISTOTLE AS A CRITIC, 190-221; life of Aristotle, 190-1; his vast authority; opposition to his authority in England, 192-3; main principles of his criticism: (1) object of Poetry, Imitation, 193-6; (2) object of Poetical Imitation, the Universal not the Particular, 196-209; examples of the Universal in Poetry, Scott's *Heart of Midlothian,* 200-1; Jane Austen's *Pride and Prejudice,* 201-2; examples of attempts to imitate the Universal by means of analysis, Ben Jonson, 204; Balzac, 204-5; absence of the Universal in modern novels, 206-9; (3) test of true Imitation,
Universal Pleasure, 209-10; disregard of Social Pleasure as principle of Fine Art by modern artists, 211; Naturalists, and Impressionists, 211-13; Aristotle's critical defects; exaggeration of Logical Analysis, 213-16; want of poetic sensibility, 216-18; distinction between Aristotle's Universal Laws of Art and his Bye-Laws, 218-19; misrepresentation of Aristotle's *Poetics* by the scholars of the Renaissance, 219-20; elucidation of the treatise by modern scholars, 220; Professor Butcher's edition of the *Poetics,* 221
Aristotle's Rules, 279-84, 331-2
Arnold, Matthew, 7, 9, 15, 20, 23-4, 42, 111, 135-8, 269, 437-8
Ars Poetica, 43, 117, 210, 237
Art Poétique, Boileau's, 238-43
Art Poétique, Verlaine's, 116-17
Atalanta in Calydon, 139
Atticus, character of, 56
Aubigné, 226, 289
Ausonius, 99, 100
Austen, Miss, 201-2
AUTHORITY IN MATTERS OF TASTE, 3-33; Professorship of Poetry, 3; indefinite functions, 4; founder of Chair; his life and character, 4-5; holders of Chair, 6-8; denial of authority in taste, 8; tendency of self-culture, 9; *De gustibus non est disputandum,* 10-13; necessity of authority in taste, 13; various courts of authority in taste, 13-19; the Academy, 13-16; the Coterie, 16; Public Opinion, 16-18; the Press, 18-19; defects in these courts of authority, 19; education of taste, 20; essential qualities in criticism, 20; consequences of unjudicial spirit in criticism; Croker and Keats,

446 INDEX

20-23 ; consequences of judging by private standard, Matthew Arnold, 23-4 ; final authority in taste, the works of great artists, 24-5 ; as having stood the test of time, 25 ; and as being representative of humanity, 26 ; education in taste at the English Universities, 27-29 ; the School of English Language and Literature at Oxford, 29-30 ; aim of lectures, 31-33
"Authority," Mediæval, in Church and State, 335-9
Aylmer's Field, 413-4

Bacon, 340, 373-4, 375, 378
Balzac, 149, 203, 204-5
Beaconsfield, Lord, 160
Beaumont and Fletcher, 280
Beauty, 166, 173, 180-2
Beethoven, 164, 253
Birkhead, Henry, 4-6, 11
Blackmore, 102
Blake, 396
Boccaccio, 320, 323, 364, 365
Boileau, 237-43, 349, 394
Bolingbroke, 375, 377, 378, 381
Bosanquet, Bernard, 161, 166, 439
Bourget, Paul, 207-9
Browning, Robert, 58
Brunne, Robert of, 316
Buckingham, Pope's lines on death of, 87
Bürger, 265
Burke, 23, 172
Butcher, Professor, 70 (foot-note), 215, 220-21, 432
BYRON as a representative of Law in English Poetry, 388-407 ; Macaulay's theory of decline of Poetry, 388 ; examined, 389-90 ; Lyric Poetry product of self-conscious stage of society, 391 ; Rousseau, pioneer of European self-consciousness and Romanticism, 391-2 ; distinction between Shakespeare's self-consciousness and Rousseau's, 392-3 ; effect of self-con-consciousness on creative art of Rousseau, 393-4 ; reaction from Absolutism to Romanticism in Europe, 394-5 ; checked in England by constitutional system, 394-5 ; progress of Romanticism in England, 395-7 ; Byron the most self-conscious of poets, 397-8 ; examples of his self-consciousness, 398-9 ; mixture of aristocratic feeling with his Romantic self-consciousness, 399 ; effect of the mixture on his poetry ; failure in epic and dramatic constructiveness, 400-1 ; his lyric self-consciousness the vehicle of expression for universal feelings, 402-3 ; uses epic, dramatic, and satiric forms lyrically as vehicles of self-consciousness, 403-4 ; his power of poetical expression, 405-6 ; Macaulay's description of his mixed and representative genius, 406-7

Cædmon, 300, 301, 304, 315, 316
Callimachus, 98-9, 109
Cambridge, University of, 28
Canada and "Our Lady of Snows," 145
Canadians, 145
Cain, 399, 401
Canterbury Tales, The, 318-28
Caravaggio, 91
Cartwright, William, 5
Cassandra, 118
Castelvetro, 279, 282
Castiglione, 21
Centuries, the drama of the, 420
CHAUCER, as representative of Law in English Poetry, 299-328 ; question as to Chaucer's title to be called Father of English Poetry, 299-300 ; mixed character of English Poetry begins with Chaucer, 300 ; mixture of races in England reflected in his birth and education, 301-4 ; in his language and versification, 304-15 ; charge against Chaucer of corrupting the language, 304-6 ; natural changes in Saxon grammar, 306-8 ; natural changes in Saxon versification, 308-9 ; Chaucer's combination of Saxon and French in his verse, 309-15 ; mixture of English and Continental culture reflected in Chaucer's Poetry, 315-24 ; domination of ecclesiastical influence in Saxon Poetry, 315-6 ; Chaucer contrasted with Langland, 316-23 ; Chaucer's mixture of secular and religious interests, 318-20 ; of art and morality, 320-1 ; of insular and continental ideas, 321-4 ; Chaucer's humour representative of English genius, 324-5 ; the "universal" character of Chaucer's genius, 326-8
Childe Harold, 403, 404, 405
Chivalry, 379-80
Christian, The, 206
Christ's Death and Victory, 369
Cid, The, 234-5
Clarissa Harlowe, 74
Classes, decline of, 128-35
Classical authority, 24-7
Classicists, French, 242-3, 248, 249
Cleveland, John, 5
Cobden, 425

INDEX

Coleridge, 63, 82
Comedie Humaine, 204-5
CONCLUSION, 419-44 ; survey of professorial period, 419 ; political coincidences, 419-20 ; the Nineteenth Century, its character, 421 ; spirit of individual liberty, 421-4 ; optimism, 422-3 ; pessimism, 423-4 ; examples of consequences of *laisser faire* in commerce, religion, art, 425-7 ; consciousness of aim in the State, 427 ; survey of lectures, 428-31 ; necessity of recognising Law in Taste, 427-8 ; Law of the Universal, 431 ; authority of Aristotle's *Poetics*, 431-2 ; law of national character, 432 ; authority of representative national critics, 432-3 ; authority of humanist education, 433-4 ; Sir Richard Jebb on Humanism in Education, 434-6 ; humanist education in the Universities, 436-7 ; self-culture in the University of Oxford, 437-8 ; its results, Professor Saintsbury's view, 438-9 ; taste and morals, 439-40 ; reaction against humanism in education, Lord Rosebery's view, 440-1 ; true aim of University education, 441-2 ; imperial culture, 442-3 ; the Law of Liberty in Education, 443-4
Confessions, Rousseau's, 391-3
Contraries, reconciliation of, 292-3
Contrat Social, 395
Corneille, 231-5, 252, 260
Correctness, 361, 381-2, 384-5
Corsair, The, 401
Cosmopolitanism, German, 263
Coteries, 16, 109-10, 297
Cowley, 106-8, 129, 370, 378, 380
Cowper, 396
Crashaw, Richard, 371-3, 376, 378
Criticism, 20-4, 37-8, 159-61, 183-9, 256
Croker, 21-3
Cromwell, 244-6
Culture, 9, 135-8, 437-43
Cursor Mundi, 316
Cynewulf, 315, 316

Dante, 67, 106-7, 335-9, 348, 351
Decadence. *See* Poetical
Defence of Poetry, 69-70
Deformed Transformed, 401
Degeneration, 111
De gustibus non est disputandum, 10-13, 426-7
Deism, 375-7, 396
Della Crusca, 109
De Monarchia, Dante's, 337
De Quincey, 361

Dichtung und Wahrheit, 255
Diderot, 231, 242
Difficile est proprie communia dicere, 48, 57
Discordia Concors, 367, 373
Discourse on the Three Unities, Corneille's, 231-4
Discourses on Painting, 25, 292
Divine Comedy, 67, 322, 333, 335-9, 355
Dolci, Carlo, 91
Döllinger, 28, 443
Dolores, 82
Don Carlos, Schiller's, 261
—— *Juan*, 404, 405
—— *Quixote*, 252, 325
Donne, 129, 378
Dryden, 41-2, 87, 281, 309
Dürer, 252

Elegy, Gray's, 57, 264
Emilia Galotti, 260
English Bards and Scotch Reviewers, 399, 403-4
English Character, 285-6
—— Drama, 101-2
—— History, 287-8
—— Language, 286-7
—— School of Language and Literature at Oxford, 29-31, 442
Ennius, 305, 325
Epic Poetry, 94-7, 102, 241-2, 347-9
Epistle to Arbuthnot, Pope's, 381, 385
Erasmus, 27, 291
Essay on Criticism, 237-8, 278-84, 292, 361-2
Essay on Man, 297, 378, 394
Euripides, 103-4, 105, 127, 178, 217
Every Man in his Humour, 195
Every Man out of his Humour, 195
Excursion, 76

Faery Queen, 102
Faust, 253, 266-7, 295, 400
Feudalism, 289, 318, 336-9, 430
Filostrato, Boccaccio's, 323
Flaubert, Gustave, 249
Fletcher, Beaumont and, 280
—— Giles, 369-70, 378
—— Phineas, 368-9, 378
France, Anatole, 250
Free Trade, ideal of, 425
French Character, 224
—— Drama, 172, 230-7
—— History, 224-5, 288
—— Language, 286
—— Metres in English, 308-15
—— Poetry. *See* Idea
—— Revolution, 60, 225, 248, 394-7
—— Words in English, 306-8, 313, 314

Fürstengruft, Die, Schubat's, 264-5
Gautier, Théophile, 246-8, 249
Georgics, Virgil's, 100, 195
German Character, 253-5, 274-5
—— Drama, 258-62
—— Empire, 274-6
—— Language, 257-8, 262
—— Literature, 255-6
Gifford, 110, 396, 406
Goethe, 174, 255, 259, 261-2, 266-7, 270, 271, 272, 290, 400
Grand Cyrus, 227, 380
Gray, 57, 264
Gregory the First, 351
Grenvill, Bevill, 5

Hamburgische Dramaturgie, 172, 259
Hamlet, 207-9, 291, 296, 297, 334, 402-3
Handel, 253
Hartmann, 181-2, 183
Hegel, 175, 180, 181
Heine, 253, 261, 267-72
Hellenising, 138-41
Hercules Oetaeus, 105-6
Herder, 263-4
Higden, 307
Hippolytus, 105
History of Æsthetic, 161, 169-75
Hogarth, 172
Holbein, 252
Homer, 49-50, 148, 149
Horace, 21, 43-5, 65-6, 78, 117
Horace, Corneille's, 236, 260
Hours of Idleness, 397-8, 403, 407, 409
Hugo, Victor, 244-6, 304
Humanism, 130, 294, 357, 395, 430, 434-43
Humanists, 27, 289, 291
Hume, David, 160, 378

IDEA OF LAW IN ENGLISH POETRY, 278-98 ; Pope's view in *Essay on Criticism*, 278 ; examination of Pope's view, 279-84 ; English national character, 285-6 ; English language, 286-7 ; English character compared with French and German character, 287-91 ; main characteristics of English character the reconciliation of contrary principles, 292 ; character reflected in English Art and Literature ; Sir Joshua Reynolds's definition of Art, 292-3 ; examples of reconciliation of contraries in English Poetry ; *Vision of Piers the Plowman*, 293 ; *The Canterbury Tales*, 293-4 ; *Satires* of Pope, 294 ;
poetry of Byron and Tennyson, 294 ; test to be applied in judging contemporary poetry, 294-8 ; popularity and singularity both inadequate tests of genius, 294-7 ; the Universal truth of classic English Poetry lies in the just mean between the two, 297 ; examples of characteristic expression in English Poetry, 298

IDEA OF LAW IN FRENCH POETRY, 222-51 ; difference in the development of Greek art and the art of modern nations, 222-24 ; French national character and history reflected in French literature, 224-5 ; French literary parties, 225 - 6 ; party of the chivalrous aristocracy, its qualities, 226-7 ; party of the bourgeoisie, its qualities, 227 ; Molière, 228-9 ; La Fontaine, 229-30 ; French character reflected in French drama, 230-1 ; Corneille, *Discourse on the Three Unities*, 231-7 ; French character reflected in French criticism, Boileau, 237-43 ; conflict between Classicists and Romanticists, 243-4 ; Victor Hugo, Preface to *Cromwell*, 244 - 5 ; resemblance between *The Cid* and *Cromwell*, 246 ; Théophile Gautier, *Émaux et Camées*, 246 - 7 ; resemblance between ideals of Boileau and Gautier, 247-8 ; conflict between Classicists and Romanticists continued between Naturalists and Impressionists, Gustave Flaubert, Anatole France, 249-50

IDEA OF LAW IN GERMAN POETRY, 252 - 77 ; results of German art, 252-3 ; German character described by Tacitus, 253 ; exhibited in their representative men, 254 ; individualism in German history, 254-5 ; absence of national principle in German literature, 255-6 ; Klopstock's *Messiah* contrasted with *Paradise Lost* and *Paradise Regained*, 256-8 ; German character in German drama, Lessing, Schiller, Goethe 258-62 ; German genius for lyric poetry, 262 ; cosmopolitan tendency in German literature of the eighteenth century, Herder, 262-3 ; futile attempt to express civic ideas in German lyric poetry of eighteenth century, Frederic Schubart ; *Die Fürstengruft* contrasted with Gray's *Elegy*, 264-5 ; German genius for lyric poetry reflected in *Faust*, 266-7 ; in Heine's

INDEX

songs, 267-72; Wilhelm Müller, 273; question as to the future of German Poetry, 274-7
Ideals for Middle Class, 135-45
Idylls of the King, 413
Iliad, 49-50, 94, 353
"Imitation" in Fine Art, 63, 152-3, 163-4, 193-6
Imitations of Horace, Pope's, 43, 382, 384
Impressionists, 59, 142, 211-13, 249-50
Individual, The, 44, 67-8
Individualism, 9, 136, 148-9, 254-5
In Memoriam, 87, 412, 418
Inspiration, 44-7, 154

Jebb, Sir Richard, 434-5
Jerusalem Delivered, Tasso's, 348-9
Johnson, Samuel, 367, 406, 433
Jonson, Ben, 17, 68, 195, 203-4
Justinian, 337
Juvenal, 55

Kant, 173, 179-80, 253, 254
Keats, 21-3, 40, 81
Keble, John, 7
King Lear, 205, 236, 296
Kipling, Rudyard, 141-5, 153
Klopstock, 256-8
Kubla Khan, 81

La Fontaine, 239-30, 251
Laisser faire, 422-7
Langland, 308, 315, 316-18, 319-20, 321, 323
Laocoon, 172
Laodamia, 76
Lara, 401
Latin element in English, 314
—— Poetry, 100-1
Law, William, 396
LAW IN TASTE, 159-189; English dislike of Criticism, 159-60; how far reasonable, 160-2; question as to the object of Fine Art Imitation, 163-4; correctness in Imitation, 164-5; Æsthetic Pleasure, end of Fine Art, 166; Mr. Bosanquet's contrary view, 166-7; question as to connection between Art and Morals, 168; history of Æsthetic Criticism, 169-75; history of Philosophic Enquiry into Æsthetic Law, 175-81; failure of Æsthetic Philosophy to throw light on artistic practice, 181-4; Law in Art and Taste to be looked for in the greatest works of Art, 184; the Absolute in Art variously reflected, 185; law of

National Character in Art, 185-6; National Criticism, 186-9
Lay of the Last Minstrel, 46-7, 71 149
Layamon, 307
Legend of Good Women, 322
Leibnitz, 394
Leonora, 266
Lessing, 172, 253, 259-60, 290, 433
Les Tragiques, 226
Liberty in Matters of Taste. See Authority
—— Political and Individual, 60-1, 423-27
Life in Poetry, 38-44, 58-62, 89-90, 124-6, 188
Literæ Humaniores, School of, 30, 441
Locke, 367, 375, 378
Locksley Hall, 407, 409, 410
—— *Sixty Years After*, 410
Logic in Art, 249-50
Longinus, 170
Lorris, William de, 225, 304
Lovelace, 380
Lowth, Bishop, 6
Luther, 253, 254, 352, 358
Lutrin, 247
Lycophron, 118
Lyly, 21
Lyric Poetry, 389-91

Macaulay, 330, 343-7, 388, 389, 406
Macbeth, 233, 258, 291
Malherbe, 226, 238
Mallarmé, 115
Manfred, 401
Mannerism, 297, 413-14,
Marino, 369
Marino Faliero, 413, 416
Marlowe, 71-72
Marot, 225, 289
Maud, 407, 410, 413
Measure for Measure, 291
Medal, Dryden's, 41
Men and Women, 417
Mengs, Raphael, 172
Messiah, Klopstock's, 256-8
Metaphysical Poetry, 5, 367-73
Metre, 73-78
Meung, John de, 225, 304
Middle Class, The English, 131-5
Middlemarch, 417
Mill, John Stuart, 85, 422
Millais, 183-84
Milman, Dean, 6
MILTON as a representative of Law in English Poetry, 329-359; popular dislike of Milton's Theology, 329; not to be taken into account in judging his genius, 330-1; Addison's criticism on *Paradise Lost*, its merits

450 INDEX

and defects, 331-2 ; *Paradise Lost* regarded (1) as an imitation of the Universal in Nature, 332-4 ; (2) as an imitation of the age and character of the time, 334-43 ; comparison between *The Divine Comedy*, as the mirror of the thought of the Middle Ages, 335-39 ; and *Paradise Lost*, as the mirror of the thought of the Renaissance and the Reformation, 339-43 ; *Paradise Lost* regarded (3) as harmonising opposite principles of Art, 343-357 ; Macaulay's contrast between the styles of Dante and Milton, 343 ; examined, 344-7 ; contrast between the epic method of Tasso and Milton, 347-50 ; Milton's reconciliation of Christian and Pagan principles in machinery of epic action, 349-51 ; of Christian and classical ideas and images, 351-5 ; faults in *Paradise Lost*, 355-6 ; *Paradise Lost*, viewed in relation to contemporary circumstances, 356-8 ; its reflection of English Character, 359
Minot, Laurence, 322
Mistress, The, Cowley's, 380
Modern Painters, 161
Molière, 228-9, 251, 252
Montrose, 380
Moral Essays, Pope's, 381
Morality and Art, 168, 177-81, 320-1, 438-40
Morice, Charles, 119-20
Morris, William, 80-81
Mozart, 253
Müller Wilhelm, 273

Nævius, 305
National Character in Art, 185-9
Naturalists, 211-13, 249-50
Nineteenth Century, the, 421-4
Nordau, 111-14, 123, 147
Norman Conquest, the, 302
Nouvelle Heloïse, 395

Ode on Immortality, 76, 391
Œdipus Rex, 105, 258
Optimism, 394, 422-3
Oratory and Poetry, 85, 139
Orlando Furioso, 252, 349
Othello, 74
Oxford, University of, 1, 28, 29, 437-44

Palace of Art, 411
Palgrave, Francis, 8
Painting and Poetry, 39-40, 41, 94-97, 246-48, 411-13

Paradise Lost, 45, 46, 129, 252, 256, 332, 333-4, 339-43
Paradise Regained, 256-7, 369
Paradiso, 45, 337
Parliament of Foules, 322
Pater, Walter, 10
Pathos, 52
Pessimism, 423-4
Pericles, 33
Περὶ ὕψους,
Phædra, Seneca's, 105
Philologists, 30, 300, 306
Piers the Plowman, Vision of, 293, 305, 316-18
Plato, 169, 170-71
Pleasure, 38-9, 63-4, 166-7, 175-81
Pleiad, 226
Poe, Edgar, 81
Poems by Two Brothers, 407
Plotinus, 170
POETICAL CONCEPTION, 37-62, Nature of, 42-4 ; Horace's principle of, 43, 48 ; Universal and Individual in, 44-7 ; Homer's method of, 49 ; Virgil's, 50-1 ; Statius', 52-5 ; Juvenal's, 55 ; Pope's, 56 ; Browning's, 58 ; existing difficulties in way of, 58-62
—— DECADENCE, 89-122 ; illustrated in history of Greece, Rome, and England, 90 ; symptoms of (1) decline of the Universal, 92-102 ; (2) exaggeration of the Individual, 102-108 ; (3) abdication by Society of its right of judgment, 108-10 ; Nordau's view of, 111-14 ; signs of, in French school of Poetical Symbolism, 115-120 ; question as to contemporary, 120-2
—— EXPRESSION, 63-88 ; Horace's rule for, 65-6 ; Universal and Individual in, 67 ; metre the vehicle of, 68-73 ; Wordsworth's theory of, 73-78 ; test for determining propriety of, 78 ; Walt Whitman's, 79 ; William Morris's, 80 ; Coleridge's definition of, 81 ; in *Kubla Khan*, 81 ; in *Dolores*, 82 ; existing difficulties in the way of, 82-86 ; examples of just, 87-8
Poetics, Aristotle's, 191-3, 213-220, 223, 432
POETRY AND THE PEOPLE, 123-156 ; connection between the life of a nation and the life of Art, 125-6 ; question as to extent of decay in national life, 127-8 ; decay in schools of art contemporaneous with decay of ruling principles in the classes of a nation, 128-9 ; the decay of the power of

INDEX

the Crown, 128 ; of the power of the Aristocracy, 130-1 ; of the power of the Middle Classes, 131-5 ; ideals of Culture and Poetry suggested by modern critics, Matthew Arnold's, 135-8 ; Mr. Swinburne's, 138-40 ; Mr. Kipling's, 141-5 ; pursuit of Novelty in Poetry, 145-6 ; causes of decline in Modern Poetry, Herr Nordau's pathological theory, 147-8 ; Self-conscious Analysis in Poetry, 148-9 want of Cultivation in public taste, 150-1 ; necessity of the Universal in Poetry, 153-4 ; National ideal in Poetic Imitation, 154-5
Polymetis, 172
POPE as a representative of Law in English Poetry, 360-87 ; value of the *Essay on Criticism*, as the critical work of a poet, 361-2 ; main principles in the *Essay on Criticism*, 362-87 ; (1) "Follow Nature," 362-5 ; different conceptions of Nature in pre-Christian Society, in the Middle Ages, and in the post-Renaissance period, 362-5 ; (2) "Avoid False Wit," 365-73 ; "Wit," the result of the theological conception of Nature in the Middle Ages, 365-7 ; examples of False Wit in English Poetry, 367-73 ; Phineas Fletcher's *Purple Island*, 368-9 ; Giles Fletcher's *Christ's Death and Victory*, 369-70 ; Crashaw's lyrics, 370-3 ; Pope's conception of Nature, 373-82 ; his attempt to reconcile Roman Catholic and Protestant ideas, 374-5 ; Catholicism and Deism, 375-7 ; his rational conception of the Universal contrasted with the False Wit of the seventeenth century, 377-8 ; his exclusion from poetry of the scholastic elements, 379 ; of the Romantic element, 380; (3) "Imitate the Classics," 379-85 ; Pope's assimilation of the classic and civic spirit of antiquity with modern life and action, 379-81 ; restricted scope of his poetical conception, 382-4 ; limitation in his principle of correct poetical expression, 384-5 ; his supremacy in ethical, satiric, and didactic verse, 386-7
Popularity, 295-6
Prelude, 76
Preraphaelites, 183-4, 276
Pride and Prejudice, 201-2
Professorship of Poetry, 3-8, 31-3
Public Opinion, 18-19, 151-2, 295-6
—— Service and Universities, 29, 437
Puritanism, Milton's, 352, 357-8

Purple Island, The, 368

Quarterly Review, 20-23
Quintilian, 24, 433
Quintilius Varus, 108

Rabelais, 227, 289
Racine, 252
Rambouillet, Hôtel de, 226, 227, 229, 239, 250
—— Marquise de, 226
—— Mdlle. de, 249
Rape of the Lock, 381
Realists in Art, 203-9
Reformation, the, 130, 289, 291, 293-4, 342, 352, 357, 420, 437
Religio Laici, 41
Renaissance, the, 138, 140, 171, 249, 290-1, 341-2, 358, 364, 373, 374, 383, 392, 395, 421, 441
Renan, 14, 250
Reynolds, Sir Joshua, 25, 292, 343, 356, 383
Richardson, 74, 396
Richelieu, 14
Robbers, Schiller's, 261
Rollinat, 118
Romance, 61-2, 380-1
Romance of the Rose, 225, 280, 322
Romanticists, French, 243-9
Ronsard, 226
Rosebery, Lord, 440
Rossetti, 112
Rousseau, 391-5, 407
Ruins of Time, Spenser's, 42, 83
Ruskin, 23, 161

Sannazaro, 380
Sardanapalus, 399, 401
Sarpedon, 26
Sartor Resartus, 9, 417
Schelling, 174-5
Schiller, 173-4, 253, 259, 260-1
Schlegel, Augustus, 159-60, 162
Scholar Gipsy, 138
Scholastic Logic, 335-9, 379
Schopenhauer, 182, 423
Schubart, Frederick, 264
Scott, Sir Walter, 46, 71, 200-1
Scudéry, 242, 380
Self-consciousness in Art, 148-9, 154, 388-90, 391-4, 414-18
Semiramis, 172
Seneca, 104-6, 118, 231
Serious Call to a Devout Life, 396
Shakespeare, 68, 86, 90, 91, 113, 172, 183, 195, 232, 392-3, 400
Shelley, 61, 69-71, 397
Sidney, 69-71, 280-1, 359, 380-1
Simonides, 170, 172

Singularity, 296-7
Skinner, 306
Society, authority of, 11
Socialism, 276, 425
Songs before Sunrise, 139
Sophocles, 26, 101, 104, 105, 119
Sophron, 200
Spectator, the, criticism in, 63-4, 123, 129
Spence, Joseph, 6, 172
Spenser, 42, 83, 1 ?, 359
Statius, 52-5
Stephen, Leslie, 362
Sublime and Beautiful, Burke's, 172
Swinburne, 82, 138-41
Swift, 375, 383
Symbolists, the French, 110-20

TENNYSON as a representative of Law in English poetry, 406-18 ; Tennyson's earliest poems imitative of Byron, 407 ; his later self-analysis, 407 ; adaptation of Byronic soliloquy, 408 ; difference between Byron's self-consciousness and Tennyson's, 408-9 ; *Locksley Hall, Maud*, 409 ; Tennyson's philosophic doubt, 409-10 ; his self-consciousness representative of that of society, 409 ; examples of, 410 ; seeks perfection of external form ; *Palace of Art*, 410-11 ; genius akin to painter's and musician's, 411 ; word-painting ; *In Memoriam*, 412 ; metrical music ; *Maud, The Daisy, The Northern Farmer, Battle of Brunanburh*, 412-13 ; want of epic and dramatic genius, *Idylls of the King, Aylmer's Field*, 413 ; *In Memoriam* a mirror of universal self-consciousness, 417
Tacitus, 253
Tasso, 347, 363
Taste, 8
Taylor, Jeremy, 23
Tertullian, 291, 351, 352

Tempest, 73, 195
Thamyris, 148
Thebais, 52-5
Theocritus, 97, 358
Theology, 335, 379, 381
Thesmophoriazusæ, 93-4
Thyrsis, 138
Τὸ Βέλτιον, 165, 199, 201, 209, 213
Τὸ Καλόν, 165
Trachiniae, 105
Two Foscari, The, 401

Unities, The, 231-6, 281-3
Universal, the, 44, 62, 92, 154, 196-209, 294, 328, 332-42, 377-8, 386, 415-8
Universities, 27-28, 291, 436-40, 442
Usus, 21

Varus, Quintilius, 188
Verlaine, 116-7
Verstegan, 306
Vineta, 273
Virgil, 50-2, 72, 118
Voltaire, 172, 231, 242

Wagner, 183
Wallenstein, Schiller's, 261
Walt Whitman, 79
Warton, Thomas, 6
Werther, Sorrows of, 295, 395
Wesleys, the, 396
William Tell, Schiller's, 261
Winckelmann, 172, 290
Wit, false, 362, 365-7
—— true, 374
Wordsworth, 49, 61, 63, 73-8, 86-7, 422-3, 424
Wragg, 7

Xenarchus, 200
Xenophon, 69-70

Zola, 14, 207

THE END